EXECUTIVE'S GUIDE
TO MOTIVATING PEOPLE

Executive's Guide to Motivating People

How Freudian Theory Can Turn Good Executives into Better Leaders

Abraham Zaleznik

Bonus Books, Inc., Chicago

94 93 92 91 90   5 4 3 2 1

Library of Congress Catalog Card Number: 89-82693

International Standard Book Number: 0-929387-11-2

Bonus Books, Inc.
160 East Illinois Street
Chicago, Illinois 60611

Printed in the United States of America

To My Teachers

In Psychoanalysis

Lydia G. Dawes, M.D.
Joseph J. Michaels, M.D. *
Helen H. Tartakoff, M.D. *
Arthur F. Valenstein, M.D.
Grete Bibring, M.D. *

In Business Administration

Franklin E. Folts *
Richard S. Meriam *
George Albert Smith, Jr. *
Melvin T. Copeland *
John G. McLean *

In Social Science

George C. Homans *
Paul F. Lazarsfeld *

In Human Relations

Fritz J. Roethlisberger *

And to my old friend and comrade-in-arms, who taught me how to teach

C. Roland Christensen

* Deceased

CONTENTS

PREFACE

Dear Reader,

You probably bought this book because you are interested in motivating people. Any executive, or aspiring executive, should be concerned about what makes people tick and how to get them keenly interested in their jobs, their companies, and their work associates. But as with all practical questions, you have to do a lot of work before you're in a position to affect how people think and feel.

The first thing you have to do is to get a better handle on your own motivation. The more you know and understand yourself, the more you will be able to know and understand other people. Now I would be writing under false pretenses if I suggested this book is meant as a "self help" or personal therapy book. I don't believe such books are too useful, although at times they seem to provide comfort for people in a quandary.

When I say get a better handle on yourself, I am referring at the outset to the ideas you already have about human motivation. In a sense, all of us are experts when it comes to figuring out what drives people to act the way they do. The trouble is that mixed in with good common sense are a lot of false ideas, wrong assumptions, and wishful thinking.

Let me give you an illustration. One of the simplest, as well as sophisticated, ideas that most executives I have met hold as a fixed truth is that if you set a clear goal, show people how to achieve that goal, establish in advance an incentive, and reward them if they meet the goal, you have a sure-fire method for motivating people. This idea (call it a theory of motivation if you prefer) comes from behavioral psychology. Much evidence supports it, which is probably the reason executives believe it and the texts on management parade it through their many pages.

The problem with this theory is it oversimplifies and leaves out some crucial elements. For example, does an employee's relationship with his or her supervisor have a bearing on how the employee perceives the goal, the path, and the incentive? Does this perception have an effect on the employee's attitude and willingness to accept the goal and work hard toward attaining it?

People have the habit of loading meaning on to their experience. What happened in the past, and the inferences attached to past experience, determines how people look at themselves and at other people, particularly authority figures. Therefore, a simple interchange in fixing a goal and providing incentives reverberates with the history that is condensed in the relationship between who is talking and who is listening. You can choose to ignore this history, and sometimes it is wise to do so, but you should be aware of what you are doing and why.

In my experience, it's what you don't know that will hurt you. The stronger your grasp on the human condition, the wiser you will become in the human dimension of your job as an executive.

I wrote this book for my students in the MBA program at the Harvard Business School. Originally called Social Psychology of Management, and more recently, the Psychodynamics of Leadership, this course introduced Harvard MBA candidates to Sigmund Freud's theories of the mind. His was a depth psychology that established the importance of unconscious motivation in human behavior.

It was never my intention to make psychoanalysts out of executives. In fact I cautioned my students that interpreting someone else's motives, conscious and unconscious, was poor practice in everyday life. The practice of psychoanalysis is a specialty requiring expert training and is used selectively for patients who can benefit from the treatment. But psychoanalytic psychology is available for general enlightenment, and in this case, for executives who are taking responsibility for the use of power in human relationships.

Over many years of teaching, I have tried various introductions to psychoanalysis among the course materials. I found that business school students need a somewhat different introduction. Most introductions assume that the reader is a mental health professional or has some interest in clinical practice. This orientation is foreign to most executives in business. So I wrote this book trying to keep the perspective of a curious, if not skeptical, executive who wants to learn about people, but is not especially concerned about the problems of mental health as such, let alone the difficulties in curing mental illnesses. I concentrated on what we have learned from psychoanalysis and not on how this knowledge is revealed, and also examined, on the clinician's couch.

You will read in this book about transference and may wonder if it was wise to avoid the clinical perspective. Transference is an important finding in psychoanalysis and is a link to the notion that history plays an important part in human interchange. Briefly, transference occurs when a person experiences in the present some aspects of a relationship with a figure from his or her past. Authority figures are natural targets for transferences of unconscious ideas and emotions contained in the history of relationship to one's parents. Transference is a discovery straight out of the clinical situation. In fact it is the lever that makes it possible to undo many of the adverse effects of past experience on character, perceptions, and behavior.

I do not dwell on the clinical aspects of transference in this book. Instead, I try to show how transference occurs in everyday life, and how it affects human relations in organizations. You will get a clue that transference is underway in yourself, or from another person to you as the object, if you have an uncanny sensation that you are on a stage performing in a drama that on the surface appears novel, but draws you beyond the reality of events into some dim past in which you were both actor and observer. This uncanny sensation is not too different from what you feel while in the grip of great drama in the theatre. Perhaps all I'm really suggesting is that life does imitate art. In connection with that thought, let me tell you about the variety of ways we learn about unconscious motivation, other than in the clinical situation.

Most of what we learn in life comes on an installment plan. It's a piece at a time. It's never all or nothing. I have encountered executives, and students who want to be executives, who seem to have a natural gift for understanding the human condition. This gift extends to the ability to sense aspects of unconscious motivation in self and others. They appear sensitive to the idea that dreams mean something beyond their manifest content; they realize that defenses are a part of everyone's psychological makeup; deep desires, fears, and the more apparent reactions of greed and envy as these voracious affects permeate human relationships.

In my trade, we say that such people are psychologically-minded. Like any other acuity, it can be honed through reflection on experience, as well as observation of people and the world around. Attachment to the arts and letters is another good way to develop psychological-mindedness. More to the point, literature and art afford much pleasure as well as proximity to some interesting truths about human nature.

I wasn't long into teaching The Psychodynamics of Leadership before I realized that it was silly to limit exposure to case studies, and even to books such as this one, which I hope I'm enticing you to read with care and deliberation. Good case studies are good narratives. They are expensive to research and difficult to write, especially in trying to tell the story while remaining true to the facts. I'm a pretty decent case writer, but I still asked myself, "Why not take advantage of some of the rich literature so many genuinely talented writers have provided to deepen whatever degree of psychological-mindedness we possess?''

So alongside case studies and chapters in this book, my students and I read Herman Melville's *Billy Budd,* to fathom the likes of seaman Billy, Master-at-Arms Claggert, and Captain Vere, who commanded Her Majesty's ship "The Rights of Man" as she ploughed the seas during the wars with France in 1797.

We read and discussed two of Arthur Miller's plays, *A View from the Bridge* and, of course, *Death of a Salesman.* Luckily, Dustin Hoffman's portrayal of Willy Loman is available on videotape, so we could see the play acted as well as read its text.

When we turned to group psychology—that's chapter 8 in this book—I called on Woody Allen for help and showed his film *Interiors.* It too is available on videotape, and I recommend strongly that you view it, especially in conjunction with chapter 8. In fact, a good way to read this book is to find some like-minded friends, and even work associates, who are as curious about human motivation as you. Seeing a film or two, reading a play, a novel, a biography, while reading chapters in this volume will provide many stimulating hours of discussion. I think it might deepen some of these friendships and associations. By the way, for the business man or woman among my readers, you might want to read Cary Reich's splendid biography of Andre Meyer, the remarkable financier of the firm of Lazard Frères. Meyer explained investment banking as ''5 percent finance and 95 percent psychoanalysis.'' I'll leave it to you to figure out what he meant. For the politically-minded, read Donald Regan's memoir on his life as it led up to his joining the Reagan administration first as Secretary of the Treasury and then as the White House Chief of Staff. While we're on politics, don't overlook Garry Wills' *Reagan's America* for a psychologically astute analysis of the great seduction of the 1980s. Back to business, while reading this book glance at John Sculley's *Odyssey.* He's the CEO of Apple Computer. You can entertain yourself trying to puzzle out how this marketer goes about working on people's heads.

When it's all said and done, you will probably end up accusing me, as have many of my students in the Harvard Business School, of burdening your life with the notion that nothing is to be taken for granted, even though Freud once commented that sometimes a cigar is just a good cigar. To this charge I plead guilty. But in my own defense, I can say that while I stressed the art of decoding in the human context, I also differentiated between thinking and acting. Using words out loud is a form of acting. You and I can think anything we want, analyze to our hearts content, even speculate for a moment or two. But so long as we keep these thoughts to ourselves (except in a classroom or discussion group), we are enjoying the privilege of freedom of thought. Once words float through the air, conditions have changed. Action has occurred, consequences must be paid. You should never, I repeat *never,* give voice to your thoughts about someone else's unconscious motives, even if, in a prideful moment, you believe you know what you are talking about. Lovers especially should not go after one another's unconscious mind at the risk of creating the nightmare portrayed in Edward Albee's *Who's Afraid of Virginia Woolf?* Intimacy offers no license. When you speak, speak as a human being from your heart as well as your mind, so that even in angry moments you are not using the intellect as a weapon.

Earlier, I mentioned that I wanted to avoid preoccupying your mind with questions that clinicians argue at length. Yet as you get into this book, you'll discover the clinician's interest in pathology. There are a couple of chapters on neuroses, what they are, how they differ, and how they originate in early childhood. You may discover as you read these, and other, chapters that you are susceptible to what medical students experience in their early encounters with pathology. You begin to see the diseases in yourself. That's a bit unsettling, but it passes as you continue reading. The reason for the emphasis on pathology is simply that's what the material is about. Anyway, psychoanalysis doesn't worry a whole lot about what is "normal", and "abnormal." When you read the chapter on development, you will discover that however we appear as mature adults, count on the fact that any progression in life is through conflict. You know the old saying, "Scratch a man and find a boy." Well, to reach maturity is to struggle with neurotic conflict. To clinch my case for pathology, think about this: is it possible to discover much about the human condition if one sets out to study health? Along these lines, I'm more than a little concerned over the fact that many of my colleagues at the Harvard Business School are going about looking for "positive role models" whom the students can be encouraged to emulate. To me, today's heroes in business are tomorrow's potential bums. Just look at the problems facing Lee Iacocca as the Chrysler Corporation enters a new crisis with the weakening of the automobile market. Will the lessons he applied in his first turnaround of Chrysler apply in this second turnaround? Along the same lines, aren't you curious about what the historians will have to say about Walter Wriston, the hero of the banking industry who led the way into making large loans to underdeveloped countries on the theory that nations never go bankrupt? In my view you learn more from mistakes than you do from seemingly correct actions.

I don't want to detain you much longer with this letter. But I need to remind myself that although writing (and psychoanalyzing) is lonely work, many wonderful people have filled my life with kindness, understanding, and practical help. First of all, I've dedicated this book to my teachers, most of whom are dead. I wish you'd look this list over carefully. You may not recognize names, but I hope you catch the idea that to have been enlightened by so many fine teachers (I could have added many more names to the list) is to have received a gift, which I hope to pass on to you, even in small measure, through this book.

On the practical side, I want to thank Elizabeth Altman, my research assistant over many years at the Harvard Business School, for her help in preparing chapter 2. Sharon Kleefield carefully accumulated, digested, and summarized materials on evaluations of psychoanalysis as a science and a therapy. I intended to write a chapter using this material, but decided to hold it for another time and book. Sharon's work on the history of consulting appears in chapter 11. I thank her for all her help and enthusiasm for the work.

Yuzuru Suzuki, currently a doctoral student at the Harvard Business School, elected to take my course during his second year in the MBA program. He undertook some scholarly work for me in studying the various schisms and schools in psychoanalysis. I intended to use his work for an appendix, but I ran out of time. I assure him I will use his work in subsequent writing.

I sincerely appreciate the help I received from Susan McWade, Linda Bowers, Elaine Journey, and Johnna Tipton. In turn, they worked hard in moving this manuscript from my various antiquated and modern word processors to their IBM's. While doing this, they kept their eye on my other responsibilities. I am grateful for their help.

I want to tell you something about my wonderful family. My wife of forty-five years, Elizabeth Aron Zaleznik (I call her Bibs) has watched, helped, criticized, edited, and generally helped me learn how to write (not that I feel accomplished in that art). She never lost interest in what I was doing even while she pursued her own career as a school psychologist and administrator. It was my lucky day in 1943, when I arrived at Alma College in Michigan and met this beautiful, gracious woman for whom the glass of life has always been half-full. My daughter, Dori Zaleznik, M.D., besides being a gifted physician, teacher, and clinical researcher in infectious diseases, has shown me by her example of thoughtfulness, decisiveness, courage, and commitment, what it means to take responsibility. I love her dearly! My son, Ira Zaleznik, J.D., early on taught me the virtues of deliberativeness, care, and knowing one's own mind. As a litigator, he makes me proud, especially in carrying out his vow never to lose a case for lack of preparation. I forgive him for beating me so badly as a youngster in our chess games, and for never having taught me how to swing a golf club properly. My daughter-in-law Janet has added so much sweetness and warmth to our family, she is a joy to us all. My grandson, Daniel, soon to be followed by others, is my treasure. He is about to experience what we psychoanalysts, with a sigh of recognition, regard as one of life's travails in being displaced by newly arrived siblings. Daniel, don't worry! With your Zayda's policy of how to raise grandchildren (bribe them!) you'll soon learn the art of creating opportunity.

Finally, I owe a lot to the Harvard Business School and thank the Dean, John H. McArthur, for the School's support over the years. I don't imagine there are many professional schools with the courage to allow me to pursue my life's work, which didn't exactly mesh smoothly with the agenda of this venerable institution.

I'll sign off now and let you turn to Chapter 1. I'll return with a "PS" after you've finished this book. If you want to sneak a look at this postscript beginning on page 226 before you read the book, it's OK with me.

Sincerely yours,

Abraham Zaleznik

Palm Beach, Florida
January 1990

WHERE FREUD FITS

Psychoanalysis, a theory and therapy of the mind, ranks among the most significant contributions to knowledge in the twentieth century. Only rarely is it possible to link a watershed in man's understanding of himself with the work of a single individual. But such is the case with psychoanalysis and its discoverer, Sigmund Freud.

Informed and intelligent people have a number of reasons for attending to the observations and theories of psychoanalysis. First, psychoanalysis has had a profound impact on psychiatry and medicine on the understanding and treatment of mental illness. Second, from it, a theory of the mind has evolved that has altered academic psychology, particularly in its approach to human motivation and development. Third, psychoanalysis has shaped Western civilization during the last fifty years. Literature and the arts, philosophy, history, and the social sciences of the twentieth century bear the imprint of the psychoanalytic perspective. Indeed, the impact of Freudian psychoanalysis on Western culture has been likened to that of Copernican and Darwinean findings. Copernicus discovered that the earth is not the center of the universe. Darwin demonstrated that man, rather than being a distinctly unique species, is part of an evolutionary chain. Freud transformed man's image from the predominantly rational being sixteenth- and seventeenth-century philosophers had supposed him to be to a multifaceted being governed by a range of irrational forces over which he struggles for control. In this discovery Freud, together with Copernicus and Darwin, undermined man's sense of grandiosity.

Psychoanalysis changed medicine, psychology, and culture. These three contributions secured a position in history for Freud and psy-

CHAPTER

1

choanalysis. Another contribution may yet be realized in the further application of psychoanalysis to the professions. Among the professions, the practice of management and leadership have much to gain from the applications of psychoanalytic thought.

Leadership concerns people. It consists of the art of motivating people to apply their talents and best efforts to secure desired goals. Leadership therefore is also concerned with the context of human action—with the promises and demands of organizations. The applications of leadership arts occur most frequently in formal organizations. The basis for understanding these organizations begins with a working knowledge of human characteristics. Only from such a base is it possible to consider the transactions between individuals and organizations and between leaders and followers.

The purpose of this book is to present to people in positions of power and authority a statement of the observations and theories of psychoanalytic psychology. While it will take all of this book to provide the information the reader wants as an introduction to the main concepts, theories, and observations of psychoanalysis, the remainder of this first chapter will construct a bridge that will enable those in executive roles to visualize what they can legitimately expect from psychoanalytic knowledge and its implications for their thinking and practice.

Executives readily accept the proposition that their role involves relationships with other people. In fact, the most common definition of the executive's job is getting things done through people. What is less clearly understood is the fact that executives use beliefs about human nature to guide their organizational actions and decisions. The beliefs can range from very sophisticated ideas about human motivation to fantasies that resemble wishful thinking. Individuals cannot act without bringing into play their beliefs, both conscious and unconscious, about human nature and motivation.

The rationale for this book is to present a systematic view of human beings, one based upon careful observation, as a possible substitute for the unsystematic layers of ideas that arise intuitively as a result of personal experience. There is some reason to believe that these layers of ideas, often unexamined, contain as many inaccurate notions as correct ones. It would therefore seem to serve the executive well to examine an exceptionally comprehensive and intellectually rigorous theory of mind and personality as a means of looking more closely at and possibly revising conceptions that have come to dominate his or her own thinking.

Once accepting the proposition that it is potentially valuable to examine and reconsider conceptions of the mind, the question arises: Why choose a psychoanalytic perspective and not some other? Or, perhaps better yet, why not present a survey of various theories of the mind and allow the reader to consider alternatives, and possibly to select from among them a combination that may be personally satisfying?

A survey of theories of the mind is useful, particularly for beginning students or as an introduction to the study of personality. For more experienced people, however, whether students or executives, surveys are less than satisfying. They tend to repeat material already learned elsewhere, or to discourage attempts to gain relative mastery of a body of knowledge. Intensive work using one general theory also encourages careful evaluation both of problems the theory attempts to resolve and the relative success in solving those problems. For the intended audience of this book—executives and students in professional schools of management—intensive investigation has another advantage. It helps to overcome the tendency to use popular ideas as easy answers to complex problems. Such a practice on the part of professional people is dangerous and misleading, particularly where the object of attention is people and their relationships.

Executives should be equipped intellectually to distinguish among descriptive, explanatory, prescriptive, and ideological theories. Most expositions on management and human relationships contain a mixture of all types of theory. As a result, they are less than satisfying. It pays to be conservative in dealing with ideas—that is, to exert care in understanding and evaluating theories and the observations underlying them. Intensive investigation of one general theory helps cultivate this approach. People who hold positions of power and responsibility should have sound knowledge of theories and findings about human nature. They should also be capable of evaluating these ideas in relation to their intuitive reactions and experience.

The psychoanalytic view of the individual is based on four major premises: (1) that all behavior is determined; (2) that unconscious mental life is an important determinant of behavior; (3) that the world outside the individual is represented internally and these internal representations, together with internally generated impulses, lead to behavior; and (4) that the past determines present behavior for the individual. The use of the term "behavior" in these four premises, and throughout this book, means not only visible actions but also thinking and feeling that may be evident only to the individual and not to other people.

PREMISE 1: DETERMINISM

The concept of determinism signifies that an individual's behavior is a result of a variety of forces not necessarily within the individual's awareness, let alone control. The conceptual opposite of determinism is free will. This means the individual has control, and even unlimited control in the extreme, over his actions. Are free will, in the form of choice, and determinism contradictory? If they are contradictory and if the premise of determinism is central to psychoanalytic psychology, then it would seem that this psychology would be of limited interest and value to people concerned with action.

Let us assume that individuals have free will and that how they behave is a function of their choice, subject to imposed restraints. If one follows this premise, then the only way to explain behavior is to deal with the calculus of choice. This assumption is close to the rationalist's position, which depends upon one other assumption: that people behave in such a way as to maximize gain (or pleasure) and to minimize cost (or pain). But note that the free will premise, framed according to the principle of rationality, also implies causality: the rational individual weighs costs and benefits and arrives at a calculation.

The deterministic exploration of what causes behavior is directed at how individuals perceive these costs and benefits and how they calculate the net effects of actions. If an observer perceives that an individual is not acting in his or her best interests (as in the case of a person who is phobic and thereby restricts life activities to ward off improbable dangers), one could reach two conclusions: either the individual is acting irrationally, or there are considerations not perceptible or comprehensible to the observer. The notion of irrationality, in turn, suggests random action or action that cannot be explained by ideas in the mind of the observer.

From a perspective based on explanation, it is best to avoid framing discussion of behavior in terms of random or chance occurrence. Using this premise—anything I don't understand occurs randomly or by chance—inquiry would be foreclosed. However, by accepting the distinction between rational and irrational behavior according to the criterion of maximizing pleasure and minimizing pain, it may still be possible to explain the so-called irrational behavior. That is to say, the irrational behavior is "determined" or caused by a complex of motives not yet comprehended by either the observer or the individual actor. We are then in the position where we must continue to inquire before we are able to comprehend. In order to inquire it helps to assume that behavior is determined.

At this point let us enter a modification of the notion of determinism or causality. Caution would suggest that it will seldom be possible to link a specific motive with a particular action. It might be possible to link simple cause and effect in the case of animal experiments where, for example, one establishes conditions such that the animal is not rewarded unless it performs a particular act. In the case of the human being, it would appear improbable to follow the same approach. It is true that an individual eats because he is hungry, but what he eats, where he eats, and with whom are subjects of further inquiry. Actions are surrounded by a complex of motives; and consequent behavior, we assume, is a result of more than one motive. To put this assumption another way; any given action is a result of a compromise among a variety of motives, and the gains resulting from behavior are attributed to multiple motives.

PREMISE 2: UNCONSCIOUS MOTIVATION

To work within the premise of determinism and the multiplicity of motives, we must deal with the problem of awareness, or lack of awareness. If an individual were totally aware of the causes of his or her behavior, without necessarily ascribing total control over an array of actions, it would be relatively easy to work within the deterministic premise. Behavior then would be viewed as being caused by the motives the actor attaches to his or her actions. But suppose an individual cannot attribute motives to those actions, as, for example, when he or she forgets an important date and misses an appointment. If the person were questioned about it, the response would probably be that he does not know why he forgot, and he might indicate how mortified he felt by the memory lapse. This example could lead us back to the notion of random events and chance occurrence: the missed appointment was an unlucky event. Another approach is to suggest that the behavior was caused, but by motives that lie outside the awareness of the actor. Here we assume that behavior is caused by unconscious motives. The only basis for making such a weighted assumption is that the evidence demands it.

      The premise of determinism may be made for logical purposes, but the premise of unconscious motivation requires a foundation in observation and facts. Abundant evidence existing for the premise of unconscious motivation will be described in chapters 2 and 3. But once the evidence is accepted, the basis for the premise is established, leading to further observations that would otherwise be unavailable.

PREMISE 3: THE INTRAPSYCHIC POINT OF VIEW

Individuals are confronted with two kinds of reality: first, the reality that the external world presents; and second, the reality of the inner world. External reality, while seemingly objective, is colored by the perceptions of the individual. Objectivity concerning the real world should not be taken for granted. Rather, because it is mediated constantly by the way individuals take in and use their perceptions of the real world, it is to be under continual scrutiny. The inner or psychic reality of the individual is the aggregate of all the sensations connected with the stimulation that arises within the mind and body of the individual. The most important aspect of inner stimulation occurs in connection with bodily need and impulses.

The intrapsychic point of view in psychoanalysis establishes the inner world of the individual as the locus of investigation. This perspective does not neglect or diminish the importance of external reality. It simply denotes that the frame of reference is the individual and that observations occur in relation to what goes on under the skin, so to speak. Much of the inner reality that interests us is unconscious mental activity. The individual has little or no awareness of its content. This content also involves conflicting motives. Individual action can thus be viewed as a consequence of one's best efforts to mediate among conflicting forces generated both from within and from the environment. But once again, the forces generated from outside are taken in and responded to from within the existing state of this inner world.

PREMISE 4: *THE PAST DETERMINES THE PRESENT*

The fourth premise underlying psychoanalytic theory is that present behavior is determined by the past. The power of this premise lies in its relation to the intrapsychic point of view. The past determines the present in individual behavior because the individual retains all the residues of past experience. In this way, current stimuli acting upon the individual from external reality combine with the residue of the past to establish the motivational set that determines how the person will act. Notice that there is no implication that the residue of the past will be or should be available to consciousness; memory of the past may be, and frequently is, unconscious. How can the past be outside of awareness and yet determine behavior? This, of course, is a question central to psychoanalytic theory and inquiry.

As with the premises of unconscious motivation and the intrapsychic point of view, the premise that the past determines present behavior results from empirical observation. It is not a logical premise in the same sense that the premise of determinism is. In this context, logic signifies the postulation of a premise for purposes of making inferences. The value of this logical premise is established in the verification of the inferences derived from the set of empirically derived premises. By assuming that all behavior is determined and is not a result of chance, what appears inexplicable is a result of inadequate observation and interpretation since, for purposes of exploration, we assume that behavior is caused and therefore can be explained.

This book is organized into ten chapters in addition to this introduction. Chapter 2 presents information on the life of Sigmund Freud and the paths he followed in arriving at his major discoveries of the causes of mental illnesses, the workings of the unconscious, and the nature of individual development. Since the observations on unconscious mental life are so basic to psychoanalytic psychology, chapter 3 presents both observations and the theory of the unconscious. Chapter 4 describes the neuroses, with detailed material on the phenomena of symptoms and how they are manifested. Chapter 5 explains symptom formation as a compromise of forces in conflict within the psyche and also as a new version of conflict experienced in earlier stages of life, especially the formative years of infancy and childhood. Chapter 6 provides a detailed view of psychological development from infancy through adulthood, with emphasis on the shifts that occur in instinctual drives and relationships with others. Chapter 7 considers the concept of defense and describes the role of mechanisms of defense in neuroses as well as in development.

Chapter 8 focuses on the psychoanalytic theory of groups and the relation between individual and group psychology. Chapter 9 broadens the focus of the theory beyond groups to large organizations and to society. Chapter 10 delineates the connections between psychoanalysis and the problems of power, authority, and leadership. Chapter 11, the concluding chapter, addresses the role that psychoanalysis can play in changing organizations.

SIGMUND FREUD AND THE ORIGINS OF PSYCHOANALYSIS

It has become fashionable in recent years to describe Freud's psychoanalytic theory as outmoded, elitist and sexist, and based on work with abnormal patients whose neuroses reveal little about normal behavior. Such criticism, by no means restricted to the present, overlooks the fact that Freud arrived at his theories, often with great reluctance and resistance, only after years of being confronted with the compelling evidence offered to him both by the patients he treated and his daily observations and reflections upon the human condition.

By his own admission, Freud had a powerful predilection for "speculative abstractions" and often feared that he would be mastered by them. He thus consciously and carefully aligned himself with objectivity, observation, and the discipline of a natural scientist.

The debate over the issue of whether psychoanalysis is a science continues. Within the field of psychoanalysis itself practitioners argue about the theory. Some claim the indivisible nature of the theory; others adopt the position that parts of the theory are useful while other parts are speculative, if not unsound. Some philosophers of science criticize psychoanalysis on the grounds that its propositions do not lend themselves to experimental test and cannot therefore be verified. Freud's own opinion is worth noting:

> I have repeatedly heard it said contemptuously that it is impossible to take a science seriously whose most general concepts are as lacking in precision as those of libido and of instinct in psychoanalysis. But this reproach rests on a complete miscon-

ception of the facts. Clear basic concepts and sharply drawn definitions are only possible in the mental sciences in so far as the latter seek to fit a region of facts into the frame of a logical system. In the natural sciences of which psychology is one, such clear-cut general concepts are superfluous and indeed impossible. Zoology and Botany did not start from correct and adequate definitions of an animal and a plant; to this very day biology has been unable to give any certain meaning to the concept of life.... The basic ideas or most general concepts in any of the disciplines of science are always left indeterminate at first and are only explained to begin with by reference to the realm of phenomena from which they were derived; it is only by means of progressive analysis of the material of observation that they can be made clear and can find a significant and consistent meaning. I have always felt it as a gross injustice that people have refused to treat psychoanalysis like any other science. This refusal found an expression in the raising of the most obstinate objections. Psychoanalysis was constantly reproached for its incompleteness and insufficiencies; though it is plain that a science based upon observation has no alternative but to work out its findings piecemeal and to solve its problems step by step.[1]

Freud's unique background as well as the cultural and intellectual milieu in which he lived had important effects on his ideas and the way in which he arrived at them. His theory and method thus can only be understood in their historic context.

Sigmund Freud was born on May 6, 1856, in Freiberg, Austria (now Pribor, Czechoslovakia). He died in London on Sept. 23, 1939. When Freud began his life the Crimean War, which changed the balance of power in Europe and led inexorably to World War I, had just ended; Charles Darwin was writing his *The Origin of Species,* which he reluctantly and with grave misgivings finally published in 1859; and Karl Marx celebrated his 38th birthday. When Freud's life ended, Great Britain was on the verge of declaring war on Germany. Freud's 83 years thus spanned a period of extraordinary change. Technological discoveries transformed industrial and business life. Science was heralded as the means of unlocking the secrets of nature and alleviating the suffering of mankind even as the fruits of the industrial revolution were shocking the sensibilities of many.

Freud's father, Jacob, was a man of gentle disposition, humor, and free-thinking skepticism. The little evidence available suggests that to his son he was "kindly, affectionate and tolerant, though just and objective."[2] Jacob Freud married twice, and Sigmund Freud was the first son of the second marriage. At birth he was both the youngest sibling in a family of two stepbrothers and the oldest child of the new family. John, the son of the elder of the two stepbrothers, was a year old when his Uncle Sigmund was born. The two children were inseparable companions until Sigmund was three and the Freuds left for Vienna. The older boy was often hard on the younger, and Sigmund tried to respond courageously in a manner befitting his avuncular status. John left a lasting imprint on Freud's early life. They loved and fought each other with such an intensity that John's personality remained "unalterably fixed" in Freud's unconscious memory.[3] An intimate friend and a hated enemy became indispensable to his emotional life, and at times the two were again fused in one person as they had been in his ambivalent relationship with his nephew John.[4]

Freud's mother, Amalie Nathansohn of Vienna, was a woman full of gaiety, spirits, and wit. She unashamedly loved her first born "*goldener* Sigi" more than any of the other eight children who followed him. Freud suffered displacement, jealousy, and then grief and deprivation when Julius, the second son, was born eleven months after his own arrival and then died eight months later. But his mother's adoration for her oldest son counterbalanced these painful losses. Many years later he wrote, "A man who has been the indisputable favorite of his mother keeps for life the feeling of a conqueror, that confidence of success that often induces real success."[5]

In 1859 the warmth, security, and familial confusions of Freud's life in a small Austrian town were ended when Jacob decided that the family must leave. In the 1840s a railroad had been built from Vienna to the north with a bypass around Freiberg. From a flourishing trade center, the town became a declining backwater. The resulting economic dislocation, aggravated by the rise of Czech nationalism, led to the failure of business and the rekindling of anti-Semitism. In the face of this double danger, the Freuds left for Leipzig and then, a year later, for Vienna. The train ride from Freiberg to Leipzig through the blazing gas jets of the industrializing countryside left Freud with a painful phobia of traveling by train that was to last until his self-analysis at the end of the century.

Another reason for going to Vienna was to give Sigmund the best education he could acquire. Well into the twentieth century, children of European upper classes were given a strictly regimented and thorough education based on belief in the power of rationalism and the values of the Enlightenment. Freud's mother and then his father had been his first teachers, and he had shown a remarkable intelligence during those years. His family held his intellect in such esteem that his siblings had to tiptoe through their activities in order not to disturb the young scholar at his studies. His teachers at the gymnasium in Vienna were almost equally impressed by the gifts of this young student. He graduated *summa cum laude* at the age of sixteen, a year ahead of his classmates.[6]

The role of Judaism as faith and ritual in the life of the Freud family is not easily documented, although Freud himself was deeply imbued with his Jewish heritage. Although he only belatedly acknowledged the enduring effect of the Bible on his thinking, even his earliest writings show evidence of it. He knew all the Jewish rituals and customs and showed a more than scholarly interest in his ancestry. The characteristic quality of his interest in speculative thinking and the riddles of the universe suggests that it was nourished by the rabbinical tradition as well as that of the Enlightenment and nineteenth-century rationalism.

On a more mundane level, Freud was acutely sensitive to anti-Semitism in any form. His first great disappointment in his revered father involved an instance of it. When Freud was twelve years old, his father told him that a Gentile had once knocked off his fur cap and shouted at him, "Jew, get off the pavement." The young Freud was indignant and ashamed when his father added that he had complied. When he himself encountered anti-Semitism at the University of Vienna where he was expected to "feel inferior and alien," he refused to do so. He used his enforced isolation as a means of obtaining "a certain degree of independence of judgment."[7]

Freud's Jewishness directly affected his choice of career, since in the Vienna of his day a Jew could only succeed in business, law, or medicine. Although he never felt an attraction to a career as a practicing physician, Freud decided on medicine, hoping thereby to satisfy his research interests.[8]

Given his personality and experience, it is not surprising that Freud found, in 1876, "rest and satisfaction" in a physiology laboratory while pursuing his medical degree. There he worked under the first of his great mentors, Ernst Brucke. Of Brucke, Freud later said, "He carried more weight with me than any one else in my whole life."[9] It was Brucke's intellectual integrity and strict adherence to scientific standards and procedures that first attracted Freud. The two men soon became close friends. Brucke supported Freud at critical points in his career, long after he left the laboratory. They remained friends until Brucke's death. From him Freud learned the rigorous scientific methods he later applied to the study of mental phenomena.

Freud remained at Brucke's Institute for six years, and left it only because of economic necessity. At the age of twenty-six Freud was still depending on support from his aging and financially burdened father. Hopes for an assistantship in Brucke's Institute were unrealistic. Brucke, who was forty years older than Freud and the same age as his father, gently told his friend that he should abandon his theoretical career and stop relying on his father's "generous improvidence."[10] The advice came at a timely moment. Freud had just fallen in love with Martha Bernays and could not marry her until he was self-supporting. Martha's mother and father had endured eight years of being engaged. The young couple had no desire to imitate their example.

Accepting the inevitable, Freud applied for a position at the General Hospital of Vienna. As a junior physician he served in various departments and once again found a mentor of outstanding stature in the person of Theodore Meynert, the distinguished Viennese anatomist. In Meynert's clinic he acquired his first experience in psychiatric work. Freud was again tempted to pursue a theoretical career—this time in cerebral anatomy—but once again financial considerations determined his decision to study nervous diseases. He spent fourteen months in the Department of Nervous Diseases although he was revolted by the condition of the wards and the superintendent's determination to keep costs down by doing as little as possible and restricting the number of patients.

In 1885, with Brucke's enthusiastic support, Freud was awarded a much-coveted traveling bursary. This allowed him to take a step that had profound effects on his future and on the development of psychoanalysis. Freud used the grant to go to Paris to study for four and a half months under the celebrated and somewhat infamous Jean-Marie Charcot—celebrated for his undeniable brilliance and ability; infamous for focusing on the unpopular topic of nervous disorders and taking hysteria and hypnosis seriously. Charcot had made Salpetriere, Paris' ancient and substandard hospital for the care of women, his laboratory. In his memorial tribute to Charcot, Freud described Salpetriere as a "wilderness of paralysis, spasms and convulsions."[11] It was neither a pleasant nor prestigious place to work.

Charcot's method of working was to look at what was before him, to "look and look again at the things he did not understand, to deepen his impression of them day by day, till suddenly an understanding of them dawned on him."[12] This approach frequently brought him into opposition with colleagues who accepted current theories. On one occasion he was criticized by a student for contradicting a newly established theory of considerable merit. Charcot replied, *"La theorie, c'est bon, mais ca n'empeche pas d'exister,"* ("Theory is good, but it doesn't prevent things from existing."),[13] a response that left an indelible mark on Freud's thinking and method.[14]

Freud described Charcot as "a man whose common sense is touched by genius," a compelling combination of qualities for Freud. He soon found himself turning away from neuropathology and toward the newer and less accepted field of psychopathology. Until Charcot began his study of hysterical patients, hysteria was thought to be either female malingering, undeserving of a respectable physician's attention, or a special disorder of the womb, correctable by the administration of the odor of herb or by extirpation of the clitoris. Charcot dismayed the medical world by using hypnosis to bring on artificial hysteria that mimicked spontaneous hysteria in every detail. His recognition of male hysteria aroused the utmost scorn and ire.

Freud absorbed most of Charcot's methods and discoveries. One particular remark of the neurologist, made in passing, lay dormant for many years before Freud recognized its significance. Charcot remarked emphatically to one of his assistants that certain nervous disorders are always a question of *"la chose genitale",*[15] an insight the significance of which Freud later felt even Charcot did not understand. Charcot's influence on Freud was unquestionably and immeasurably huge. Freud was always happy to acknowledge his indebtedness to the great neurologist. It was otherwise with Dr. Josef Breuer, whose influence on Freud began before he left for Paris and ended in a final break between the two men in 1896.

Freud had met Breuer in Brucke's Institute in the 1870s. The two men became close friends and colleagues. Breuer, fourteen years older than Freud and already an established and highly respected Viennese physician, relieved Freud's chronic poverty with frequent and generous loans. Shortly before Freud left for Paris, Breuer had confided to him an extraordinary case he had been treating for hysteria. It was the case of Fraulein "Anna O.," the remarkably intelligent Viennese woman, Bertha Pappenheim. Having cared for her father during the prolonged illness that preceded his death, she developed an array of severe symptoms after he died: her limbs became paralyzed; her sight and speech were disturbed; she had anxiety attacks, terrifying hallucinations, and suicidal impulses; and eventually she was unable to take any nourishment. Anna O. fluctuated between her "normal" self and a "bad" self. Her experiences during the transition between these states excited Breuer's interest in the case. In the late afternoons Anna O. would fall into a somnolent state, followed by a deeper sleep she called "clouds," and then a hypnotic state. In the final hypnotic phase, she began to verbalize her torments and hallucinations. In the aftermath of this period she became calm and could look forward to a day or more of cheerful normality before her symptoms began to return.

Breuer, perceiving the rich possibilities of ameliorating symptoms through verbalization, began to encourage Anna to talk and then augmented her verbalizations by inducing hypnosis. When Anna O. was hypnotized, he led her to talk about the origin of each of her symptoms. To his amazement this caused them to disappear. He referred to the process as "catharsis." Unfortunately the joy of Breuer's discovery was marred by two subsequent developments. First, despite Breuer's persistent belief that the symptoms disappeared, his patient was never entirely cured. The second event concerned Breuer's emotional reactions and was charged with consequences for the development of psychoanalysis.

Breuer became aware of the fact that Anna O. had fallen in love with him. Evidently unable to tolerate and even investigate this fact, Breuer terminated the treatment. He abruptly announced his decision to Anna O., who up to that time had been improving rapidly. Breuer shortly thereafter was summoned to his patient's house with the alarming news that her condition had taken a sudden turn for the worse. Upon observing his patient, Breuer suddenly recognized that she was simulating pregnancy and childbirth and surmised that in her fantasy she was delivering his child. Breuer, who looked upon his patient as being asexual and completely reticent about sexual matters, fled the house.

Fascinated with Breuer's story, Freud tried to interest Charcot in its implications, without success. Charcot continued to use hypnotism to induce rather than alleviate hysterical symptoms. Both hypnotism and catharsis demonstrated that ideas played a powerful role in neuroses. Freud became increasingly aware of the potential importance of the sexual content of these ideas in understanding hysteria and possibly other neuroses. Many years were to pass, however, before Freud could establish the way sexual ideas and feelings resulted in neurotic suffering.

When Freud returned to Vienna in 1885 he resumed his close relationship with Breuer and his wife Matilde. The first sign of a change in Breuer's manner came in the form of an outburst against Freud's approaching marriage. To Freud the four years of his engagement were too long by far; to Breuer they appeared too short. He seemingly resented this sign of independence in his protege. Freud took another step toward independence from his benefactor by accepting his last loan from Breuer nine months before he married Martha Bernays in September of 1886, although the final break was still a decade away. After the marriage the two families maintained their close ties and the Freuds named two of their children after members of the Breuer family.

The two men continued to discuss and exchange ideas on hysteria. In applying Breuer's cathartic technique to his own patients, Freud had discovered that not all patients could be hypnotized and that even in those cases where hypnosis was induced, catharsis was not assured. After pondering the significance of these two facts, Freud began to concentrate his efforts on discovering the bases and mechanisms of all neuroses rather than on removing the symptoms of hysteria. His observations forced him to recognize that sexual factors were repeatedly associated with the onset of a neurosis. Further, he found that different types of sexual problems produced different pictures of neurotic disorders. He used these distinctions as a means of classifying neuroses.

In discussing these issues with Breuer, Freud tried to revive the older man's flagging interest in hysteria with a view to a joint publication of their findings. Breuer remained curiously resistant to the idea until Freud realized that Breuer's reluctance seemed to be associated with his embarrassment and sense of responsibility over the events that terminated the case of Anna O. To reassure him, Freud told him of one of his own patients who had suddenly flung her arms about him at a critical point in the therapy. Freud said the two incidents were examples of transference, the process during psychoanalytic treatment whereby patients develop toward their physicians emotional reactions that reenact their relations with previous love objects. Breuer, apparently reassured and relieved by this explanation, agreed to the joint publication, but differences in scientific ideas and the widening personal rift between the two men made the task a painful one. Freud's "initial satisfaction" with the undertaking turned into "uneasiness." When he wrote to his new friend Wilhelm Fliess, a Berlin physician and biologist, in 1893 to announce the publication of the first joint effort, he said, "It has meant a long battle with my partner." Nevertheless, *Studies in Hysteria* was published in 1895.

The scientific issues that drove Breuer and Freud apart centered around their differences concerning the role of sexuality in creating the intolerable conflicts that produce pathogenic effects. Breuer was ambivalent at best and often completely unwilling to accept Freud's belief that sexual problems were the essential causal factor in a neurosis. He was also disturbed by the conclusions Freud was drawing from his investigations of his patients' sexual lives. Breuer's negative responses to his discoveries became intolerable and Freud turned to Wilhelm Fliess, who had an intense interest in scientific problems.

Freud and Fliess had met in 1877, ironically through Breuer. They were mutually attracted at once and the friendship soon became intense. Fliess was two years younger than Freud and possessed a love of speculation and imaginative intellectual play that Freud tried so hard to control and channel in himself. Fliess set no limits on his own flights of imagination, building an elaborate structure of theory on his discovery of sexual periodicity in men, women, and the universe.

Freud endowed Fliess with even more qualities of insight and brilliance than that unquestionably remarkable man actually possessed in order to turn him into a mentor and much-needed confidant. Fliess thus offered the support that Freud could no longer find from Breuer. Their friendship was approaching its most intense stage in 1896 when Freud made his final break with Breuer. Freud confided to Fliess that he had developed a violent antipathy for his former friend, supporter, and mentor.

Ernest Jones, relying on Freud's letters to Fliess rather than on Freud's later reconstruction of the causes of his differences with Breuer, believed that in the 1890s Freud suffered from a "very considerable psychoneurosis," and that Fliess was essential to him as a means of alleviating his intense suffering, which usually took the form of paralyzing self-doubts. These were also the years during which Freud did his most original work. In 1895 Breuer wrote to Fliess, "Freud's intellect is soaring at its highest. I gaze after him as a hen at a hawk."[16] A year later Freud and Breuer made their final break.

Fliess served as a catalyst for Freud's ideas as well as a source of emotional support. Freud wrote to Fliess in 1895, "one cannot do without people who have the courage to think new things before they are in a position to demonstrate them."[17] But intellectual differences soon began to disturb the closeness of the relationship, and Fliess' inability to tolerate criticism of any sort might have led to their final break in 1900. By this time Freud had found a new source of strength in himself. In 1897 he had begun the painful and difficult process of analyzing his own unconscious. He had no precedent to follow, and in the initial stages it drove him even more toward a dependence on Fliess. By the century's close, however, Freud reached an emotional and intellectual maturity that remained with him permanently. An important offshoot of his own psychoanalysis was his massive work, *The Interpretation of Dreams,* published in 1900.

Relieved of his overwhelming need for mentors and the repeated reenactment of the love-hate relationship of his childhood, Freud began to consolidate his ideas and hypotheses into a theory of psychoanalysis. Since his ideas were radical, unconventional, and often shocking to his colleagues, he needed to support them with convincing evidence. To provide supporting evidence for his hypotheses and discoveries, Freud wrote a series of case studies that presented at least a small portion of his vast reservoir of observations and findings. But to write the case studies meant overcoming unusually formidable obstacles.

First, there was the problem of confidentiality. Freud knew that his patients would not speak openly of their most closely guarded secrets if they feared their intimacies might one day become public property. In addition, the closely knit fabric of Viennese life required that he disguise perfectly the identity of the patients whose cases he wished to use. Paradoxically, he found that it was "far easier to divulge the patient's most intimate secrets than the most innocent and trivial facts about him; for, whereas the former would not throw light on his identity, the latter by which he was generally recognized, would make it obvious to every one."[18] Yet it was precisely these trivial details that were of great importance for the intelligibility and coherence of the material.

Second, the kind of material that Freud elicited by prodding his patients' psyches was both extremely complex and highly unusual. The most significant matters arose from the unconscious—a level of the mind dismissed entirely, or at best considered suspect, by most of his medical colleagues. Moreover, the materials supplied by his patients alternately revealed the past and present, the conscious and unconscious, fact and fiction. Many of their verbalizations were contradictory and were cloaked in varying forms such as dreams, fantasies, memories, associations, and symptoms. The meaning of these multifaceted materials could only be discovered through an equally complex and unusual form of analysis.

Third, the analyst was not an objective observer and reporter. Rather, he was the object of intense feelings on the part of the patient and had to examine with care his own reactions to each patient. Freud often presented in his written cases this interplay as a combat of wills by which he tried to convince his patients and his readers that the knowledge and technique of psychoanalysis could explain and remove neurotic disorders. Freud also used the theme of combat of wills as a literary device with an eye on the reading audience. To write in a reasonably compact and readable format, Freud compressed and synthesized in his case studies an overabundance of materials collected over many months and years; he countered or anticipated attacks on the credibility of his technique and theory; and he interpolated theoretical remarks, general comments, historical and other digressions, and suggestions for further investigation.

What Freud had to leave out was equally dismaying. He wrote at one point to Fliess:

> It is a regrettable fact that no account of psychoanalysis can reproduce the impressions received by the analyst as he conducts it, and the final sense of conviction can never be obtained from reading about it but only from directly experiencing it.[19]

It took all of Freud's considerable literary powers to overcome these obstacles and weave the diverse components into an exposition that served his many purposes, while remaining convincing, readable, and interesting. He found he could not use a straightforward narrative form or, to use his words, "Linear presentation is not a very adequate means of describing complicated mental processes going on in different layers of the mind."[20] He sometimes despaired of finding an adequate form, writing to Jung in 1909, "How bungling are our attempts to reproduce an analysis; how pitifully we tear to pieces these great works of art Nature has created in the mental sphere."[21]

But he persisted in his efforts and eventually published six lengthy case histories. That he was keenly aware of their limitations in serving as scientific evidence is apparent in many of his passing remarks. In the introduction to his case on obsessional neurosis, he wrote:

> The crumbs of knowledge offered in these pages, though they have been laboriously enough collected, may not in themselves prove very satisfying; but they may serve as a starting point for the work of other investigators, and the common endeavor may bring the success which is perhaps beyond the reach of individual effort.[22]

Freud adjusted the written presentation of the six cases to the neurosis, subject, circumstances, and purposes of each situation; in general, however, they followed a similar pattern. Each began with an introduction, comprised of comments on the technical difficulties of the particular case, his primary and secondary purposes in presenting it, and brief remarks on his method and theoretical assumptions. This was followed by a presentation of the clinical picture, interlaced with biographical and other materials, and an analysis of the case. He ended his cases with a discussion that might touch again on matters of theory, with supporting arguments for his points or whatever seemed in need of further investigation. A brief description of the purpose and special characteristics of each of these six cases will shed some light on how this general format and aims were realized in practice.

Dora (1905) was the first case Freud published after developing his free association technique. He began his treatment of Dora in 1900, the year that he published *The Interpretation of Dreams,* but vacillated for five years before allowing it to be published. His hesitation was apparently due to professional discretion as well as to his fears that the case might provoke undue scandal or criticism. Moreover, it was merely a fragment of a case, since Dora had broken off the treatment abruptly after only three months, a circumstance Freud explained as being due to his failure to master her transference to him of emotions she originally directed toward her father. As a result, the treatment was unsuccessful and the picture of her disorder incomplete.

Nevertheless Freud felt this case merited publication because it showed, however imperfectly, the internal structure of a case of hysteria and, more important, "how dream interpretation is woven into the history of a treatment, and how it can become the means of filling in amnesias and elucidating symptoms."[23] Freud used his "Postscript" to the case to discuss the theoretical and practical implications of transference.

His *Analysis of a Phobia in a Five-Year-Old Boy,* known familiarly as the "Little Hans Case" (1909), is unusual in that information was elicited from the small patient by the father, under Freud's tutelage. Little Hans' father had kept a record of the development of his cheerful and amiable child from the age of three, coming to Freud when the child was five with the disturbing news that his son had developed a phobia preventing him from leaving the house: Hans feared that a horse would bite him if he ventured on the street. The two men thus became partners in their joint effort to relieve Hans of his fear and were eventually successful in their endeavors.

The case was of special interest to Freud since it illustrated both theory and technique. It supported his hypothesis regarding the existence and importance of infantile sexuality and it illustrated the way in which a phobia, identified by Freud as a symptom that forms part of a neurosis, can develop. Its major significance in regard to technique was related to the part played by suggestion in determining the course of the analysis. In the case of Hans, who often had to have help from his father to verbalize his thoughts and feelings, the hypothesis that suggestion played a major role seemed plausible. Freud, however, argued that there were many instances in which Hans had shown considerable independence in his ideas. To cap this argument he confessed he deliberately omitted telling Hans' father that the child would approach the subject of childbirth by way of talking about the excretory function, a prediction based on Freud's previous analytic experience. Hans, without any hints or promptings from his uninformed father, fulfilled Freud's expectations and thus innocently offered confirmation of this hypothesis.

Freud's third case, *Notes on a Case of Obsessional Neurosis,* or "The Rat Man" (1909), was also a fragmentary case, due to the medical discretion in this instance rather than incomplete analysis. It is unique among the cases in that Freud's original notes, recorded on a daily basis, were found in his papers after his death. Their subsequent publication thus allows the reader insight into the processes by which Freud chose, condensed, and organized the materials into a case study. Freud modestly remarks in his "Introduction" that the case allows him to make "some disconnected statement of an aphoristic character upon the genesis and finer psychological mechanisms of obsessional processes."[24]

The case shows Freud's free association method in its purest form. Initially it was only when his patient showed resistance that Freud interrupted his monologue of free associations to remind him that "overcoming resistances was a law of treatment."[25] Later he offered his patient some principles of psychoanalytic theory, interpretations of obsessional ideas, and conclusions regarding the precipitating cause of the neurosis in order to elicit and test his patient's reactions.

Freud's *Psychoanalytic Notes on an Autobiographical Account of a Case of Paranoia,* or "The Schreber Case" (1911), is noteworthy because the source of the materials analyzed by Freud was an autobiographical memoir published in 1903. The author, Dr. jur. Daniel Paul Schreber, once a presiding judge on the Court of Appeals in Germany, wrote, in the interests of scientific and religious truths, an account of the incapacitating mental illness that led to his being discharged from his duties and being treated for many years in an asylum. The memoir was a valuable source because, as Freud said in his introduction, access to patients suffering from paranoia was possible at the time only to analysts attached to public institutions, and that such patients had the useful but unusual peculiarity of disclosing, in a distorted form, what other patients tend to keep carefully secret.

Freud used the materials in the memoir to present a picture and analysis of paranoia, as well as to present some ideas that he was to explore in greater detail in later years, including comments on repression, the nature of the instincts, and narcissism. In his "Postscript" he remarked that the case might well "serve to show that Jung had excellent grounds for his assertion that mythopoeic forces of mankind are not extinct."

When Freud wrote his next case, *From the History of an Infantile Neurosis,* or "The Wolfman" (1918), he was already deeply involved in a controversy with Carl Jung and Alfred Adler, two of his most devoted followers, that soon led to a final rift. Freud used the case to argue against divergences he felt were incompatible with the principles of psychoanalysis.

"The Wolfman" allowed Freud to trace the origins of his patient's current and severe neurotic symptoms back to an infantile neurosis. It permitted him to study infantile neurosis without the limitations imposed by Little Hans' inability to verbalize easily and to follow its erratic development into adulthood. Even Freud found many of the details related to him by this patient to be extraordinary and incredible, but he was delighted that they confirmed so many of his hypotheses about infantile sexuality. He concluded that the precipitant of the original neurosis was his patient's observation of his parents' sexual intercourse at the age of one and a half, which had led to an overwhelming fear of being devoured (seduced) by his father, a fear that took the form of being afraid he would be eaten by a wolf. The patient had long forgotten this "primal scene," as it was later called, but it had left an indelible mark on his life, leading him to build and rebuild complicated defenses against a strong homosexual tendency that had been stimulated by the incident. Freud also considered issues such as memory of events and fantasy in the infantile neurosis in presenting this elaborate, difficult, and important case.

Freud's sixth and last case, *The Psycho-genesis of a Case of Homosexuality in a Woman* (1920), was far simpler in form and content. Its outstanding characteristic stemmed from the fact that the patient submitted herself to treatment only to please her parents and had no desire to be "cured." Freud used the case to discuss ego eroticism, or narcissism, and the determinants and characteristics of various forms of homosexuality.

The case studies formed the core of observation upon which Freud constructed a psychoanalytic psychology. The method employed to elicit these observations—psychoanalysis—involved the cooperation of patient and psychoanalyst in an effort to alleviate the pain and suffering resulting from psychological conflict.

During the years 1915 to 1917 Freud gave a series of lectures on psychoanalysis to an audience composed mainly of medical students of the University of Vienna. Aware that he had a particularly skeptical audience and one that expected to be able to see the phenomena with which they were dealing, Freud introduced his subject by speaking of the difficulties his audience would confront in believing in psychic phenomena. He placed part of the responsibility for the inability to comprehend the unseen on their training, which always focused their attention on the observable aspects of anatomy, physics, chemistry, and biology and never on the psychical life "in which, after all, the achievements of this marvelously complex organism reaches its peak." Then characteristically, he disarmed his listeners by saying that their next difficulty was the fault of psychoanalysis itself, for two of the hypotheses on which it was based "are an insult to the entire world and have earned its dislike. One of them offends against an intellectual prejudice, the other against an aesthetic and moral one."[26] The first hypothesis states that a large portion of mental processes are unconscious; the second is the assertion that sexual impulses, both in the narrower and wider sense of the word, play an extremely large part in the causation of nervous and mental diseases.

These two hypotheses lay at the heart of the problem Freud faced in developing a method. He needed to find a technique capable of eliciting from a subject information that he or she did not even recognize as existing. Moreover, the source of such information was not localizable. Only a few scientists at the end of the nineteenth century were willing to postulate its existence, although the concept had enjoyed some popularity earlier. Finally, the elicited material, which took the form of thoughts, feelings, attitudes, internalized objects, dreams, fantasies, was meaningless without interpretation.

Breuer's cathartic technique had provided limited access to such materials and had shown dramatic therapeutic effects. These effects were explained as arising from the discharge of emotional energies that previously had been "strangulated" and thus appeared in the distorted form of symptoms. Once the discharge, or "abreaction," of this energy took place through verbalization, the symptoms disappeared. But Freud found that the cathartic method affected only the symptoms. It failed to get at the root of the patient's neurotic disorder, which he believed arose from the whole network of underlying and interlocking ideas and emotions. Oddly enough, one of the difficulties with the cathartic method was that it worked too easily; hypnosis allowed patients to bypass their normal control over painful matters that had been deeply buried.

More important therapeutically and theoretically than abreaction was the investigation of resistances to unconscious materials. Once this network of underlying unconscious emotions was revealed, it could be replaced with conscious acts of judgment that recognized and then either accepted or condemned what had formerly been repressed.[27]

After some experimentation with alternative techniques for carrying out this type of investigation, Freud adopted the method of simply asking his patients to lie on a couch in a comfortable position free from distractions and try to say whatever came to mind, without censorship or selection. In listening to his patients' associations under these conditions, Freud noted gaps in their narratives. He believed they were caused by selective amnesia, and he directed his patients' attention and concentration to filling them in. The patients then became anxious and uncomfortable and energetically resisted the unwelcome memories. By examining the form such resistance took, he found he could begin to construct the pattern of the underlying conflicts.

He soon discovered that these patterns revealed themselves in an even more illuminating way when patients began to transfer to the physician the emotional attachments they had originally established with their parents or other intimates. To demonstrate to his patients that these networks of emotions and patterns of response appeared in their resistances in the transference, in every new relationship they established, and even in the most trivial aspects of their lives, Freud had to interpret them. This "art of interpretation" drew upon the theoretical system Freud had constructed over many years of clinical work. In making his interpretations, Freud did not simply throw hypothetical constructs at the back of his patients' reclining heads. Rather, he used his hypotheses to guide his own observations of the emerging materials, to point out and explain determinants that his patients failed to recognize, and, in some cases, to question his patients on particular points.

Freud, as earlier mentioned, had a penchant for imaginative speculation and metapsychological theorizing. Reading about Freud's complex and closely interwoven theory without access to the mass of his unrecorded cases and without working through some 600 papers and books in which he recorded his observations and interpretations, a reader might be tempted to believe that Freud indulged in his bent for speculation while constructing his theory. Certainly as early as 1916, and especially after 1923 when Freud's life was first threatened by the cancer that eventually killed him, he went through what he himself called "a phase of regressive development." During these last years of his life his interest returned to questions that had fascinated him from an early age. He had set them aside in order to make a "life long detour through the natural sciences, medicine and psychotherapy."[28] But Freud's theory was almost completely formed before that date and was therefore the end result of his strictly controlled and disciplined "detour."

Some of the elements of Freud's thinking that create the greatest difficulty for modern-day readers seeking to understand his theory consist of the residues in his thought of the scientific and philosophical beliefs of his century. Freud attributed his decision to go to medical school to the impact of Goethe's "Fragment on Nature." That acknowledgment was only one of many that Freud and his contemporaries made regarding the powerful sway that Goethe and the German Romantic movement, which included such disparate and individualistic thinkers as Hegel, Lamarck, and Kant, held over their early education. As a school of thought it can be characterized briefly by its adherents' belief that they possessed the key to the secrets of nature in the form of "speculative physics." They believed in a nonmaterial vital force, not subject to investigation, which controlled the activities of the organism; they held that Nature is one vast organism made up of forces in constant conflict; and they often expressed their beliefs in a highly emotional, mystical language. In medicine, the beliefs of *Naturphilosophie* led to reforms in the direction of optimistic and compassionate care of the ill and insane.[29]

Before the middle of the nineteenth century a reaction against these romantic notions of nature and science was forming. Brucke was a member of the small group in Germany that began an emotionally charged crusade against the ideas of *Naturphilosophie*. Members of this group took a pledge to do all in their power to demonstrate the truth that "no other forces than the common physio-chemical ones are active in the organism" and that these were "reducible to the force of attraction and repulsion."[30]

The most prominent member of this circle, which soon constituted itself as the Berlin Society of Physicists, was Hermann Helmholtz. Helmholtz is probably best known for his formulation of the law of conservation of energy, which he presented to the group as a contribution to physiology. Helmholtz attacked the *Naturphilosophie* belief in a transcendental vitality with such violence that it suggests he was tearing out the roots of his own earlier conviction. In place of a vital force controlling the organism, he saw organic functioning as a matter of energy transfer and used classical mechanics to describe its operation.

The quantitative, mechanistic, materialistic, and deterministic concepts of this group of physicalistic biologists dominated the teaching of the University of Vienna during the years Freud was associated with it. He was strongly attracted by their ideas and called Helmholtz, whom he regretted never meeting, one of his idols. In an 1892 footnote to one of his published works, Freud revealed that he himself had had the temerity to interrupt the great Charcot with the comment, *"That cannot be possibly so; it contradicts the theory of Young-Helmholtz,"* which evoked Charcot's memorable comment, mentioned earlier, *"La theorie, c'est bon, mais ca n'empeche pas d'exister."*[31]

Evolution, in its Darwinian formulation, was the other great concept of the second half of the nineteenth century. Belief in Lamarckian evolutionary theory had been a part of *Naturphilosophie*. The new school, however, rejected Larmarckian ideas in favor of an approach that shared many of the beliefs of the Helmholtzian circle. Rejecting any notions of vital forces, essences, and transcendental purpose, the new theorists interpreted evolutionary development in terms of physical energies. In addition, they emphasized that the phenomena of life could not be understood without a study of the developmental history of the organism.[32]

Freud was exposed to both these streams of thought—that based on physical energy and that based on organismic development—while working in Brucke's Institute, but it was Meynert who first applied them experimentally in the field of neurology and psychology. Meynert believed that human thought and behavior were governed by inflexible laws, and that our illusion of free will is due only to our ignorance of how such laws operate in controlling the most minute details of the mental processes. One of his favorite phrases was the "mechanics of the brain."

An understanding of these two influential conceptualizations of the nineteenth century is important because Freud made them his own by giving them new meaning and direction. Some acquaintance with their original intent and meaning is also necessary because their residues in Freud's writings were crucial for his own creative purposes. Freud transformed these conceptualizations by following Charcot's advice to "look and look again at the things he did not understand." By so doing, Freud created a theory that, for all its time-bound aspects, transcend the limitations of the original formulations.

In a manuscript that remained lost among Fliess' letters from Freud for fifty years before it was discovered and published as *A Project for a Scientific Psychology,* Freud allows us a glimpse of the process by which he absorbed the ideas of his age, began to transform them for his own purposes, and finally, rather as if he had eaten too rich a dish, turned away on the edge of disillusion. He wrote the manuscript in feverish haste in 1895, the year of his joint publication with Breuer. Shortly after he had begun it and was "positively devoured" by his ambition to "explain something from the center of nature," he wrote to Fliess:

> I am vexed by two intentions: to discover what form the theory of physical functioning will take if a quantitative line of approach, a kind of economics of nervous force, is introduced into it, and, secondly, to extract from psychopathology a yield for normal psychology.[33]

He used all the armor he could muster from the intellectual currents of his time, added his own "imaginings, transpositions and guesses" in an effort to describe quantitatively the impact of the environment on an organism's nervous system and thus discover the determinants of consciousness.

In this manuscript Freud used two general principles to explain the functioning of the neuronal system. The first, the principle of "inertia," states that when the nervous system receives stimuli from the external environment, its primary task is to discharge the quantity of energy carried by the stimulus. This "flight from stimulus" allows the organism to return to a state of inertia. The second principle, that of "constancy," works in relation to the discharge of stimuli received from the interior of the organism—stimuli that give rise to the major needs of hunger, respiration, and sexuality. Unable to withdraw from such stimuli, the organism seeks to restore the lowest possible level of energy through discharge. Freud anticipates many of his later ideas in this essay, which is difficult, abstruse, and lacking in supportive evidence.

While writing the *Project,* Freud was frequently overcome by feelings of elation. "Barriers were suddenly raised, veils fell away," and he felt that he was on the verge of fitting all of his ideas together in a way that would allow him to understand the determinants of consciousness.[34] He sent his hastily composed manuscript off to Fliess in a fever of excitement, but once he had delivered it to the care of Fliess, a reaction set in. Freud returned to an examination of some of the doubts he had about the deficiencies of the idea of abreaction and the quantitative, biological model he had described in this work.

Rather than abandoning the idea of determinism, a central tenet of physical science, he took this principle, which assumes that all natural phenomena can be explained by assembling and ordering facts and constructing a theory encompassing these facts in the most concise manner, a step farther by demonstrating the importance of understanding *psychic* determinism. Psychic determinism assumes that all behavior is motivated and goal directed and that the origin of motives is to be found *within* the organism and not simply in response to external stimuli. The practical consequence of this belief is to take very seriously *all* behavior and not to dismiss what one does not understand because it seems bizarre, idiosyncratic, or unworthy of study.

Through the close observation and careful evaluation of facts, Freud began to realize that his initial theory of neuroses was inadequate to explain the complexity of the mind. In many ways this was a painful process, but in carrying it forward Freud was able to reach a major turning point in the history of psychoanalysis.

His early theory of the etiology of neuroses held that they are caused by the displacement of large amounts of excitation in the unconscious; these sums of excitation are, in turn, the result of holding an undischarged memory of an event in the unconscious. The event can always be traced back to early childhood, even though memory of it is reactivated by experiences in puberty or adulthood. Consequent displacements take the form of symptoms, which are attempts at dissipating noxious memories. Such displacements are never successful since they carry the excitation along abnormal paths. Further, Freud had been convinced by his clinical experience that traumatic childhood experiences involved sexual seduction, usually in perverse forms, by a parent or other grown-up person.[35]

Freud at first found it difficult to accept that such a large number of these incidents occurred in the lives of his bourgeois patients, but he believed his patients' dreadful tales. Later he explained his credulity by pleading that "this was a time when I was intentionally keeping my critical faculties in abeyance so as to preserve an unprejudiced and receptive attitude toward the many novelties which were coming to my notice every day."[36] In his own self-analysis, undertaken in reaction to his father's death in 1896, Freud uncovered seduction memories of his own. Recognizing the impossibility of such an event in his own childhood, he was compelled to consider the possibility that other tales of seduction were equally unreal. His discovery that this was often the case and that fantasized seductions could produce later neuroses struck at the heart of his original theory.

At first Freud felt "helpless bewilderment" in the face of his finding and was tempted to give up the whole work as Breuer had done.[37] Yet his letter of Sept. 21, 1897, in which he confided to Fliess his uncertainties and their implication for the fate of his theory, ended on a note of muted elation. Somewhat misquoting II Samuel, Freud wrote, "Certainly I shall not tell it in Dan or speak of it in Ashkelon, in the land of the Philistines. But in your eyes and my own I have more the feeling of a victory than a defeat."[38]

Freud soon felt he had no right to despair simply because he had been deceived in his expectations; he merely had to revise those expectations. The new fact that emerged from these reflections was that fantasy is a psychical reality with force equal to that of a real event. He then analyzed the reason for such childhood fantasies and discovered that such fantasies "were intended to cover up the autoerotic activity [usually masturbation] of the first years of childhood, to embellish it and raise it to a higher plane."[39] He came to feel he was on the right track at last and that he had been saved from an error that might have had "fatal consequences" for his life's work.[40]

Yet eight years were to pass before Freud published these discoveries in his *Three Essays on the Theory of Sexuality.* Caution, a need for further confirmation, and Freud's own unwillingness to accept completely the existence of infantile sexuality appear to have contributed to the long delay. Later he was to wonder at his own hesitation in accepting facts readily recognized by discerning pediatricians and nursemaids but denied by almost all other members of society. He explained this astonishing circumstance as being the effect of the amnesia that hides the infantile experience of the majority of adults.[41]

The book created a sensation. Its contents were judged to be shockingly wicked; its author was deemed to be a man with an evil and obscene mind. Few people at the time were objective enough to note that it demonstrated Freud's freedom from the domination of his intellectual antecedents. He had replaced his biological, mechanistic model of mental functioning with a psychological model that allowed for the complexities of intrapsychic dynamics. Psychoanalysis had come into being.

Endnotes—Chapter 2

1. Sigmund Freud, *The Standard Edition of the Complete Psychological Works of Sigmund Freud,* translated from the German under the general editorship of James Strachey (London: The Hogarth Press, 1968 ed.), 24 Volumes. Volume XX, 57–58.

2. Ernest Jones, *The Life and Works of Sigmund Freud* (New York: Basic Books, Inc., 1957), 3 volumes. Volume I, 7.

3. Sigmund Freud, *Standard Edition,* Vol. V, 424.

4. *Ibid.,* 483.

5. Ernest Jones, *Life,* Vol. I, 5.

6. Sigmund Freud, *Standard Edition,* Vol. XX, 8. Ernest Jones, *Life,* Vol. I, 20.

7. Sigmund Freud, *Standard Edition,* Vol. XX, 9.

8. *Ibid.,* 28.

9. *Ibid.,* Vol. XX, 253.

10. *Ibid.,* 10.

11. *Ibid.,* Vol. III, 11.

12. *Ibid.,* 12.

13. "Theory is good, but it doesn't prevent things from existing." Freud elsewhere revealed that it was he himself who challenged Charcot. *Standard Edition,* Vol. I, 139.

14. *Ibid.,* 13.

15. *Ibid.,* Vol. XIV, 14.

16. Ernest Jones, *Life,* Vol. I, 242.

17. *Ibid.,* 297.

18. Sigmund Freud, *Standard Edition,* Vol. X, 156.

19. *Ibid.,* 103.

20. *Ibid.,* Vol. XVIII, 160.

21. Jones, *Life,* Vol. II, 264.

22. Sigmund Freud, *Standard Edition,* Vol. X, 157.

23. *Ibid.,* 166.

24. Sigmund Freud, *Standard Edition,* Vol. X, 155.

25. *Ibid.,* 166.

26. Sigmund Freud, *Standard Edition,* Vol. XV, 21.

27. *Ibid.,* Vol. XX, 29–30, see also Vol. VII, 249.

28. Sigmund Freud, *Standard Edition,* Vol. XX, 71–72.

29. Robert Holt, "Sigmund Freud," *International Encyclopedia of the Social Sciences,* edited by David L. Sills, (The Macmillan Co. and the Free Press, 1968). Vol. 6, 6.

30. Ernest Jones, *Life,* Vol. I, 40–41.

31. Ernest Jones, *Life,* Vol. I, 208; Sigmund Freud, *Standard Edition,* Vol. XX, 13, No. 3.

32. Ernest Jones, *Life,* Vol. I, 42. Robert Holt, "Freud," *International Encyclopedia of the Social Sciences,* Vol. 6, 6.

33. Sigmund Freud, *Standard Edition,* Vol. I, 283–284.

34. *Ibid.,* 285.

35. Sigmund Freud, *Standard Edition,* Vol. I, 147–148.

36. *Ibid.,* Vol. XX, 34.

37. Sigmund Freud, *Standard Edition,* Vol. XIV, 17–18.

38. *Ibid.,* Vol. I, 260.

39. *Ibid.,* Vol. XIV, 18.

40. *Ibid.,* Vol. XX, 33.

41. Ernest Jones, *Life,* Vol. II, 12.

THE UNCONSCIOUS

A twenty-eight year old management information and computer specialist had the following dream:

I was a young person, maybe sixteen, seventeen or eighteen years old. The dream had to do with work, industry and technology. I was in an office or a laboratory. I was working at the XYZ computer company in their township laboratory. The people I saw there were working for the computer company, but the place didn't look like the company or the township laboratory.

There was an assembly line and a row of desks and benches. The room had a low ceiling and I could see the slant of the roof. Above the benches there were large wooden boxes with electronic equipment. I could see the titles, but I was curious, and I wanted to know exactly how to use the equipment. I wanted to impress the people that I could use this equipment. I was a newcomer to the plant and lab. I wanted to convince them that even though I was young and inexperienced, I could do it.

This computer specialist had this dream on a Saturday night. Before going to sleep and having the dream, he had the following experience. There was a party at his house. He felt disappointed in the party, and felt excluded. He wanted to sleep. He had busied himself in the kitchen instead of joining the folk singing. His wife sent a messenger for him, a woman; she didn't come herself. He wanted his wife to take him into a room, put her arms around him, tell him everything was fine, and then to come join the folk singing, but she didn't do that. He left the party early and went to bed. He felt pangs of guilt that as host he had left the party, but then he had the thought, "Fuck it and fuck them; it's my house and I'll do just as I please."

The young computer specialist had a series of thoughts in connection with the dream. The thoughts and the sequence in which they appeared are as follows:

When I was at _____ college, I would get confused about how old I was. When I was twenty years old and people would ask me how old I was, I would get confused and tell them I was seventeen. In fact I was twenty. I guess I had a lot of growing up to do. Thinking of age reminds me of Mr. X [the name of an older man]. I used to work with him at the ABC company in their lab. I'm thinking of the discussions I had with one of our customers over at the plant. The work isn't going well over there. I remember now going to Sunday school and to church. I would stare into the light for a long time until I desensitized my retina, and then I would have an after-shadow. I would play at injuring my eyes, and even thought that I would go blind. Then my father would have to help me. While I was at Sunday school and in church my father would be out playing golf. When I was in college I tried so hard to go out of my way to establish contact with my professors. But if I was successful, I would knock them down and discredit them in my eyes. There was Professor X. I would call him by his first name and we would go on outings together. I tried to see him as perfect, but then I found fault in him and I would knock him down because he didn't meet my standards.

This dream sequence illustrates the vast chasm that exists between the seemingly chaotic and incomprehensible imagery of a dream and the thoughts that occur in association to the dream. Nowhere in the dream does there appear to be feeling or passion. The stillness of the dream, its quiescence, is striking. Yet in his associations to the dream, the young computer specialist presents thoughts of loneliness, longing, and thematically unites the content of the dream with his underlying wish for a strong father who would guide him and take care of him. Characteristic of unconscious mental life, however, is the appearance of a theme opposite to the wish in the dream for the strong, caring father. The rejection of this father is also an apparent theme in the form of the computer specialist's habit of knocking down in his own eyes the idealized father figure such as the professor whom he erected to represent this wish.

The question which we shall address in this chapter is the nature of unconscious mental life and its relation to conscious thinking, motivation, and behavior.

The concept of unconscious mental life is the nucleus of psychoanalysis. This chapter will examine the unconscious from several vantage points to demonstrate its fundamental position in psychoanalytic psychology. The place to begin is with a paradox: How can mental life or some part of it be unconscious? We can liken this paradox to the philosopher's problem with the tree that has fallen in the forest.

If no one is present, did the noise of the crashing tree occur? Thoughts and feelings that are outside of awareness or consciousness is a fundamental definition of unconscious mental life. If thoughts and feelings exist outside of awareness, or are unconscious, then they are not susceptible to ordinary methods of observation.

At the outset, we can dispose quickly of one way in which unconscious mental life exists. It would be impossible for people to function in a state of *total* consciousness. To be aware of all possible perceptions available at any moment would make thinking and attention impossible. The commonsense notion of concentration presumes that is is possible to erect and use screens or barriers to keep perceptions arising from the outside and from within so they cannot reach consciousness. The economics of attention—the process by which people are able to concentrate— suggests the existence of different levels of awareness and consciousness. If while reading these sentences the noises of fire engines became audible from their distant position, they probably registered in one's mental awareness but were easily discarded. If the engines approached and even came down the street, their presence would overwhelm attention to reading and indeed would cause these words to recede from consciousness and enable one to attend to the possibility of imminent danger.

Ideas, perceptions, and feelings existing outside of consciousness, but easily drawn into the act of attention are, strictly speaking, part of unconscious mental life. But this part of the unconscious accounts for only a small portion of experience and one of lesser importance in this examination of motivation. Mental life outside of consciousness at any given moment but easily available to conscious awareness is called *preconscious*. The purpose of distinguishing *preconscious* from *unconscious* is to allow room for the more significant use of the concept of the unconscious as it determines behavior.

Unconscious mental life operates outside of awareness and is not easily brought into the realm of consciousness; it is certainly not brought into awareness at will. There are at least three conceptual pathways for exploring the unconscious. The first is *phenomenological* or *descriptive;* the second is *functional;* and the third is *structural.*

PHENOMENOLOGY

The initial problem we face is to discover the evidence of unconscious mental life. Is the concept of the unconscious simply a convenient construct to allow for logical progression in investigating the problem of motivation, or does it refer to facts about human behavior that can be observed, described, and classified? Even if the unconscious were a construct used in logical inquiry and explanation, it would not in any sense be trivial. But the claim psychoanalysis makes is that the unconscious, at the outset, refers to facts about the human mind and how people think and act.

The presence of unconscious mental life is evident first in the fact that certain individuals function in different and dissociated mental states. One of the earliest recorded cases in psychoanalytic literature is the report of Josef Breuer's patient, Anna O, appearing in the volume co-authored by Josef Breuer and Sigmund Freud entitled, *Studies on Hysteria.*[1] Anna O. developed disturbing physical symptoms, such as impaired vision and paralysis of her arm, without distinct physical causation. Such symptoms, involving functional impairment without organic cause, are referred to as hysterical. In addition to these symptoms, Anna O. experienced two distinct states of consciousness. In one state, she appeared normal, capable of recognizing her surroundings, and in control of her faculties. In the second state, she had hallucinations, displayed a violent temper, and was unreasonable. In either state, Anna O. had no awareness of the existence of another state of consciousness: what was apparent in one state was unconscious in the other.

Different states of consciousness appear also in connection with hypnosis. The treatment of mental disturbances through hypnosis preceded the development of psychoanalytic therapy. It is still used today as a therapy but also as a means to modify behavior such as smoking or overeating. In hypnosis it is possible to put certain types of people into a light sleep and to suggest behavior when they return to consciousness. In experiments with hypnosis, the suggested behavior takes place at a pre-suggested signal. Throughout the action, the subject is unaware of the suggestion and is not able to explain why he did what he did (such as turning on the television set when the hypnotist knocks on the table). The subject literally forgets the suggestion given under hypnosis but still acts on it because of its continued influence on his unconscious mental life; he is motivated to act because of the force of unconscious ideas.

The existence of dreams that occur during sleep provides important information on unconscious mental life. Experimental work on sleeping and dreaming, in which different stages of sleep are described by characteristic brain waves, has established that about 25 percent of sleeping time is devoted to dreaming and occurs during a particular state of sleep called REM (rapid eye movement). Despite the frequent occurrence of dreams during sleep, most people are unaware of their dreams and probably would be surprised to discover that they indeed dream each night.

Dreams are important for the examination of unconscious mental life not only because of their general value as evidence of unconscious states, and their revelations of how the unconscious works (more phenomenology), but also for their information about the function and structure of the mind. Later we shall deal with function and structure, but for the moment we concentrate on describing unconscious mental life.

A question arising from the evidence thus far is: Are different states of mental life distinct and discontinuous? From observation of patients suffering the effects of dissociated states, it appears that there is only consciousness, but of different kinds—as though one state disappears upon being displaced by the other. This seems plausible until one recognizes that it is possible to recover the "disappeared" state of consciousness while in the other state. In the case of Anna O., for example, she was able to recover the angry and abusive state as a result of talking associatively. She was also able to determine the meaning of her hysterical symptoms by recapturing memories. In doing so, she found that her symptoms disappeared, although not necessarily permanently. Anna O. referred to this procedure for recovering unconscious thoughts seriously as "the talking cure" and jokingly as "chimney-sweeping."

The capacity of unconscious ideas to enter consciousness by one means or another suggests that unconscious mental life is continuous. It is not restricted to sleep states or extraordinary mental conditions in which the same individual has totally different personalities alternating in their appearance and influence. The existence of unconscious mental life thus is not an attribute solely of people who are mentally disturbed. The discovery of the unconscious as a universal quality of the mind is what permits psychoanalysis its claim as a general psychology, as well as a theory of and therapy for mental illness.

The capacity to forget, the disturbing experience of slips of the tongue, or the performance of odd acts all provide strong evidence of the continuous effects of unconscious mental life and its position in normal psychological processes. While jokes about forgetting one's spouse's birthday abound, the embarrassment and awareness of the implied hostility in this lapse of memory should be taken seriously as indications that motives for action are not necessarily the domain of consciousness, nor subject to will and control. The saving grace in most of these lapses or parapraxes, as they are technically known, derives from the fact that they often are very funny. While a good joke had best be left alone as just a good joke, the force of humor comes from the sudden explosion into awareness of the condensed and multiple meaning of the event. It is a form of speaking the unspeakable.

Alternate states of consciousness, dreams, and parapraxes provide evidence of the existence of unconscious mental life. All of these phenomena, including hypnotic states, are usually unavailable to conscious awareness. While it is true that everyone occasionally remembers a dream from the night before, much more regular dreaming occurs than one remembers. The evidence of unconscious mental life therefore remains somewhat opaque and indirect. These facts are much farther removed from observable experience than the falling apple that ultimately led to the theory of gravitational force.

A more direct encounter with the quality of unconscious mental life occurs in the experience of people subject to hallucinations and what are commonly recognized as thought disorders. Such people are usually in the throes of psychotic episodes in which the sense of reality that anchors individuals to their surroundings has been badly impaired. Another way of describing psychotic experience is to suggest that the perceptions emanating from the individual's inner world dominate and overwhelm the perceptions from the outer world.

Hallucinations may be visual and auditory experiences. To the individual they appear the same as perceptions from outer reality. The quality of hallucinations and the manifestations of thought disorders provide the basis for distinguishing between two types of thinking. The first type is characteristic of the unconscious and is called *primary process thinking*. The second type is called *secondary process thinking* and is descriptive of conscious and rational thought.

It is easier to grasp the distinction between primary and secondary process thinking by starting with what is familiar: logical or rational thinking. Rational thinking generally can be said to follow a five-stage sequential pattern:

(1) Awareness of a problem occurs, followed by organizing the problem according to its elements, examining the connection among the

elements, and introducing facts from the real world as evidence to test inferences.

(2) Attempts to develop alternative solutions to the problem are then begun, and may be derived from remembering past experience in which similar problems appeared and were solved.

(3) Next, alternatives may be weighed and scaled according to their usefulness, much in the manner of what is familiarly known as cost-benefit analysis, and the best or most satisfying solution may then be adopted.

(4) Thought turns next to how best to implement the solution—a stage that may reveal weaknesses in the solution so that a fresh pass at solving the problem rationally may occur.

(5) At some point, action occurs and actual results may be compared with anticipated results.

This familiar description of stages in the rational approach to solving problems characteristic of secondary process thinking may become more interesting if we consider the conditions necessary for such a logical process to occur. The most important condition would seem to be the ability to focus attention on the task at hand. The seemingly automatic ability in rational thinking to put aside extraneous perceptions and thoughts further presumes that perceptual screens and barriers not only are in place but can be successful in blocking out the multitude of perceptions available both from the outside world and from the psyche.

This blocking effect necessary for secondary process thinking becomes even more important when one considers that perceptions from reality and from the psyche are continuous. The useful analogy in this connection is that of a dam that holds back the flow of water but does not stop the stream. An inappropriate analogy would be that of a digital instrument operating on the principle of a switch with an "on" or "off" position: secondary process thinking does not occur by switching on logical thought patterns of consciousness. Nothing discussed to this point provides any indication of how the damming occurs that prevents unconscious images from entering into consciousness and interfering with logical thought patterns. What we do know is from observing the pathetic condition that occurs when the psyche is overwhelmed and little exists but the manifestations of the unconscious and of primary process thinking. For these troubled people, the dam does not exist or it has collapsed.

Primary process thinking occurs often in visual form. It is concrete rather than abstract. Visions appear real, whether in the form of dreams or outright hallucinations. Ideas may substitute for one another freely and be equivalent in significance and content. There is no regard for time in primary process thinking; everything occurs in the present. The stream of thoughts may jump from one topic to another and appear to the individual as connected; only to an observer are the ideas disconnected, jumbled, and without sequence. Disparate ideas become equivalent, and one thought may easily displace another, carrying along with it the value and emotion attributed to the idea that has been displaced. A thought may represent its opposite, as in a dream in which an individual sees himself in a passive, quiescent state but associatively discovers himself in an aggressive and agitated state. Ideas or images become symbols and may represent a variety of other ideas and images, some of which are contradictory. An individual may dream of a gang of youths threatening him, only to discover that the gang represents part of his psyche that has been displaced and is symbolically represented in the visual image.

Among many intriguing questions about the unconscious, one concerns the relation between thought and feeling. We have used words such as thoughts, images, and ideas to designate the content of the unconscious. Can feelings or emotions also be a part of unconscious mental life? Empirical evidence suggests that the emotions, frequently referred to as "affects," are very much part of the unconscious. When some emotions are unconscious, the individual experiences their derivatives. Take the case of anxiety—a conscious feeling of discomfort that does not necessarily focus on the ideas that do make or should make one feel distraught. It is often accompanied by physical reactions such as sweating, shortness of breath, a tight feeling in the stomach, and even heart palpitations, sometimes to such a marked degree as to arouse further fears that one is in the midst of a heart attack. Other stressful feelings, such as sadness and anger, may be totally outside of awareness.

Another example of unconscious emotion is the sense of guilt. The derivatives of such guilt may be in conscious feelings of anxiety, reduced self-esteem, and even depression. But with all of these accompanying affects, the root of the sense of guilt may exist only in the unconscious: the individual has no awareness of it.

Other feelings, however, may also be unconscious. Individuals who, in the personality they project onto the outer world, appear passive and compliant, may unconsciously harbor anger, and even murderous impulses. Similarly, erotic feelings may exist in the unconscious even though, or especially when, the individual feels revulsion rather than pleasure toward sexual situations or seductive behavior.

In one of the early cases in the psychoanalytic literature, Freud reported on the experience of a young woman who felt the utmost disgust when an older man kissed her. The disgust was not a transitory state since it entered into a chain of reactions that led to significant psychological symptoms.[2]

Unconscious mental life consists of ideas and affects outside of awareness. Only under particular circumstances can they come to conscious attention. The quality of unconscious thoughts and feelings is irrational, primitive, and designated as primary process thinking. Secondary process thinking, which is familiar and rational, is characteristic of conscious mental life. The evidence for the existence of unconscious mental life is in observation of dissociated states, experiments in hypnosis, dreams, parapraxes, hallucinations, and thought disorders. The overwhelming evidence of the existence of the unconscious comes from clinical psychoanalysis wherein, through free association, the relationship between manifest symptoms and unconscious thoughts and feelings becomes apparent, with beneficial effects for the patient.

While these forms of evidence are usually within the domain of specialists in therapy or in investigation of the mind, the existence of the unconscious is a general phenomenon. It applies to individuals relatively free of psychological symptoms, as well as to those who seek therapy to alleviate painful conditions. And the distinction between levels of pain, or between what is normal and abnormal, is often difficult to draw; the line is so subtle that for our investigative purposes it can conveniently be ignored. The relevant claim in this context is that unconscious mental life affects all thinking and behavior, is omnipresent, and has powerful effects in everyday life.

The difficulty of proving this claim is that demonstration or validation requires special tools and capacities for observation. The observer encounters the problems of deciphering the language of the unconscious. For conditions or phenomena that originate in irrational forms and are blocked from free access to conscious attention, the process of observation cannot rely on ordinary approaches. In short, the link between primary and secondary process thinking is interpretation. Unconscious mental life and its derivatives in conscious attention and in behavior, have keen significance and can be interpreted. The rules for interpretation begin with an understanding of the *function* of the unconscious—the ways in which it operates.

FUNCTION

The question with which to begin the exploration of how the unconscious functions is: Why is unconscious mental life so inaccessible to conscious attention? The corollary is: What regulates the flow of unconscious material to conscious attention and awareness?

The unconscious at its base is nonverbal and closely linked to the biological nature of the human being. Well before thought and language, the individual exists in relation to biological needs such as hunger, thirst, and elimination. These needs are periodic rather than continuous, and their gratification, while assuring survival, also establishes the condition known as pleasure—the quenching of appetite. Prolonged need is the opposite of pleasure and is a cause for individuals to act in such a way as to diminish, if not satiate, appetite to achieve the state of mind and body called pleasure.

In its most primitive form, the unconscious is the mental derivative of appetite. The chain of perceptions, thoughts, images, and affects attendant upon the heightening of tension associated with appetite and the reduction of tension associated with satisfaction, is the core of the unconscious. Appetite is the engine that drives the psyche toward a predominant aim—the state of pleasure. Pleasure is thus the endpoint of a cycle that begins with heightened tension in the condition of need, followed by action and reduced tension.

If the unconscious is the mental derivative of appetite, it is also channeled in the service of pleasure. It impels toward direct action as a means of achieving the state of pleasure. The human infant, however, is severely limited in the action it can take to secure the state of pleasure, even though the unconscious directs its energies toward action. The most an infant can do in its state of heightened need is to cry and thereby alert a caretaker who, in turn, can act to secure for the infant the state of pleasure. But between the time of intense need and the securing of gratification, the unconscious floods the psyche with images and affects derived from its state of arousal and even pain. Just what these images and affects are is beyond the reach of what we are capable of observing and recording. In fact, we depend on the capacity of individuals to communicate in words what they feel and imagine in order to capture even an approximate and rough picture of what unconscious mental life is about.

Some students of psychoanalysis, beginning with Freud, hypothesized that very early in life, during the preverbal period, the infant's images while in the state of heightened need contain hallucinations of the action associated with securing the state of pleasure. If, for example, sucking at the mother's breast is the action necessary for satisfaction, it is hypothesized that the infant will hallucinate the breast and the act of sucking. While no one knows factually whether such hallucinations occur, it is convenient to assume that they do, in light of other facts about the mind such as its ability to produce psychological symptoms. We can further infer that the unconscious consists of the storehouse of images associated with securing pleasure from the state of pain connected with intense appetite.

The predominant position that the satisfying of appetite holds for survival is the reason for postulating the unconscious as the expression of a principle of mental function called the pleasure principle. The human organism, from its inception, behaves according to the pleasure principle. It is dominated by forms of thinking characterized as primary process thinking. The pleasure principle is a more abstract way of defining the aim of unconscious mental life, which is to move in the most direct line to satiate appetite. The most direct line means the mode of action equivalent to instant gratification.

Appetite and the mental derivatives that form the unconscious do not, initially at least, inhibit action; the capacity to delay gratification occurs as a consequence of development, although it is highly probable that the mechanisms for delay are biologically determined. The closest one may come to experiencing instant gratification is during earliest infancy with an alert and responsive caretaker. But even here, some gap in time always exists between heightened need and pleasure. While we have speculated that hallucinations of the pleasurable activity occur during periods of frustration, we are on firmer ground when observing infants simulating the gratification of appetite by sucking on parts of their own bodies. Such introverted activity probably contains mental representations that form part of the unconscious and that contribute to body image. Using one's own body for pleasure, or its simulation, probably also contributes to the capacity for delay of gratification.

While survival depends upon gratifying appetite, it also depends upon the increasing capacity of the developing human being to tolerate frustrations and to delay pleasure. Tolerance of continued tension associated with heightened appetite permits the elaboration and complexity of mental faculties to emerge. The ultimate aim of delay is to allow thinking to substitute for action and to permit a second principle of mental activity to control behavior. This second principle, the reality principle, is another abstract way of conceiving the balance of forces assuring survival of the human being.

The reality principle assumes that secondary process thinking ultimately dominates psychic activity. But here one must ask the question: Toward what aim? The pleasure principle is not compromised but ultimately served by the reality principle. Because the aim of secondary process thinking is to secure gratification of appetite and the promise of pleasure that goes hand-in-hand with relaxing tension, the reality principle accommodates pleasure but allows for the hard fact that the quest for instant gratification will assure destruction rather than survival.

Gaining pleasure requires mental work. And this work tends to take into account the conditions of reality as well as the demands of appetite. Efficient mental work assures maximum gratification with the least psychic cost. The ability to think as a precursor of action serves both the pleasure principle and the reality principle. The more that action allows for multiple gratifications with the same expenditure of energy, the greater the efficiency of both thinking and acting.

The concepts of the reality principle and the efficiency of mental work point to the capacities of the human being for delay, for inhibition of appetite, and perhaps most important, for the transformation of desire into aims that will satisfy appetite while being congruent with the conditions of reality. In the end, hallucinatory activity and the introversion of desire ill serve the pleasure principle. Some forms of delay must occur so that the human being begins to attend to the outer world and to fashion modes of thinking and feeling suitable to reality.

The reality principle could become dominant under two conceivable conditions. The first would be to expunge the unconscious as much as one erases a blackboard to clear away unwanted material. The accumulated evidence about the unconscious suggests that the opposite occurs: instead of being expunged, the unconscious endures. The accumulation of experience adds to and overlays the images and thoughts connected with early and archaic states of the mind. A memory cannot be erased; rather, it can be forgotten. To forget is not to eradicate all of the residues of experience we have come to call memory.

The second condition that would meet the requirements of the reality principle is the taming of the unconscious. Forgetting the past suggests that memory persists, but that it attracts little energy and therefore makes little demand upon the psyche. For a memory, or to put it another way, for images, ideas, and feelings associated with memory, to enter consciousness presumes that it is capable of attracting energy to enable it to enter consciousness. If, by whatever causes, unconscious derivatives attract increasing quantities of energy, they will press toward conscious attention and toward activity. To maintain the state of consciousness without the intrusion of unconscious material that has attracted psychic energy requires the reinforcement of barriers to attention and the further suppression of the material pressing toward consciousness and action.

The barriers to consciousness and activity are those quantities of psychic energy that oppose the movement of unconscious material toward attention and activity.

Quantities of psychic energy are called *cathexes,* a Greek word that is difficult to translate literally to fit the sense in which it is used in psychoanalytic theory. In psychoanalytic usage, cathexis refers to a quantity of energy capable of being attached to other persons, to mental representations of other persons, or to one's body and inner representations of it. When a mental representation is invested with psychic energy, or *cathected,* it seeks to enter consciousness or to find its way directly into action. The sum of psychic energy directed toward preventing unconscious materials from entering consciousness or finding discharge through action is called *countercathexis.* Without countercathexes, there would be nothing to prevent unconscious materials from gaining direct access to conscious mental life, with disastrous results. The flooding of consciousness immobilizes the individual or forces such frenetic behavior that one cannot survive without special care. The condition wherein the barriers to consciousness have been substantially destroyed is psychosis. People with psychotic disturbances display bizarre thought patterns, withdraw from the world around them, and sometimes act in destructive ways.

To elaborate the significance of cathexis and countercathexis, we can refer to dreaming. The meaning of a dream is seldom clear. Certainly dreams do not foretell the future, nor do they present solutions to the rational problems and conflicts one encounters in daily experience. Rather, a dream presents the psyche's best solution to satisfying lingering wishes that have gone unfulfilled and remain cathected, perhaps for many years. These unfulfilled wishes are subject to the attraction of fresh energy in conjunction with, or as a result of, current experience. The function of a dream is to preserve sleep. It can only do so if the expressions of inner wishes appear in the dream images in highly disguised forms. When disguises begin to fail, the unconscious breaks through to consciousness and disturbs sleep; the countercathexes have failed. At the extreme, nightmares occur as a consequence of unconscious material overpowering the barriers to consciousness. The fact that nightmares occur during sleep indicates that the forces protecting consciousness diminish in intensity.

The flooding of consciousness with unconscious material can overwhelm the psyche and undermine the capacity for rational thought and action. Nothing we have considered to this point, however, except for the notion of quantity, clarifies why unconscious material is so threatening and therefore must be contained within relatively safe boundaries.

But quantity alone is difficult to grasp in relation to the problem of maintaining mental balance. Even if one were awakened by a bad dream or a nightmare, it is usually not difficult to restore the balance and even return to sleep. It appears as though the gateways to consciousness are carefully guarded and the contents of unconscious mental life are censored, even in the case of dreaming, to prevent awareness of unconscious thoughts and images.

Consideration of both quantitative and qualitative aspects of the unconscious in tandem is necessary to grasp the built-in human resistance to becoming conscious of what is unconscious. The quantitative aspect refers back to the helpless state of the individual during infancy. Because the infant is dominated by appetite, the flooding effect is purely the result of desire and the infant's incapacity to restore equilibrium without the intervention of a figure likely to place the infant's needs ahead of his or her own. Perhaps this primary condition of anxiety leaves a trace of what it means to be threatened by desire that emanates from within when the means to deal with the tensions of the desire are absent. And perhaps the state of helplessness results in a tendency of the psyche to "overkill:" to treat the pains of unfulfilled desire in the adult with mechanisms that originated in an earlier primitive stage of development.

It should be clear by this time that we are dealing with a model of the mind that views the unconscious as a force subject to counterforces. Together with their quantitative aspects, unconscious forces and counterforces have crucial qualitative dimensions: they tell a story and they have meaning. But the story and the meaning, which for any one individual is his or her subjective experience, must be interpreted. And human stories are neither obvious nor easily told.

STRUCTURE

We have thus far considered the unconscious from the perspectives of description and of function. Description, or phenomenology, attempts to discover the contents of unconscious mental life through the idea of appetite and the comparison of primary and secondary process thinking. Function attempts to clarify the controls that prevent unconscious mental life from flooding and consequently dominating consciousness. Positioning the existence of barriers attempts to deal with quantity or amount. Censorship attempts to deal with quality or content of the images that appear in conjunction with the forces of the unconscious.

In this chapter's final section, we shall examine the unconscious and consciousness from the perspective of structure. Although organization of the mental apparatus can be approached in several ways, the view of structure developed here fits well with the notion that the unconscious has both quantitative and qualitative features. An elementary but nonetheless significant way to portray the structure of the mental apparatus is to assume that the mind can be divided into regions or layers. The resultant topographic picture of the mind would then have to take account of the existence of the unconscious and conscious thoughts both quantitatively and qualitatively.

The first structural model of the mind developed in psychoanalysis was based conceptually on such a mental topography. Although a revised structure appeared later in Freudian psychoanalytic theory to account for important facts and relationships more fully, the later structural model did not invalidate the earlier one. The reason for presenting the early model in this chapter, while reserving the revised model for later consideration, is pedagogic: one learns more readily about the unconscious and the dynamics of the mind by starting with a topographic model.

The topographic model establishes three regions of the mind— the unconscious, the preconscious, and the conscious: as psychological abstractions, these three regions describe neither anatomical nor biological entities. The unconscious region, or layer, is susceptible to stimulation from the impulses that arise within the human organism. The impulses appear in the unconscious as urges to act, which are characterized in terms of quantity, and as mental images associatively constructed from all prior experience with impulses and the drive toward pleasure, which are characterized in terms of quality. According to this model, the conscious region of the mind is susceptible to direct stimulation from the outer world. Information from, and perception of, the outer world activates the human organism to perform work in the conscious region.

The preconscious region is positioned between the conscious and the unconscious. It contains all of the perceptions and their associative images not necessary for conscious attention at any given moment, but which may easily move into the conscious region when necessary. It is this realm, however, that also acts as the barrier to prevent unconscious material from entering consciousness. The mental function of censorship occurs in this region.

The ability of the preconscious to function as the barrier or gateway to consciousness is based on an important presumption. To serve as a censor, the preconscious must have psychic energy available that can be attached to unconscious material, thereby allowing it to enter consciousness. The attachment of energy to ideas (the cathecting of mental representations), originates either in the unconscious or through perceptions coming from reality to the conscious region of the mind. In much the same way, the preconscious must have available energy to prevent unconscious imagery from entering consciousness. As mentioned, this barrier effect of the preconscious is known as countercathexis, or the attachment of energy to functions that can prevent the flow of unconscious material toward the conscious region of the mind.

Implicit in placement of the preconscious in an intermediary position between the unconscious and the conscious regions of the mind is the function of censorship. This function relates directly to the qualitative aspect of the unconscious, consisting of thoughts or mental representations of energic aspects of the psyche. When one is hungry or sexually aroused, numerous mental images are evoked, based on memory, associations, and the characteristic way the mind works under conditions of heightened tension connected with appetite. The preconscious can permit the flow of unconscious material to consciousness by accepting and rejecting certain symbols that represent the contents of the unconscious. By condensing, displacing, and representing one idea or image for another, the derivatives of the unconscious can enter consciousness. What enters consciousness, no matter how disguised or symbolically distant from the unconscious material, permits action to take place with several results, including pleasure, the performance of elaborate and sometimes highly creative work, and the maintenance of mental equilibrium often under conditions of stress.

The traffic between the unconscious and the conscious regions of the mind is always imperfect. The impulses and derivative images that seek to enter consciousness include much that is intolerable to the psyche. Again this noxious material has both a quantitative and qualitative aspect. The sheer strength of the impulses seeking discharge and the content of the associated images may be a source of both distress and disequilibrium.

The indications of distress, themselves exquisite reflections of how the unconscious mind works, brings us to the original question that impelled psychoanalytic investigation: Why do people become victims of mental illness?

Endnotes—Chapter 3

1. Sigmund Freud, *Standard Edition*, Vol. II, 21-47.
2. Sigmund Freud, "Fragment of an Analysis of a Case of Hysteria (Dora)," *Standard Edition,* Vol. VII.

THEORY OF NEUROSES: SYMPTOMS

The chief executive officer of a large corporation who is in his early fifties found that he was losing energy and interest in his work. He became somewhat distant from his subordinates, in sharp contrast to his close working relationship with them. He began to drink heavily and would often not appear for meetings, and when he did appear it was clear that he was unable to concentrate and in some apparent distress. Several key subordinates tried to approach him with sympathetic concern for his changed behavior, but he rejected all such friendly approaches. One of the senior vice presidents called a member of the board of directors to report the chief executive officer's change in behavior. The board convened in executive session to consider what action the board should take in the face of this evidence that something was wrong with the CEO. They delegated a respected attorney, who was a member of the board, to approach the CEO to inquire into what had happened. The attorney met with the CEO, and the CEO reported that he was very unhappy, unable to concentrate, and that he would seek psychiatric consultation. The psychiatrist placed the CEO in a hospital, and the board placed the CEO on a leave of absence. After a short period of time in the hospital, the CEO returned to work, met with the attorney and reported that he had been depressed and was taking medication, and expected to be back to his old self in a very short period of time. The CEO threw himself into his work, but soon after returning, began drinking heavily. The attorney met with him once again, and the CEO was angry and refused

CHAPTER

4

to acknowledge that he had a problem with alcohol, among his other difficulties. One of the janitors in the building reported to the attorney that he was removing empty liquor bottles from the CEO's office. The attorney approached the CEO once more, and again was met with an angry response. The board then convened upon the recommendation of the attorney. They discharged the chief executive officer.

This kind of self-destructive behavior is examined in this chapter.

To study neuroses—a broad class of mental disturbances—is to venture into the realm of psychopathology. The immediate question that comes to mind is: What can one extract from the study of mental illness that will illuminate a general psychology? It might seem convenient to restate this question and to ask how abnormal psychology relates to normal psychology. One should hesitate before drawing sharp distinctions between abnormal and normal. Often the distinction turns on the decision to consult a specialist rather than on the presence or absence of psychological impairment. Whereas it is especially difficult to separate normal from abnormal in analyzing neuroses, the distinction is more easily drawn with the class of mental illnesses known as psychoses, because of the severity of the symptoms.

Neuroses arise from mental conflicts without organic causes that produce suffering and impair an individual's capacity to function. They do not involve the massive distortions of reality and the dominance of primary process over secondary process thinking characteristic of psychoses, nor do the impairments they produce overwhelm the individual's capacity for rational thinking and reality testing.

In contrast to physical illnesses, the causes of neuroses cannot be easily isolated; no foreign bodies, such as bacteria or viruses, cause neuroses. Because neurotic illness involves the total personality, approaches to treatment differ from those used for purely physical illness. A doctor cannot prescribe a specific remedy for a neurosis. Rather, the therapeutic approach relies on engaging the patient in a cooperative effort to ameliorate symptoms and to alter the structure of personality that gives rise to the neurotic condition.

Persons suffering from neuroses are not always inclined to change. They frequently arrive at a position where they "live with" their problems, enduring the suffering and even drawing those close to them into the web of their conflicts to support the structure of the neurosis. What may finally drive people to change, apart from painful symptoms, are the pressures of life, such as a choice of vocation or career, psychological accidents, such as loss of a job, or intimate relationships with others, such as falling in love. In the absence of painful symptoms or pressures and accidents that originate in one's experiences with other people and with other aspects of reality, there may be little motivation to alter the conditions within the psyche that give rise to, and sustain, neuroses.

One claim that can be made for studying neuroses is their prevalence. We are all likely to encounter neurotic patterns within ourselves and in others; to be forewarned is therefore to be forearmed. Another claim, however, takes priority: the way the mind works to produce neurotic symptoms is similar to the way it works when there is no apparent evidence of psychological conflict. A related claim can also be made: it is easier to learn about the mind by starting with pathology than by starting with health.

Attempts to define or describe mental health, let alone to understand the conditions that promote health, have yielded little knowledge about the dynamics of the mind. Often the study of mental health leads to misconceptions about people and the human condition. To make matters worse, theories of mental health sooner or later establish ideal conceptions of what people should strive to accomplish. Setting up such ideals and standards or prescribing goals and aims inadvertently makes people aware of how they are falling short of what they are supposed to achieve. Most of these standards have little to do with the human condition. Paradoxically, therefore, mental health efforts may, in the end, contribute in some degree to the causes of mental illness.

Since Freud's initial formulation of the theory of the neuroses, attempts to describe neurotic conditions and to classify the various syndromes that belong within the broad spectrum of neuroses have proliferated. The classification prepared by the American Psychiatric Association in the 1980 edition of *The Diagnostic and Statistical Manual* (DSM—III) lists five categories of neurotic disorders. As John Nemiah (1978) states in his summary of psychoneuroses, "We must remind ourselves once again that [neuroses] are only syndromes: clusterings of symptoms and signs that though sometimes sharply differentiated from one another more often than not have unclear boundaries, frequently so blurred as to be undetectable."[1]

It is not uncommon for psychiatrists to diagnose their patients' problems as "mixed neuroses." Although certain syndromes, such as obsessive-compulsive neurosis and conversion hysteria, appear distinct, many more neuroses consist of symptoms that appear in several categories. For example, people who consciously value independence and simultaneously deal harshly with their desires to have someone take care of them, may develop psychosomatic disorders, such as stomach ulcers and asthma. The same constellation of conflicting desires may also be involved in depression, but without the appearance of psychosomatic symptoms. It may appear as well in the syndrome known as "anxiety neurosis."

To complicate matters further from a scientific standpoint, cultural influences may alter the prevalent clinical picture. For example, the syndrome known as "conversion hysteria" (in which psychological conflicts become manifested in physical symptoms and functional impairments) was once fairly common. Today conversion hysteria seems to be less prevalent, perhaps as a consequence of cultural changes, higher levels of education, and less restrictive attitudes toward sexual expression.

Within the past ten or fifteen years, interest has shifted away from classical categories of neuroses to syndromes known as narcissistic personality disorders and borderline states. Narcissistic personality disorders, according to those who argue that this syndrome is both distinctive and new, are afflictions characterized by self-absorption and lack of inner cohesion and identity. Borderline states are illnesses that stand somewhere between neurotic disorders and psychoses. Theoretically the reason for insisting on the validity of these diagnoses is to fit a treatment mode to specific illnesses. From a scientific point of view, questions of diagnostic validity and modifications in treatment procedures are still unclear and unresolved.

A further difficulty presents itself in considering neuroses from a purely descriptive and taxonomic point of view. A number of specialists observing the same patient may arrive at different designations of the specific neurosis they think they are observing. Psychiatry on the whole lacks solid epidemiological studies that provide information on the frequency and prevalence of types of mental illness. Finally, the malaise called "neurosis" is so close to everyone's experience that it can easily appear to be a condition of life rather than an illness. The logical extension of this point of view is to focus on society rather than the individual as the locus of illness, particularly in the concern for the causes of human suffering. The fact that society still values both the individual and the treatment of illness prevents the complete shift of focus onto society.

Neuroses are the products of mental conflicts. For this discussion it seems reasonable to accept the proposition that the locus of neurotic suffering is in the individual. Even if it were possible to "treat" societies, it is still a worthwhile endeavor to understand how mental conflicts play themselves out in the human mind and how they become manifest. We shall omit in this discussion the important consideration of how neuroses are treated. For readers not primarily concerned with clinical psychoanalysis and psychotherapy, this omission may not be too serious.

Historically, of course, understanding of neuroses emerge from the attempts of physicians, psychiatrists, and psychoanalysts to treat people with neurotic disturbances. The discipline advanced simultaneously as treatment method and theoretical investigation fused in the one activity. The only way this fusion could have taken place successfully was for the therapists to understand the varying perspectives from which the patients perceived them and to use this knowledge in the course of the treatment. Once this understanding established its roots in the psychoanalytic method, the demand for sharply defined and accurately differentiated syndromes could be relinquished. The focus shifted to what the patient said and how the patient felt.

This focus provides us with a rationale for considering neurotic symptoms apart from the preoccupation with diagnostic categories. Rather than presenting the clustering of symptoms or the syndromes found in standard diagnostic categories, which is the tradition in psychiatry, we shall attempt to cut into the problem in another way: by reference to how symptoms appear.

MODES OF SYMPTOM DISTURBANCE

All neurotic disabilities become manifest through symptoms. Sometimes the individual alone is aware of them; in other instances the symptoms are apparent to others. These symptoms—which are signs of mental conflict—appear as disturbances or distress in five modes: (1) behavior; (2) mood; (3) thought; (4) body function; and, (5) character. It is worth repeating that the appearance of symptoms in one mode does not preclude the appearance of symptoms in other modes. As we consider each symptom mode, we shall refer to simultaneous manifestations in other modes. Although this approach does not elucidate the differences between, for example, obsessional and hysterical neuroses, it does provide comprehensive coverage of most neurotic symptoms.

Behavior

Sexual dysfunctions rank among the most important forms of behavioral symptoms indicating neurotic conflict. In the case of the male, sexual dysfunction appears as the inability to gain or hold an erection or as premature ejaculation. In the case of the female, sexual frigidity, or the inability to become aroused, is a common symptom. The experience of pain during intercourse so that it becomes impossible to complete the act is also indicative of neurotic conflict, unless a physiological condition exists that would otherwise account for the pain. A more controversial sign of female dysfunction is the absence of orgasm during intercourse. Before this condition can be classified as a neurotic symptom, however, it would have to be a consistent experience of sexual intercourse. Failure to achieve an orgasm while masturbating is more clearly a neurotic symptom. The controversy over what is or is not a neurotic symptom in female sexuality centers on whether vaginal orgasm is the expected climax of sexuality in the female, whether it is independent of or different from clitoral orgasm, and whether clitoral orgasm is subordinate to vaginal orgasm. In the case of the male, the failure to gain or maintain an erection and premature ejaculation are clearly neurotic symptoms.

Various sexual perversions also are sexual dysfunctions. Perversions consist of the inability to proceed from foreplay to genital intercourse as a fixed condition of sexual experience. Much of foreplay involves acts that also appear in perversions. The difference, however, is in the aim of the sexual activity. Sexuality is perverse in the symptomatic sense when foreplay is the exclusive aim of sexual pleasure and when it becomes a way of avoiding genital intercourse. Sexual activity that leads to genital intercourse is not perverse.

Controversy surrounds the question of whether homosexuality is a perversion and, therefore, a sign of neurotic disturbance. At one time members of the psychiatric profession viewed the choice of someone of the same gender as a sexual partner as sexual inversion, which, in turn, signified psychopathology. In abandoning the arena of scientific discourse to determine the answer to this and related questions, the issue has become politicized.

One method of determining whether homosexuality is or is not a symptom of neurosis is to assess how the individual feels about his or her homosexual behavior. For some people, homosexual activity is accompanied by overwhelming shame and anxiety and is the cause of considerable suffering. Moreover, homosexual activity may be a means of dealing with severe anxiety and depression, especially when it is episodic and promiscuous. The following examples are illustrative.

> A man who appeared to be very effective in his work, to be happily married, and a devoted father of several children periodically found a male stranger with whom he had sexual relations. The precondition for this activity was that no previous relationship existed between the men and that they were not to see each other beyond the scene of the sexual encounter. The man felt dreadfully ashamed after each meeting, suffering deep remorse and self-hatred because he could not stop the activity.

That his homosexual activity was symptomatic of neurotic conflict became clear when he sought treatment for his symptoms and the underlying conflicts.

> A young professional woman experimented with homosexual relationships although she did not abandon her interest in men. Consciously the experiments provided her with a sense of freedom from convention so she could consider these relationships to be apart from her major problems. Unconsciously she was afraid that she would fail in her profession and not be accepted by people who were important to her.

Whether her homosexuality was symptomatic should be judged in the light of her limited ability to be alone, to endure competition with other women, and to tolerate her depressive reactions.

Whether sexual activity without a partner is a neurotic symptom is, like homosexuality, a controversial subject. Masturbation begins early in life and does not originate, as it was once thought, during puberty. Masturbation may continue during adulthood when a partner is temporarily absent or after sustaining permanent loss. It is clearly symptomatic when it is compulsive and accompanied by guilt or shame. Masturbation is especially important as a symptom when it occurs in conjunction with sadomasochistic fantasies. Its compulsive quality may, in fact, be a consequence of limited capacity to be with people because of the interference of angry thoughts and fantasies.

Fantasy almost always accompanies sexual activity. The behavior, therefore, functions as the language of the psyche, reflecting many underlying desires and also fears. Sexual fantasy is usually not restricted to periods of sexual arousal when with a partner. It accompanies other symptoms. The further the symptoms are removed from sexual behavior, the more difficult it becomes to connect them to sexuality.

An example of behavior that is in part sexually driven and yet, in appearance, is far removed from sexuality is ritualism. Ritualistic and repetitive behavior consists of involuntary actions that are without apparent motive or purpose. One of Freud's case studies, the "Rat Man," still ranks as the best description of a patient dominated by ritualism and a need to repeat his actions. This patient, referred to as the "Rat Man" because his fantasies involved punishment carried out by gnawing rats, felt compelled to undertake elaborate rituals in connection with repaying real or imagined debts. For example, when he took a train trip, he worked out an elaborately circuitous route and constantly repeated certain actions. This irrational behavior disguised hostile attitudes toward authority, particularly his father, who still exerted enormous influence over him even though he had been dead many years. The patient felt that his father prevented him from marrying and from having sexual pleasure. The compulsive rituals limited his freedom and his enjoyment of life but held at bay his hostile wishes toward his father.

Ritualism and strict adherence to form as preconditions for action are commonly observed in children, although many adults also feel they can act only according to ritualized steps. In children, the dominance of ritualism is generally short-lived. When acted out in a group it plays some part in socialization. The neurotic component is evident in the tendency of children to repeat what they observe passively in movies and television, particularly if the content stimulates their aggressive and sexual impulses. The arousal of impulses is threatening because of the fear of becoming destructive and the fear of retaliation. The problem of angry feelings also leads to rituals that make visible the danger connected with anger. Children, for example, play a game in which they must avoid stepping on the cracks in the pavement because "step on the crack will break your mother's back." For adults with problems of aggressivity and anger, such mild forms of dissipating fears are less readily available. They may resort to more serious symptomatic rituals and repetitions. A few examples may illustrate:

> A man in his mid-thirties, who was married and had children, worked as a meat department supervisor in a large chain of supermarkets. He attended a popular movie about ancient Rome and felt increasingly upset while watching battles or bloody scenes of captives and slaves being tortured. While driving home from the theater he felt he had to exercise exceptional care. He felt compelled to drive close to the dividing line of the highway. When crossing a bridge he had to proceed with great caution because he was afraid he would go into the railing and off the bridge. He reported that his overly cautious driving continued for some time.

In another instance, a woman was afraid that she would infect her children with germs and they would fall ill. She therefore repeatedly cleaned her house and would wash and rewash her hands while preparing and serving a meal until the skin of her hands became raw.

Another form of restriction of behavior occurs in phobias. Whereas in ritualistic behavior one is compelled to act in certain ways to ward off disastrous consequences, in the case of phobias one must *not* do certain things in order to avoid possible but highly improbable dangers.

Another of Freud's case studies, "Little Hans," deals with such a phobia. Here, as mentioned earlier, a five-year-old boy was afraid to go out of the house because he believed he would be run down by a horse-driven wagon. In fact, he had once witnessed an accident in which a horse fell over. This accident, through symbolization and association, gave content to his unconscious fears. Although this phobic reaction to open spaces restricted his freedom and mobility, it also regulated his fears. It is important to note that Hans was not the only one restricted by the phobia. It also victimized his mother because she had to stay with him when he would not leave the house.

Besides agoraphobia (the fear of open spaces), fear of heights, elevators, and flying also restrict behavior. People will sometimes undergo hypnotic suggestion to rid themselves of their phobias, particularly when these become too restrictive or embarrassing. Phobias can often be financially costly. If an executive has a fear of flying that prevents him from attending business meetings or visiting clients, he will probably ruin his career unless he can eliminate the phobia. When a phobia is cured without understanding its cause, it is quite likely that other symptoms will appear or become exaggerated because the basic conflict remains untouched.

Sleep difficulties—either being unable to fall asleep or awakening after a brief sleep—are also common behavioral symptoms among children and older people. Insomnia may arise from fear of dying and the belief that falling asleep courts the risk of never awakening again. Sometimes parents take their infants to the pediatrician with the complaint that their babies have a sleep disturbance. Careful and tactful investigation may uncover that the sleep disturbance is in fact the parent's and not the child's, especially in the case of adults who are anxious about their capacity to be responsible caretakers.

A particular class of behavior reflects the inability to control impulses. Much impulse-ridden behavior is antisocial and includes stealing, extreme overeating, temper tantrums, and the inability to control uses of alcohol and certain drugs. Impulsive behavior often leads to conflict with authority and can be self-destructive. The most vivid illustration in the business and professional world is the case of alcoholism.

An executive, highly regarded for his work, began to drink heavily during business meetings and at sales conventions, becoming boisterous, indiscreet, and hostile. When cautioned about the effects of his loss of control, the executive vowed he would not drink at meetings. It soon became apparent that he could not refrain, and further inquiries revealed that he had a serious drinking problem not only at conventions. Although for a time he had managed to hide the problem from his associates, it became painfully apparent that he was out of control. Ultimately he lost his job.

People afflicted with alcoholism often deny that their behavior indicates a psychological problem. In fact, alcoholics are unreliable because they deny the problem to themselves and often lie to others about what they do. The board of directors of a company had to dismiss a chief executive officer who claimed his apparent drunkenness resulted from the adverse effects of prescription drugs. Whether he believed this himself is not certain, but he insisted almost to the end that he was not an alcoholic, even when confronted with incontrovertible evidence.

While little research has been done on the phenomenon of white-collar crime, acts of extortion and embezzlement in business often reflect neurotic disturbances. People commit white-collar crimes for the money, and also because they have limited control over their behavior. The impulse to act overcomes, or is not limited by, what one would conventionally consider responsible behavior and a sense of right and wrong. Compulsive gambling also illustrates a loss of control. The hope for a windfall stimulates the urge to gamble, although the individual knows the odds are against him; yet he is powerless to stop himself. To compound the problem, the compulsive gambler who runs up large debts may also commit white-collar crimes to pay off his obligations, thus adding to his and his family's misery.

Mood

The capacity to control one's behavior depends upon the ability to sustain or tolerate moods. Emotions arise from impulses or desires and from anticipation of pleasure or the dread of pain. The two dominant moods associated with symptoms of neuroses are anxiety and depression. Each of these involves an overriding emotional reaction—one likely to color not only particular actions and events but also one's total outlook on life. Single events, or anticipation of events, can call forth some anxiety, just as the shortfalls between what one expects and realizes can lead to a dampening of emotions or to disappointment. These are both corollaries of depression. Transient experiences with anxiety and depression are hardly symptomatic of neurosis; they are responses appropriate to one's experience. Indeed, the absence of awareness of anxiety and depression may be truly symptomatic when an individual works hard to deny emotions.

Anxiety presents itself as a sense of dread—the anticipation that something terrible is about to happen. Although the individual may realize intellectually that he or she is reacting without cause, the sense of impending danger cannot be shaken off by rational observation and reassurance. The fear is often accompanied by sensations of shortness of breath, heart palpitations, a hollow feeling in the stomach, possibly accompanied by a feeling of constriction in the throat. (Anxiety is so closely related to unpleasant body sensations that we arbitrarily exclude it from the class of symptoms referred to later in this chapter as impairment in body functions.) Anxiety may also precede or accompany phobic reactions, as well as some of the behavioral symptoms described earlier. Yet, at times, anxiety may be the chief symptom of neurosis and need not be connected with phobias.

Evidently anxiety is so widespread a symptom that it accounts for a large proportion of visits to physicians and the high frequency with which drugs such as valium are prescribed. The widespread use of valium and other tranquilizers that temporarily relieve anxiety indicates the degree to which people have become accustomed to anxiety, accepting it as their way of life. Only when the degree of anxiety heightens are people willing to try something different to gain relief.

> A middle-aged man reported that he always felt tense, but on one occasion the normal tension turned into a state of panic. He was having trouble getting along with his supervisor. He awakened from a nightmare and began sweating and experiencing labored breathing. He called the police who rushed him to the nearest hospital in an ambulance. Observation failed to diagnose a heart attack or other physical disorder. The event frightened the man sufficiently to impel him to seek psychotherapy, although he had enormous difficulty in acknowledging that he might be involved in neurotic conflict.

Depression as a mood appears as a reduction of energy and motivation. It is accompanied by sadness, often a deep sense of pessimism, and a low self-regard. It is not uncommon for depressed people to lose their appetites and consequently to lose weight. Mild depression often leads to sleepiness and, in its more severe forms, makes sleeping fitful and difficult. Depression occurs when one has suffered a loss through death, and is in such circumstances a normal part of grieving. It also occurs with other losses that affect one's sense of security and well being. The neurotic type of depression exists apart from experiences with actual losses in one's current life. The sadness and feelings of being unloved or worthless may exist without objective cause, just as the fears generated by anxiety exist without the presence of real danger.

Depression sometimes appears in conditions of rapid mood changes. For a period of time an individual may be depressed, but this mood shifts into its opposite, a state of elation. These sharply oscillating moods, particularly when they occur episodically and contain deep troughs of depression followed by extreme heights of elation, are not to be confused with neurotic depression. These cyclical mood states indicate manic-depressive illnesses, which are more serious than depressions that occur as symptoms of neurotic disturbance. Manic-depressive illness may be biologically determined, whereas no evidence of biological causation or family inheritance exists for neurotic depression.

Anxiety and depression are the major affective signs of neurotic conflict. The mood of emptiness in which the person feels nothing is generally regarded as symptomatic of neurotic conflict. Admittedly this mood of emptiness resembles depression and may be the mood state that heralds a depressive reaction. It differs from depression in that it appears frequently with a personal sense of being special or of grandiosity: the individual believes he or she is different from most others, if not superior. In contrast, depressed individuals acknowledge a sense of being diminished and of deserving little regard from others.

The feeling of emptiness is sometimes regarded as the exquisite form of existential despair. Albert Camus and other existential writers have raised this mood of emptiness to almost heroic proportions. In his novel, *The Stranger,* Camus describes the emptiness of his hero, a clerk in a business, who feels nothing in relation to people and little about himself. To break out of his nothingness he commits a senseless murder and then begins to feel a sense of internal vitality consequent to his murderous act.

The mood of emptiness and feeling nothing has become popularized in the notion of "turning off" and "tuning out." These moods of withdrawal are not psychotic-like because there is no impairment in reality sense or awareness. Rather, it is experienced as a loss of interest in the outside world. The "turning off" and "tuning out" syndrome, if it can legitimately be called a syndrome, seems to happen to people during their late adolescence and early adulthood. It also appears again in what is popularly known as the "mid-life crisis," although confronting middle age more often leads to depression.

Thought

The appearance of neurotic symptoms in patterns of thinking should not be confused with the dangerous mental state that accompanies psychotic disorders. In psychoses, thought disturbances appear with frequency and in forms highly visible to others. Psychotic thought disturbances include hallucinations that substitute for perceptions of reality. They also include delusional ideas of a persecutory nature and extreme grandiose fantasies. Both of these indicate paranoia.

The peculiarities of thinking in neurotic conflict are subtle, and frequently not easily accepted as symptoms. It is not unusual for thought patterns that reflect neuroses to appear ordinary both to the individual and to observers. The thought patterns are sometimes easily accommodated and passed off as simply that individual's "way."

One of the most interesting thought disturbances in neurotic conflict is obsessive thinking. Here thinking substitutes for action and is circular, persistent, and inconclusive. A sense of doubt is one indicator of obsessive thinking. Hamlet has been celebrated as the classic self-doubter whose innumerable questions locked him in his thought patterns at the cost of his ability to act. A person afflicted with excessive doubt will burden all decisions, major and minor, with weighty considerations from all sides of the question. The end result is a standoff. In back of the doubting and elaborations in thinking is a sense of ambivalence about people, substantive issues, and, of course, one's self. The close connection between ambivalence and obsessional thinking almost blurs the distinction between symptoms of mood and thought. The distinction still holds, however, in that an individual afflicted with obsessional thinking has very limited awareness of mood. The ambivalence is unconscious and appears in the form of doubting and excessive mental ruminating. In fact, obsessional thinkers characteristically force the separation between thinking and feeling. This forced division within the psyche accounts for their difficulty in communicating with other people.

> A woman in charge of a large organization was known for her brilliance and her verbal ability, but she was unable to hold peoples' attention and to convey her ideas. The reason for her difficulty in communicating was the over-elaboration of her thinking and, therefore, of her verbalization. In addition, her words lacked conviction because they were relatively devoid of feeling. This absence of affect made it difficult for people to listen to her.

People who think in obsessional ways seek an abstract level of thought. They are unable to move freely from the concrete to the abstract. Their fixation on abstract issues reinforces the quality of inconclusiveness in their thinking because the types of questions asked are virtually unanswerable. Obsessional thinking is pseudophilosophical since it lacks inherent rigor and does not observe the logical rules that characterize genuine philosophical exploration.

Obsessional thinking elaborates form at the expense of substance. Rather than solving problems involving substantive issues, the obsessional thinker becomes concerned with questions of how to solve problems. A preoccupation with methodology, although fruitful in the hands of the gifted, is a ruse generally designed to avoid reaching conclusions. Emphasis on form at the expense of substance also occurs in bureaucratic situations, or at least among those inclined toward a bureaucratic style. In bureaucracies, concern for rules and procedure often dominates in situations where common sense indicates that following the rules strictly will subvert the goals which the rules were supposed to support. What sociologists call the condition of trained incompetence—when substance becomes submerged in the preoccupation with adherence to method, procedure, and rules—is the logical outcome of obsessional thinking.

Neurotic symptoms that appear in obsessional thinking result in severe inhibitions in performance. Individuals with work blocks illustrate how obsessional thinking inhibits performance. For example:

> An executive noted for his promise and ambition performed brilliantly when called upon to give verbal presentations, particularly when he had little advance notice. But when he had to prepare talks in advance or present his thinking in writing, he could not meet the deadlines. Not infrequently he would simply fail to produce anything. Somehow putting his thoughts into writing created for him a sense of permanence, of going on record for all time as holding a particular position. When making verbal presentations he felt less committed, being able to change his mind and alter his presentation in midstream, depending upon his perceptions of audience reactions.

This same executive's reaction illustrates another quality often observed in neurotic thinking. It is not unusual to find very intelligent and rational individuals often engaging in a kind of magical thinking without being aware of its defects. Magical thinking is, on the whole, more subtle than superstition, although it has similarities to the use of a talisman to assure good fortune or to avoid disaster. People in certain occupations, such as sports and the theater, commonly adhere to superstitious rituals before performances or events. For example, members of a cast will tell an actor to "break a leg," a wish meant to ensure the actor's success and avoidance of misfortune. Athletic stars often perform religious or physical rituals before an event. Businessmen involved in risky decisions sometimes follow a ritual or adhere to a superstition as a means of assuring good luck. For instance, one executive in the retail business described how he always wore a particular blue suit on the day he opened a new store.

Such rituals and superstitions are often group oriented, designed to lift the spirits of a group involved in some risky activity. As such, they are relatively benign, and may even do some good if they succeed in raising morale. But magical thinking betrays an attempt to avoid reality and, if successful, leads to disaster. For example, a business executive who aspired for a degree of professional competence he did not possess instituted an elaborate pension and benefit program. This new program came at a time when the company faced the disastrous consequences of a new technology that the same executive had introduced without adequate testing and personnel training. By making a new "good" decision the executive hoped to undo his prior "bad" decision.

Organizations in the midst of crises are ripe for an outbreak of magical thinking. As Nero fiddled while Rome burned, so individuals resort to miracle solutions more as a means to provide reassurance to themselves than to address the realities of the problems confronting them.

Defects in thinking arising from neurotic thought patterns are not the result of low intelligence or an inability to think logically. Rather, the essence of neurotic thought is that both rational and irrational thinking coexist. As we shall discuss subsequently, the causes of the symptoms lie in the individual's attempts to secure some equilibrium in the midst of inner confusion and turmoil. Every new equilibrium that evolves from internal stresses may exact a price in the form of neurotic symptoms in any one of the ways described so far in this chapter.

Body Function

Almost everyone is familiar with the concept of psychosomatic disorders. The types of physical symptoms that signal probable instances of a mind-body alteration are stomach distress, including ulcers and colitis, certain coughs, asthma, allergies, and cardiovascular disease. Some researchers believe that heart attacks are caused, in part, by stress. There is some evidence that particular personality types are at higher risk for coronary problems than other types. The type at highest risk is the tense, impatient, hard-driving individual who may be at additional risk because this type of person also often tends to be a heavy cigarette smoker, uses alcohol immoderately, lacks exercise, and has poor eating habits.

The mind-body problem in neuroses has been called "the mysterious leap" to designate not only the fact that science has not achieved an understanding of the relationship between mental conflict and somatic disturbances but also to call attention to the lack of specificity between causes and effects of illnesses. As we suggested earlier, a variety of somatic disturbances can all be related to one common underlying conflict, such as the repression and frustration of dependency desires.

The problem may also be complicated by the real possibility that "the illness of choice" is determined not only by body tendencies of the sort that Sigmund Freud called "somatic compliance" but also by the possible interplay of cultural, individual, and biological factors. A study of key employees in a large bureaucracy revealed that cultural factors affect the types of stress symptoms individuals are likely to report. Operating in Canada, the organization's executives were English and French, the two main cultural groups in the country. The statistics on their reported stress symptoms showed that the English group presented symptoms of a psychosomatic character, such as stomach distress, respiratory disorders, and allergies. The French Canadians reported proportionately fewer psychosomatic symptoms and more emotional symptoms, such as anxiety and depression. These findings suggest that body symptoms of neurotic disorders may result from predispositions established through learning and cultural influences. Learning obviously takes place in the family, which acts as the mediator between the wider culture and the individual. In this case, the English may, through example and precept in the family, learn to sit on their feelings, which beyond a certain point will break out as a bodily ailment. In contrast, the French learn to sensitize their experience, even in exaggerated forms, and therefore suffer emotional distress.

It may be that all symptoms are part of a language of distress. To understand this language is to learn about what causes the distress. Facility with the language may also help to relieve the symptoms.

A complicating factor in considering psychosomatic illness as the language of distress is the unwillingness of the sufferer to disclose what the symptoms are trying to communicate. This is not due to willful and conscious suppression but rather to the unconscious wish to gain from the illness. Someone suffering from physical rather than purely psychological symptoms is less likely to be accused of malingering.

In addition to the disguise provided by symptoms, the sufferer may also gain some moral advantage by taking a martyr-like attitude toward enduring pain. People with physical symptoms can also gain some advantage through exhibitionism. They can often exert control over others with the certainty that they will avoid criticism and reproaches. The same cannot be said for people with apparently pure psychological symptoms. In a society that values individualism and self-reliance, it is not easy to show patience for neurotic sufferers, particularly if they have many material advantages. Little tolerance thus exists for such disorders as obsessional thinking, anxiety, or depression. The fallout from psychosomatic disorders in the form of secondary motives or gains derived from an illness may be more widespread than at first meets the eye.

> A young adult man described how as a child he discovered a way to cause swollen glands in his neck, a temperature, and other symptoms that persuaded his mother he was ill and should be kept away from school. By pinching his nostrils and keeping his mouth tightly closed while blowing out as hard as he could, the boy found his neck glands would swell alarmingly enough to convince his mother to keep him in bed. The boy played on his mother's overprotectiveness to prolong his dependency on her. His stance of excessive clinging remained a latent component of his relationship to his mother until it was dissolved when his excessive love turned to hate.

A further piece of evidence that yields some clues about the quality of psychosomatic disorders is in the widely known "placebo effect." Although statistics are not easily available, it is commonly believed that a significant proportion of visits to a physician are made in response to neurotic symptoms. Some of these are clearly physical; others are more clearly mood related. Earlier we referred to the widespread use of valium and other tranquilizers. Doctors seem to know that the disappointment a patient feels when no prescription is ordered may result in sufficient anger to worsen the patient's state of mind. In the case of suspected neuroses, giving the patient a placebo may secure temporary relief from symptoms. If together with a harmless prescription the doctor offers a sympathetic ear, much may have been accomplished in providing relief, even if only for a short time. The patient's attitude toward the doctor may be the real "cure" while the medication or neutral placebo represent the doctor's concern and desire to help.

Placebos serve another purpose in medical experimentation that offers some additional evidence about their effects on neurotic symptoms of a physical nature. It is considered vital in clinical trials of new medications to conduct experiments with a control group as well as an experimental group. Both groups have the same physical illness, but one is given the trial medication, the other the placebo. If the trial medication is useful, the experimental group should show improvement while the control group should remain the same. Placebos do not work where physical illness with clear organic and biological causes exists. In the case of physical symptoms in the absence of organic causes, placebos are apt to have at least a temporary effect in ameliorating symptoms. The placebo effect is so powerful that experimenters in clinical tests make certain there is no contamination through doctor-patient relationships. Those administering dosages do not know whether they are offering a medication or a placebo, nor do they know if the subject is a member of the experimental or the control group.

Character

Standard works on psychiatry describe two types of disturbances associated with character. The first type is referred to as character disorders, the symptoms of which were discussed in this chapter among behavioral symptoms. These symptoms include sociopathic behavior, impulse-ridden behavior, addictions, and sexual perversions. The theory of character disorders emphasizes defects in the structure of the mind, particularly those aspects of structure that regulate and control the impulses. When the regulatory structures are inadequate and lack cohesiveness, the impulse to act without regard for consequences may become overpowering. The end result is often criminal behavior and/or self-destructive behavior such as alcoholism and drug addiction. While this explanation is somewhat oversimplified it nevertheless provides important clues to the causes of character disorders.

The second type of character disturbance refers to symptoms of pathology involving the total personality. In everyday usage, the character of an individual usually refers to moral qualities. When an individual is said to have a "good" character, such qualities as being lawful, generous, observant of the golden rule, and having other socially valuable traits come to mind; opposite traits appear to describe people with "bad" characters. There are, however, a range of traits that are only tangentially related to morality but are significant when used to describe a total personality. These character traits can sometimes be identified as an individual's style—the distinctive quality that makes him or her known to others as a singular individual easily differentiated from other people.

Because character arises out of the link between the inner person and the way that person appears to other people, the range of traits to be considered goes beyond style to encompass talents, interests, appearance, and even mannerisms. Character then is the total personality the individual presents to the world. In this broad use of the term character, we are not limited merely to the development of personality from the inside. We must also consider the influences of social factors such as class, occupation, and cultural background. The appearance of these character traits in individuals who appear to be submissive, passive, withdrawn, and even depressive may not be a function of neurotic disturbance but, rather, a learned response to sociocultural influences. For example, people who are oppressed in society and forced into subservient positions will develop all of the earmarks of a depressive character neurosis. But such a diagnosis would be very misleading. Character traits in such cases are learned responses. They are designed to secure survival in surroundings hostile to the individual and to the group from which he or she originates.

Similar distinctions may be implied in considering, for example, the differences in character between men and women. Stereotypically the male is aggressive, outgoing, and more practical in his approach to life, more self-assured, and more willing to take risks than the female. Women stereotypically are less aggressive, more nurturant, sensitive, moralistic, and conservative than men. While there is evidence to indicate that differences in aggressiveness and physical strength are biologically determined in men and women, other character traits are formed in response to a society's role definitions of men and women. A society teaches individuals, through families, school, and occupation, to fit these selected definitions.

For some individuals, the ability and willingness to assume certain roles and to develop the character traits consistent with their assigned roles become a central conflict. The conflict may even interact with neurotic conflicts. The two types of conflict are distinguishable and worth keeping separate by dividing the pathological, in the sense we have been using this term, from an individual's life struggle to express talents and desires that find little hospitality in a given culture or society. This distinction is not easily drawn. Very often gifted people struggling against stereotypic roles become creative in working through their struggle but, at the same time, are deeply involved in neurotic conflicts.

The field of psychobiography has taken on the challenge of showing the interaction of talent, character, society, and neuroses in the life and works of great persons. Although psychobiography focuses on outstanding individuals who have a place in history, the problem and methodology of this new field of scholarship may also be important in understanding the general human condition. Psychobiography may provide an accurate reflection of the struggles in all our lives to deal with personal neuroses and the demands of society. A majority of the people in any culture may tilt the balance toward society in the form of conventional adjustment and the diminution of the effects of neurotic conflict. Nonetheless, the role of individual neuroses in achieving or failing to achieve solutions must be taken into account.

A factory manager in a medium-sized organization presented major problems to his immediate boss, to his peers, and to subordinates. He held very low opinions of their competence and he appeared impatient when they came to him for help. The nature of the product made in this factory required that people in sales, engineering, accounting and personnel call on him for help. The only individual the factory manager held in high esteem was the president. The factory manager thought the president was a brilliant man and the only person in the company who was worthy of respect and admiration. Although he was feared for his stern manner, shortness of temper and his willingness to tell other people how they fell short of his expectations, the factory manager had the reputation of being extremely competent, ambitious, and hard working. In short, he was a valuable man to his company, but, because he did not suffer fools gladly, his future in the company was in jeopardy. His abrasiveness and impatience led people to rebel against him. The president of the company concluded, with great reluctance, that unless the man changed, he would have to let him go.

Although this man displayed character traits classically fitting the description of the "authoritarian personality," it would be difficult to isolate the derivation of these traits in his personality.

The authoritarian personality is a product of a sociocultural milieu in which, on the one hand, a person is expected to hold rigid beliefs and to act in harsh ways toward others, particularly those who are dependent upon him. On the other hand, he or she is expected to idealize authority figures. Authoritarian cultures give rise to a belief in duty, obligation, and stern punishment for those who transgress. In American culture, the authoritarian personality is not a hero. One way of looking at the factory manager's problem is to observe the lack of fit between his sadistic, authoritarian tendencies and the expectations of the people with whom he had to interact. These people, for the most part, were the products of the American culture, which values equality and the muting of power in interpersonal relations. One could easily conclude that the conflicts presented in this case were not personal or neurotic and that the factory manager's character traits, which were so ill-fitting, derived from his cultural background and were, therefore, not neurotic symptoms. Indeed, inquiry into the factory manager's personal history revealed that he was born in an eastern European country where his social class expected authority figures to use punitive force in their interpersonal relations. To illustrate further aspects of the authoritarian personality:

> A man in charge of a retail store which was part of a large corporate chain showed similar sadistic characteristics. Subordinates complained to his boss and representatives of the personnel department about his tendencies to humiliate people when issuing directives or reprimands. He appeared especially hostile to women employees. He was in his late thirties, unmarried and, like our factory manager, a diligent supervisor who had a reputation for running profitable stores. This store manager was born in the United States and was familiar with American attitudes toward authority, yet in managing the store he could not overcome his tendency to lose his temper, to berate his employees, and to display authoritarian qualities in his approaches to people.

An inquiry into the store manager's background revealed the fact that he lost his father at a very early age and had been raised by his grandparents. He was physically punished during childhood and adolescence and could not recall ever being befriended or helped by an older male while in school or in the military. Although the evidence so far would not be conclusive, the material suggests that his character traits, mainly the sadistic ones, were formed in response to a neurotic conflict rather than sociocultural factors.

Character serves as protective armor. People who are lonely and somewhat mistrustful of friendships keep other people at a distance by being aggressive, insensitive, and sometimes cruel in their attitudes and behavior. No amount of attention to social skills will alleviate the conditions that give rise to a character armor that is meant to keep other people at a safe distance. Furthermore, people with sadistic character traits tend to be preemptive. Living with fear of being humiliated or abused by a more powerful figure, they will often attempt to act first: they attack and humiliate others to avoid becoming victims themselves.

Finally, there is a strong sexual component in sadism. For motives we need not go into here, cruelty and sexual pleasure become fused. The end result is that even in activities seemingly far removed from sexual interchanges, a strong measure of satisfaction is derived from being cruel to people, in the same way that some children gain pleasure from cruel acts toward animals.

One of the important factors that distinguishes neurotic conflict from other conflict is the presence of fantasy, usually unconscious, which supports the individual's behavior. The content and quality of such fantasies provide important clues to the motives that fuel the conflict and produce the symptoms. Character structure is one of the residues of fantasy and conflicting motives.

Thus far we have singled out character structure with marked sadistic features to illustrate the part played by neurotic symptoms in the formation of character. A number of other symptoms also cluster together to establish an individual's unique character. The opposite of the sadistic type is the masochistic character, for whom enduring an unhappy fate seems to be inevitable. The nature of these "destiny neuroses" seems to point to the innocence of the sufferer. Closer investigation usually demonstrates that the individual has a need to suffer and brings about his or her hard luck.

> A vice president of a corporation was shocked to learn that the president wanted him to resign even though his record for profit and growth was excellent. But the vice president had made a number of moves designed to threaten and test the authority of his boss, including removing his headquarters to a city remote from the business and suggesting to his peers that they join his rebellion. He refused to implement a directive, which the president finally sent after making many other attempts to reach an agreement with his vice president on the course of action needed to alleviate a major problem. The vice president dragged his heels and finally forced the president's hand.
>
> During a lengthy interview, the vice president described the devastating effect of being fired on his self-image, economic well-being, and the security of his family. He asked the interviewer, a consultant to the company, to intervene on his behalf so that the request for his resignation would be withdrawn. With some patience and careful listening, the interviewer found that on his previous job, a responsible executive position, this vice president had gone two levels above his immediate boss to complain about his superior's inadequacy and how the company would be better off if he were discharged. The vice president implied, of course, that he would be more suitable for the position than his boss. The vice president was asked to resign from this company as well.

The probability seemed high that this individual had a need to court disaster and, on this score, demonstrated the traits of a masochistic character. The need appeared to be so strong and so deeply imbedded in his character that he had to produce situations of suffering that he could view as the result of other people's insensitivity or of an unlucky fate. A further illustration:

> A young woman with a spirited personality and considerable intelligence found herself repeatedly enmeshed in relationships in which she was abused and denigrated. Whenever she found a man who might have been interested in her in a serious way, she withdrew from the relationship and turned toward someone whose proclivities for abuse soon came to the surface. On one occasion during such an affair she became so frightened that she asked the police for help.

Closer examination indicated that she was far from being the helpless victim she believed herself to be. She had developed a repertoire for engaging her lovers by teasing them and casting doubts on their masculinity. Her flirtation with danger, also an aspect of her character structure, appeared in reaction to certain depressive tendencies that were suppressed by the excitement she generated.

A final example, which by no means completes the catalog of character symptoms, is the rather common phenomenon of the passive-aggressive personality.

> A young man learned from a woman with whom he had been in love that she no longer wanted to see him. He felt destroyed but could begin to realize that his passivity had become disturbing to her. She had made remarkable strides in her career while he could not bring himself to make a choice about what he wanted to do in life. He made his passivity visible to her in other ways, including his desire that she make all the decisions.

The aggressive side of this man's character structure made itself felt but in highly disguised forms. He could not recognize the aggressiveness in his clinging and in the demands he made upon his lover. Fortunately he was able to accept the end of this relationship while he went about making some important decisions concerning his future.

One of the many intriguing qualities about the presence of neurotic symptoms in character structure is the ease with which people are able to accept the symptoms almost as a natural state. It is even possible to endow these symptoms with virtues in order to disguise any possible connection with their neurotic conflicts. Consequently, changes in character structure are quite difficult to bring about. Whereas most neurotic symptoms cause suffering to the person who has them, people with characterological symptoms usually cause more suffering to others. One of the reasons people with character symptoms try to change is that their interpersonal relations fail to such a degree that they finally must examine themselves as a source of the problem.

Neurotic symptoms arise out of conflict within the psyche. The symptoms appear as disturbances in behavior, thought, mood, body function, and character formation. It is almost impossible to describe symptoms of neuroses without delving into the dynamics that bring them about, but the emphasis in this chapter has been on description and, only by inference, on explanation. In the next chapter we will examine the causes of neuroses in the interplay of the forces that bring them about and maintain them.

THEORY OF
NEUROSES: EXPLANATIONS

The *New York Times* carried an Associated Press report of a tragedy that occurred on December 29, 1981, in Ludlow, Massachusetts. Here is the report as it appeared in the December 30 issue of the *Times:*

Young Hunter Kills Himself

After Wounding Best Friend

A medical examiner said today that a teenager committed suicide with a .22 caliber rifle after the gun discharged and wounded his best friend as they were fox hunting. Michael Fredette, a 15-year-old whose father shot himself to death November 8 while trying to persuade someone else not to fear guns, was pronounced dead at Mercy Hospital in Springfield, Mass. at 9:30 A.M. Monday. Kevin Wojcik, 15, a classmate at Ludlow High School, was admitted in critical condition to Baystate Medical Center with a gunshot wound in his head.

"The cause of death was probable suicide based on the evidence we presented and the results of the autopsy," Police Chief John Jorge of Ludlow said. Dr. William Mosig performed the autopsy at Mercy Hospital. "We're quite certain of the cause," the police chief added.

He said the police found a spent shell in the snow and another in the chamber of the rifle. To fire the rifle, it is necessary to flip a bolt up and back to eject the spent shell and push the bolt forward to lock it to load another shell, Chief Jorge said.

CHAPTER

5

> The police believe that the shootings occurred as the youths rested, he said, while a third teenage hunting companion scouted the area for foxes.
>
> Michael's rifle discharged, piercing the back of the Wojcik youth's skull, Chief Jorge theorized, then Michael turned the rifle on himself because he had wounded his friend.
>
> Their companion, 50 yards away, heard the gunshots and found the youths lying together in a field, the police said.
>
> The youths had hunting licenses and had attended a firearms safety course, the police chief said.
>
> Michael's father, Lionel Fredette, a 47-year-old gun collector and father of two boys and three girls, was killed November 8 when he put a .357-Magnum revolver to his forehead to persuade a friend of one of his daughters not to fear guns.
>
> Chief Jorge said the father asked the friend, "Do you think I would do this with a loaded gun?" and put the revolver to the bridge of his nose, pulling the trigger three times. The third time it fired, killing him, the chief said.

Unless Kevin Wojcik had survived the shooting, there would be no one who could report with any degree of certainty what actually occurred. Even if Wojcik had survived, much would remain to be reconstructed about the causes of the shootings in the woods. The main area of uncertainty would be Michael Fredette's state of mind prior to the discharge of the rifle. Undoubtedly, the police chief and the doctor performing the autopsy had many doubts about what occurred, but certainly in the interests of the injured boy's family and the dead boy's family, the reconstruction made public was the most humane interpretation that could have been offered. The tragedy, however, throws into bold relief the questions of what causes human actions and how one arrives at inferences and interpretations that depend upon some notion of cause and effect.

Those who are inclined toward external explanations of events would undoubtedly focus on social causes. The pro-gun control people would focus on the fact that guns are readily available and therefore enable people to injure others and themselves through the easy access to revolvers and rifles. People who object to the killing of animals for sport or for any other reason would probably focus on the dangers of hunting in the woods where accidents occur each year, killing and wounding hunters and bystanders. Educators interested in problems of public safety might wish to inquire into the adequacy of the firearms safety course available to the boys and to others as a way of minimizing accidents. Perhaps the content of the course or the way it was taught fell short. Had they been more adequate, one could speculate, the rifle might have been held differently while the boys were resting, and therefore would not have discharged.

But even with such external explanations, the question of state of mind will not disappear. Was the first shooting accidental? Was Michael so distraught over his father's death that he became demented, shot his friend, and then turned the rifle on himself as a kind of act of reunion with his dead father? Was he so enraged at his father that he lashed out, confusing his closest friend and his father? None of these causes, derived from reconstructing motives and a state of mind, depend on the presence of conscious intent. The motives could have been unconscious, but if so, the reconstruction of the event will leave room for doubt. There is a method for discerning unconscious motives, but obviously it cannot be applied in this case.

Explaining behavior, or finding causes for how people act, is difficult. It is complicated by lack of information and often the difficulty encountered in collecting needed data. In addition, the difficulties are compounded by attitudes. There is little reason for individuals to disclose their motives, even if they were known to themselves. Those who seek to discern or interpret motivation frequently lack the objectivity needed. They are often incapable of listening carefully because they cannot hold judgment in suspense, and cannot avoid moralistic stances, even where such stances are inappropriate. Nevertheless, it is impossible to avoid interpretations of actions and motives in human relations. For human intercourse to occur even under the most routine conditions, people automatically act in response to their definition of the situation, which includes why the other person is acting the way he is.

Building theories is not an occupation reserved to the scientist. All attempts to create a sense of order out of one's experience requires a theory. The trouble with everyday theory building is that often the results tend to be incomplete, incorrect, and misleading. Psychological intelligence assumes that individuals are capable of going beyond commonsense derivatives of conventional wisdom to apply some critical judgment in the theories they adopt for their personal or professional uses.

Here are some axioms useful as guidelines for building theories that apply to explanations of neuroses according to psychoanalytic observation and principles:

1. *Behavior is overdetermined*. This principle means that there is no one cause or explanation of behavior or a state of mind. People act

in response to multiple motives that operate simultaneously. Some of the motives are conscious, but many are unconscious.

2. *Motives need not be consistent.* While the need for consistency may be the sign of a modest intelligence, it is also a misleading way to understand human behavior. Ideas and emotions do not function according to the physical law stating that two objects cannot occupy the same space at the same time. In the mental sphere, multiple thoughts and feelings coexist even in defiance of logic. The concept of ambivalence points to the fact that individuals simultaneously experience sharply contradictory feelings toward others. The love-hate polarization is ubiquitous and not solely in the domain of the poet.

3. *Intention, motive, and meaning gain visibility through symbols.* Direct expression, while important, does not exhaust the meaning of what people do and what they think. To understand one's self and others requires some capacity for the observation and translation of symbolic expression.

4. *The past determines the present.* People are carriers of history, both personal and collective. The idea of the "here and now" can only make sense if one incorporates understanding of how it is possible for history to be omnipresent in human affairs. To interpret according to a literal definition of the "here and now" without regard for history will mislead.

5. *Most behavior and its underlying motives go beyond simple dichotomies of good and evil, egoistic and altruistic, healthy and unhealthy.* To interpret is to suspend judgment, at least long enough to gain some access to how other people think. Becoming moralistic too quickly surely closes access, just as being "pollyannish" reveals one's superficiality. A perceptive statement of this principle comes from Albert Camus' novel *The Plague:*

> The evil that is in the world always comes of ignorance, and good intentions may do as much harm as malevolence, if they lack understanding. On the whole, men are more good than bad; that, however, isn't the real point. But they are more or less ignorant, and it is this last that we call vice or virtue; the most incorrigible vice being that of an ignorance that fancies it knows everything and therefore claims for itself the right to

kill. The soul of the murderer is blind; and there can be no true
goodness nor true love without the utmost clear-sightedness.

The fundamental job of explanation in understanding neuroses is to establish the causes of psychological conflict. The various symptoms of
neurotic disturbance arise from and express the conflicts raging within
the psyche. The explanations must meet two conditions. First, they must
present a logical portrayal of how various forces within the psyche can be
in conflict and can produce symptoms. This condition of explanation
deals with the dynamics of the mind. It can be designated as a *psychodynamic* explanation of neuroses. A second condition presents an explanation of neuroses as a result of historical forces. Here the *personal
history* of the individual explains the existence in the present of neurotic
conflicts that lead to the formation of symptoms.

PSYCHODYNAMICS

The conflict of forces, or the psychodynamics of neuroses, begins with
the concept of psychic energy and the pleasure principle. Individuals experience tension derived from instinctual drives and their derivatives. The
pleasure principle asserts that instinctual energy in addition to having
quantity has direction, which is toward discharge. The aim of energy is to
seek an outlet in the form of an object that will permit or enable discharge and the reduction of tension.

Energy connected with instinctual drives can be understood as
desires for food, water, and sex, as well as the striving for satisfaction of
a myriad of needs such as achievement, power, belonging, and recognition. The theory of drives in psychoanalysis uses two categories of energy
derived from biological sources—sexual and aggressive energy. Sexual
energy, or *libido,* can be viewed broadly as life-giving and life-sustaining
energy. This is more all encompassing than what is conventionally understood as genital sexuality. Aggressive energy is destructive in that its discharge is the cause for some modification in the environment. To build a
house one must fell a tree; to gain food one must alter the soil or kill an
animal. Aggressive energy is also at the root of the propensity to make
war and to kill. There is sufficient violence to offer some validation of the
idea that man inherently has aggressive energy that seeks discharge.

The two types of energy, sex and aggression, have a common
aim: to seek discharge utilizing the environment and the objects in it. The
psychodynamics of neuroses begin with the inhibition of discharge, or
thwarting of the pleasure principle. What one desires, quantitatively and

qualitatively, is usually not available, at least not easily or in the original form in which desire exists. What inhibits the activity that results in discharge and pleasure is, on the one hand, reason and self-control and, on the other hand, morality and conscience. The interplay of desire, reason, and conscience is the condition of neurosis because the result of this interplay is the formation of symptoms. The symptoms of neurosis are the expressions of the compromises undertaken within the psyche, which is forced to do work imposed upon it initially by the presence of powerful impulses.

The idea of symptoms as a compromise, although a costly one, among the conflicting forces within the psyche needs some clarification and illustration. Take the case of "Little Hans," described earlier. Hans was afraid to go out of the house because he feared horses. This phobia was a symptom of an intrapsychic conflict. Hans wanted to dominate his mother, a wish that combines both sexual and aggressive impulses. Hans could not gratify his wish, first, because it was unrealistic, as judged by parents and other authorities, and second, because there was no ready way within his capacities for him to get what he wanted. The parental authority standing in his way was the equivalent of a bad conscience that tells him one is wrong to want what he wants and, furthermore, that persisting in these desires will result in being punished. Hans makes real this fear of punishment by the image of a horse that will bite or otherwise harm him, and is therefore in terror of going outside. He suffers the symptom of anxiety consciously associated with the idea that some harm will befall him in the form of a horse he will encounter when he leaves the house. The other side of this symptom of anxiety is another symptom— the restriction of his freedom and the limitation of his development so that he is unable to gain the pleasures available to a person his age. He is forced into a regressed position in life as a consequence of his neurosis: the conflict between his wish to have and dominate his mother, on the one side, and his sense that this is an inappropriate desire for which he can expect to be punished, on the other. But note an additional and crucial fact about the symptoms. Insofar as his phobia causes his mother to stay at home to take care of him or to be with him when he goes outside as a way of overcoming his fears, Hans gets what he wants, but in a modified and costly form.

Symptoms of neuroses involve a measure of gain. There is some satisfaction of the pleasure principle along with all of the painful aspects of the symptoms. In this sense, all symptoms are a result of the compromise of forces within the psyche—the forces deriving from desire, reason, and conscience.

While the presumption throughout this book is that most readers will have little familiarity with psychoanalysis as theory and therapy, the ideas of psychoanalysis have permeated our culture. Most readers have encountered the idea that the structure of the mind can be divided into three parts or agencies. The first is the *id,* which represents instinctual drives or what here has been termed desire. The second is the *ego,* which represents reason and the functions that permit the testing of reality. The third is the *superego,* which represents the forces of conscience and morality.

In the case of "Little Hans" just cited, it is clear that the desires he cannot readily satisfy belong to him: he wants what he wants when he wants it. It is not clear, however, that the agencies called ego and superego function as part of his personality. Rather, his parents and other authorities act as his link to reality and reality testing, just as they serve as his conscience, to show him and tell him what is right and wrong. It would seem, therefore, that the case of Little Hans would not exactly meet the conditions that define a psychoneurosis.

We have indicated that what is a unique characteristic of neuroses is that the locus of conflict is within the psyche; neurotic symptoms arise from the conflict of forces within the mind. It would appear to be more accurate to say that for Little Hans, the conflict he is experiencing is a *real* conflict instead of neurotic conflict. Real conflict suggests that the locus of the antagonistic forces are in two places: within the individual and in the forces of the real world represented by other people, institutions, and impersonal conditions. A man or woman out of a job and feeling depressed may be involved in a real conflict as opposed to a psychoneurotic conflict.

The solution to this problem of distinguishing the locus of the conflict will become clear when we discuss the way the past provides the foundation for neuroses in the present. For the time being, we shall suggest that the bridge between real and neurotic conflict is in the concept of internalization. While conscience was once personified in the presence and actions of external figures or parents as objects, the representation of the parents' moral code is taken into, or internalized, by the psyche. This internalization gives rise to the superego as an agency of the mind that exists in an autonomous way within the psyche. Real conflict, particularly during the early years of childhood, leads to neurotic conflict. Agencies of the mind that provide the forces in conflict exist within the individual.

Symptoms are the compromises resulting from the struggle among conflicting forces, denoted by the agencies referred to as id, ego, and superego. The conflicting forces involved in neurotic symptoms are mainly unconscious. If consciousness dominated during the play of forces, the resulting compromises would serve the individual's interests far better than they are served with the appearance of symptoms. It is not valid to assume that people are perverse by their nature and that they seek poor solutions to their problems. On the contrary, self-interest is a powerful force. The case to be made is simply that people do the best they can. In the face of unconscious forces that operate intrapyschically, the compromises represent the best solution available to an individual at any given time. Unfortunately, most compromises yield some measure of painful symptoms.

To illustrate the content of intrapsychic conflict, here is an associative story told in response to one of the pictures in the Thematic Apperception Test series. The respondent was an engineer who participated in a study designed to illuminate the nature of career conflicts. The particular picture to which he associated showed a solitary male figure silhouetted by an open window. The picture is devoid of content and enables the respondent to project upon this ambiguous stimulus whatever fantasy comes to mind. Here is the story the engineer produced:

> The character is an Air Force bomber pilot who has been scheduled for a bombing mission. The pilot has arisen early and is contemplating the weather in the light of the early dawn. The mission is a hazardous one and the pilot is wondering what is in store. The mission is scheduled to be the last before the crew is rotated back to the States. The bad luck of the last two crews in the same situation comes to mind, and he wonders what effect this will have on the morale of his crew and if it will affect the performance of their duties. After their briefing the pilot gives the crew a cheerful pep talk that fools no one. The mission is flown successfully with only some minor damage to the plane. However, the transport carrying them back to the States crashes on take-off and kills half the crew.

At the outset, it is important to recognize that the choice of story theme and its affective content reflect what goes on inside the skin of the respondent. The fact that the engineer chose a theme that couples aggression and danger suggests that he is preoccupied and conflicted about aggressiveness. He places his hero in a position of responsibility, and a lonely one at that, because he must uphold the morale of those dependent upon him, although no one is there to do the same for him. The irony presented in the demise of "half the crew," destroyed after facing the danger of battle and on their way home to loved ones, hints at the ubiquity of danger and at the need to detach one's self from the responsibility for the harm aggression causes. After all, another pilot crashes the plane on takeoff. Whether the hero survived or not is in doubt. The climax of destruction and death absolves the hero whether or not he survived. The hurt resulting from the free-floating aggression is left to the imagination of the reader. The impulse to hurt others finds expression, while the guilty conscience is assuaged because the harm that occurs is through no fault of the hero-pilot in the story.

One can readily interpret the neurotic struggle suggested by this story in the language of the three part structural model of the mind (id, ego, and superego). The id impulses are mainly aggressive, are elaborated in the theme of war, bombing, death, and destruction. The inference of superego controls derives from the loneliness of the pilot, his weight of responsibility, and the solution to the problem of aggression that clears the hero of culpability. The ego functions defend against guilt and anxiety mainly through the story structure and content. The writer establishes his major defensive position by distancing the story in time and place, by evoking fate, and by the uses of irony in constructing the story. The nuclear conflict at best can only be hypothesized from the story. It does not appear in a story that provides ample room for the work of censorship, both conscious and unconscious, given the situation under which it was written.

The concept of defense derives from a principle of equilibrium that applies equally well to the mind as it does to the body. Although a separate chapter in this book will examine ego defenses, it is not possible to consider the psychodynamics of neurotic conflict without introducing the concept of defense.

The biological capabilities of all organisms include the inherent mechanisms to restore the body to a steady state when attacked from within or from the outside by noxious agents or stimuli. Just as the body has signaling devices to begin a biochemical process of defense against bacteria, and the mind has its own devices of defense against the onslaughts of painful stimuli, so does the ego have defenses to deal with anxiety. If, for example, one is suddenly confronted with danger from some object, the automatic flow of adrenaline permits the individual to mobilize defenses that can lead to actions such as fight or flight. In guarding against the dangers arising from instinctual arousal that seek direct discharge, the defensive position establishes itself in response to signals. The signals initiating defenses are anxiety and other painful affects such as guilt and shame. The success of the defenses can be measured by the reduction of these painful affects. The limitations or failures of defense can be measured by the extent and severity of symptoms that appear in conjunction with the effort to restore equilibrium.

Symptoms are a measure of the costs of neurotic conflict, but also the degree to which the person is able to cope with conflict, inflicting the least harm upon himself. Whatever the set of symptoms that arise as a result of the psychodynamics of conflict and defense, it represents the effort to restore the state of equilibrium. One must always bear in mind the possibility that however painful and costly the symptoms are, there always lurks in the background a far worse solution to the problem of intrapsychic conflict. One set of symptoms guards against another set that represents an individual's potential for psychopathology.

The bomber pilot story illustrates how neurotic conflict works. It demonstrates the formation of defenses against the derivatives of aggression as they appear in destructive fantasies. One of the most difficult considerations in a theory of neurosis based in part on impulse and desire is to place aggression in the model. The same difficulty does not appear in the case of sexual drives. One would not quarrel with the idea that sex is a fundamental drive, that its roots are biological, and that the developmental changes that occur in the sex drive throughout an individual's life activate the maturation of the individual. Although a strong case can be made for the view that aggression is also an innate, biologically determined drive, several problems must first be resolved. Among them is the question of how to deal with the reactive nature of aggression.

Is aggression innate or a consequence of frustration? If the human being is thwarted in the gratification of desire, an upsurge in aggression will result. One answer to this problem of whether aggression is innate or reactive is to suggest that both positions are correct. Aggressive impulses are stimulated when the individual is frustrated and a condition of anxiety will arise consequently to block the expression of hostile and destructive wishes. On the other hand, it is probably correct to say that reactive aggression draws on biologically determined aggressive energy. The reason for this position is simple observation that aggression serves many ends and purposes and not just the motive of revenge. It is not possible to survive without the availability of aggressive energy and the capacity to use it. To build a house, one must fell a tree!

Another type of problem arises when considering energy in the explanation of neurosis. Energy connotes mechanics. A mechanistic framework tends to remove one from the human being who endures the suffering and ultimately is able to communicate the meaning and significance of neurotic conflict. Some observers of psychoanalysis, including numerous practitioners, shy away from the concept of energy claiming that mechanistic concepts prevent the development of empathy essential in understanding another human being. This tension between mechanics and humanism is inherent in psychoanalysis. It is the familiar problem of quantity and quality that permeated our discussion of the unconscious. To state the problem another way, the model of neurosis that deals with the play of forces—of instinctual drives and defenses—does not at the same time tell the story of what the intrapsychic conflicts are about. One runs the risk of losing sight of the person enduring the suffering and of being capable of listening to and making sense of the story the person wants to tell.

The other side of the coin, however, is the misunderstanding both of psychoanalysis and of the human condition that arises when the quantitative and mechanistic points of view disappear or are ignored. Sooner or later, every human situation will appear commonplace and banal. When such a time arrives, the tendency to resort to everyday wisdom both to explain and to deal with human conflict will assert itself. Much about neurosis and the human condition is mysterious. It is probable that a considerable source of the mystery derives from the effects of instinctual energy in human development. The conservative approach is to keep a path open to the probable sources of new knowledge.

A psychodynamic, or mechanistic, explanation of neuroses examines how the interplay of forces within the psyche produces symptoms. This explanation examines the forces in conflict in the present time, but underlying the focus on the present is a historical perspective. The forces in conflict in the "here and now" derive from one's personal history. Circumstances in the past create conditions in the present. In the following section the relationship between past and present will be considered in the presence of psychological conflict and the formation of symptoms of neuroses.

PERSONAL HISTORY AS EXPLANATION OF NEUROSES

One critical finding of psychoanalytic investigation is that all neuroses are derived from or caused by psychological conflicts in the past, particularly during the formative years of infancy and childhood. To call this relationship between past and present a "finding" rather than an "assumption" indicates that it is a product of observation rather than a useful or convenient construct. But asserting that the conflicts during early development cause neuroses in adults is no less controversial.

Almost from its inception, psychoanalysis has had to face important challenges in how it uses personal history in explaining neuroses. The most notable challenge to the significance of infantile conflicts came from Alfred Adler. Adler, an early worker in psychoanalysis, challenged Freud by asserting that the indications of infantile neuroses as precursors of illness in the adult were results of the regressive effects of psychological conflict in the adult. Adults with neurotic symptoms would, in the "here and now," remake the past into infantile conflicts as a consequence of their current illness. Adler's theory presented a formidable challenge to psychoanalytic theory because it attacked a critical explanatory idea as well as, ultimately, the principles of psychoanalytic therapy that sought to revive memories of childhood to cure neuroses.

Freud wrote his celebrated case "From the History of an Infantile Neurosis" or, as it is more popularly known, the case of the "Wolf Man," to address the controversy surrounding the genetic explanation of how neuroses of infancy and childhood lead to adult neurotic disturbance. The case turned on the recovery of early memories through a dream that lay the foundation for the Wolf Man's illness as an adult. The probability that the dream, which occurred during the early years and which was recovered as a memory, could have been constructed and used regressively was very low. As a result, the case presented much evidence to support the crucial Freudian link between infantile and adult neurosis.

A few clinical examples will illustrate how the past determines the present in the formation of neurotic symptoms.

> 1. A young man with marked symptoms of self-doubt and depression felt detached from his parents; he experienced neither strong love nor hate, but rather felt indifferent toward them. He recovered a memory of a close and mutually adoring relationship with his mother during his early years when his father was in military service. Before recovering this memory, he experienced a growing hostility toward his mother. The reconstruction of the childhood experiences that led to his symptoms as an adult was as follows: the young man had repressed (forgotten) the period of time in his life when he and his mother were in a close and adoring relationship. He also repressed the hostility he felt when his father returned from military service to resume his life with his family. The depression and self-doubt he experienced as a young adult resulted from his failure as a child to resolve the feeling that he had been rejected by his mother. He had responded to real events in his early life, such as the closeness to his mother and the subsequent displacement in her attention by the return of his father, by turning his anger inward, and by internalizing the guilt that resulted from his rage upon being displaced. As a young adult, whatever success he enjoyed in life fell under the shadow of this shattered relationship with his mother.

2. A middle-aged man encountered severe difficulties in his business affairs and became depressed. The nature of these business difficulties involved conflicts with regulatory agencies. He perceived these regulatory authorities much as he had his father who, in his view, had never given him approval and support. The neurotic conflict derived from childhood was generated by his longings to be close to his father. Later in life he transferred these longings for closeness to other men more powerful than he. The wish for closeness was unacceptable and ultimately displaced onto the notion that he would perform in ways designed to gain the approval of authority. When approval was not forthcoming, he felt worthless, which in turn aroused the passive and dependent longings he continued to reject from the time he was a child.

3. A man endured numerous humiliations because he could not perform sexually. He would ejaculate prematurely, leaving his partner dissatisfied and himself in a state of humiliation and anxiety. The anxiety undoubtedly exacerbated the symptoms because he anticipated he would fail in sexual activity. This man developed a fear of women early in his life that subsequent development did not overcome. The premature ejaculation, while a symptom of the early fear of women, was a means for him to get out of a situation that he unconsciously feared. His fear of women was derived from other aspects of his early development that resulted in his unconsciously ascribing to women various mysterious and dangerous powers, including the power to emasculate him.

4. A young woman had developed a very hostile attitude toward other people, including the expectation that they would reject her. This hostile attitude was derived from the fear that she would be incorporated by her mother, to whom the woman unconsciously felt both attached but angry. This fear of incorporation, as though she would be taken in by the object and therefore would disappear, masked her desire for closeness. The woman had not been able to separate from her mother, resulting in her impaired ability to establish good relationships with other people, especially those to whom she felt sexually attracted.

These illustrations of how symptoms are derived from and perpetuate earlier psychological conflicts also demonstrate some of the problems in understanding how the past determines the present. One question, for example, is whether neuroses in later life occur as a result of traumatic events in childhood. There is no question that traumatic events, such as the loss of a parent at an early age, will have a marked influence on personality and later development. But the trauma need not be limited to such drastic occurrences. More usual events can also be traumatic in the sense that they impose the requirement that some change must occur within the individual to deal with the events. Included in such commonplace trauma are the usual separations that occur between parent and child, such as those connected with the birth of a younger sibling. Another form of traumatic experience consists of the developmental changes that occur within the individual and in the individual's relationship to others. A relatively clear-cut example is seen in the changes that occur during puberty and adolescence, beginning with the effects of sexual maturation and the heightening of the libidinous drive.

In general three major conditions of infancy can cause later neurotic impairment. The first is the condition of developmental deficit that occurs during very early infancy, when dependencies are both literal and intense. If the person upon whom the infant depends fails in one way or another, the resulting short-fall in development will often affect seriously and adversely the ability to function independently, to take care of one's self, and to be available to other people.

The second condition wherein the past will probably affect the present in causing symptoms is object loss. Loss of the loved parent, in the sense used here, is not necessarily loss through death or physical separation. Rather, it is the requirement, imposed from within and from outside, that the individual relinquish a particular attachment to the parent and reconstruct the relationship. The inability to make the successive separations inherent in development results in the "loss complex" in which the individual later in life becomes vulnerable to depression, to rage reactions, and to a sense of self-worthlessness.

The third condition whereby the past affects the present is the one upon which psychoanalysis focused in its original concerns with neurosis, namely, the oedipus complex. The less-than-perfect solution to the problem of attachment to the parent of the opposite sex and rivalry with the parent of the same sex results in the vulnerability to neurosis as an adult.

All three of these conditions in the past that determine or cause later neuroses will be considered in the next chapter. Before proceeding to this discussion of psychosexual development, some further clarification of the relationship between infantile and adult neuroses is necessary.

One question that often arises in considering causation is that of prediction: Is it possible to predict from observations of infancy and childhood the outcomes in later development? The answer to this question is negative. Psychoanalysis, or any other science for that matter, cannot predict the effects of development. In fact, psychoanalysis works as a "postdictive" science in that it takes the present forms of neurotic disturbance and reconstructs the conditions of the past that gave rise to the neurosis. Just because an individual in infancy and childhood experienced marked trauma from a combination of real events and fantasy does not necessarily mean that the individual will be disabled. The most that can be said is that the trauma will have effect. But many other conditions intervene, including the ability of individuals to move forward in life despite the disabling effects of the past. Individuals may also remain relatively unimpaired until some unfortunate turn of events stirs up the infantile neurosis. Disappointment in a career or a relationship will require new efforts at adjustment and adaptation that may involve neurotic conflicts that hitherto lay dormant. In the example of the middle-aged man who suffered as a consequence of his problems with regulatory authorities, it is within the realm of imagination to suggest that he might never have fallen into his depression had he remained free of real conflict with authority in the form of the regulatory agencies.

Perhaps the safest way to conclude this chapter on the explanations of neuroses is to suggest that the conflicts in development and the ubiquitous infantile neurosis establish the potentialities for the way people might encounter neurotic disturbance later in life. One may also reverse this formula: given the fact that all psychological development occurs in a matrix of conflict, infantile neuroses also establish the potentialities for important accomplishment in the adult. The intervening variable here is talent, a subject that neither psychoanalysis nor other human sciences fully understand.

Psychosexual Development

As the Christmas holidays approached, Donald Holden felt under increasing pressure to solve a problem in the personnel department of Marigold Products. Holden, who was Chief Operating Officer of the company, disliked the alternatives facing him as well as the pressure to act during the holiday season. But he realized that the situation had to be resolved because of the effects on the people involved and other executives operating divisions within Marigold.

The Director of Personnel Administration and his Assistant Director were fighting. The Director had been with the company for over thirty years. He was the first head of personnel, and in fact had built the department as the company grew and found it necessary to expand personnel services. The director was in his fifties, married with three daughters. His wife was a successful teacher and his daughters were completing school and in the early years of their careers. The Assistant Director was in her early forties. She had graduated from high school and left her parents' farm to find a job in a city some distance from where she grew up. She was the only one of her siblings to have left home. Her brother, a little more than a year younger, ran the family farm while an older sister married a farmer and lived nearby. The Assistant Director had married and later divorced her husband. Her daughter was in college, living in the dormitory while her son was in high school and living with her. Of the two children, her daughter was "more independent," while her son "needed propping up" from time to time.

CHAPTER

6

The Assistant Director had worked as an administrative assistant before joining Marigold. The Director of Personnel had recruited and hired her as a general assistant, to replace a woman who had been his assistant but who had been asked to run personnel services for one of the large divisions of the company. This assistant left the company soon after her transfer. While the new assistant had had no personnel administration experience, she had a good record as an administrative assistant and seemed eager to work in the personnel field. Over a four-year period, the Assistant Director had increased her scope of responsibility to include recruiting management people for the company's division heads. Formerly, each division recruited its own people, but the Assistant Director had convinced division directors that she could help in recruitment and preliminary screening. Increasingly, division heads and other executives asked her to find management people to fill job openings.

As the Assistant Director became more active in working with division heads and their staffs, the Director became concerned that executives were asking his assistant for help and not coming to him. He suggested to the Assistant Director that she share this work with him, but she was reluctant to comply because she felt that the executives had confidence in her and not in her boss. The Director and the Assistant Director then pursued a number of acrimonious exchanges. The Director wanted the Assistant Director to sign a statement outlining the principle of shared responsibility for executive recruitment, but the Assistant Director refused. She proposed, as an alternative, that she should run the department and recruit for the divisions while the Director should concentrate on external matters such as community relations.

The Director believed that the conflict could easily be resolved if Holden would issue a directive outlining the responsibilities of the Director and the Assistant Director following the content of the document the Director had asked his Assistant Director to sign. The Assistant Director also believed the conflict could be resolved if Holden were to appoint her as the Director of Personnel Administration, a job she felt she could perform more ably than its incumbent. She had presented this view to Donald Holden and he asked her what she thought should happen to the present Director. The Assistant Director responded that he should be designated as the Assistant. She expressed confidence in her ability to get the Director to work cooperatively and amicably as her subordinate.

The Director and Assistant Director were barely on speaking terms. Divisional executives became reluctant to bring work to the Personnel Department sensing the prospect of being caught in the middle of a battle between the two executives in the personnel function. The Director felt under pressure to keep close to what was going on in his department while the Assistant Director resented his "looking over my shoulder and wanting to be involved" in her activity. The Director believed he was being pushed out of his job. The Assistant Director believed that the Director was not doing his job and that he felt under siege only when he observed what his assistant was able to accomplish, particularly in providing recruiting services to the divisions. Individually, the Director and the Assistant Director believed the conflict would be resolved once Donald Holden, the Chief Operating Officer, made a decision to name him or her, respectively, to be in charge of the personnel department.

This kind of case study can best be understood in terms of one of Freud's most controversial discoveries, which is explained in this chapter.

There is little doubt that the discovery of the place of infantile sexuality in the formation of neuroses is one of the monumental discoveries of psychoanalytic theory and practice. Yet infantile sexuality, both in the form of clinical findings and the theory that grew from them, created a storm of controversy.

When Freud published his *Three Essays on Sexuality* in 1905, infancy and childhood were considered to be the years of innocence.[1] The only "evil" ascribed to these halcyon years was attributed to the works of the devil. By harshly expunging manifestations of sexuality in children, parents and nursemaids were only doing what was morally necessary. Few people other than astute nursemaids and physicians could envision at the time that sexual development began in earliest infancy or that the manifestations of sexual maturation during puberty were, in fact, a continuation of developments long underway in the life of the individual.

Freud shattered belief both in total rationality and in the innocence of childhood, two narcissistic injuries for which society could scarcely find a way to forgive him. While the opprobrium cast on Freud and his reactions to the criticisms are of considerable interest in the history of science, a more important historic question requires consideration: How did Freud arrive at the discoveries incorporated in his famous *Three Essays on Sexuality*?

The answer to this question is not easily available. While it is true that Freud's observations of patients with mental disturbances had convinced him that sexual factors ranked high in the list of possible causes, it was not necessary to assume that the noxious elements were derived from the early years. In fact, there was much reason to conclude that frustrations in the sexual sphere during the adult years caused neurotic symptoms.

The cases Freud saw often presented symptoms of serious sexual conflicts that were clearly visible in "the here and now." What considerations could give rise to the implication of infantile sexuality in the origin of neuroses? And even if one were to implicate infantile sexuality in the etiology of neuroses, by what line of observation or reasoning could one conclude that a developmental line in sexuality exists in all normal human beings? For Freud, the temptation to see sexual trauma in early life as the cause of adult neurosis was almost overpowering, and, indeed, he barely managed to extricate himself from the trap of making this interpretation. But make no mistake!—the theory of sexuality in psychoanalysis postulates a line of development of all human beings that begins from birth and then proceeds through stages to adult sexuality.

Freud's self-analysis also contributed to his discovery of infantile sexual development and its crucial role in the theory of neuroses. Ernest Jones, Freud's biographer, and many other writers give considerable weight to his self-analysis in the discovery of his theory of sexuality. In the mid and late 1890s, Freud began exploring his own unconscious conflicts and tried to uncover and resolve his underlying neurotic struggles. Much of the material in Freud's book, *The Interpretations of Dreams,* published in 1901, consisted of his dreams and his interpretations of them—the basic material he used to formulate his theories of the unconscious and of the mechanisms and functions of dreams.

Granting that Freud's self-analysis undoubtedly played a large part in the formulation of the theory of infantile sexuality, it was not enough to generate the theory. There is no intent here to play cat and mouse with the reader. The plain fact is that Freud arrived at his discoveries and theories of sexuality in large measure through a leap of the imagination that most scientists seek and almost none achieve.

A close reading of *The Three Essays* will not demonstrate how laborious, painstaking, and methodical observation yields a theory of such significance as the one that appears in this small book. The work contains no statistics, no experiments, and no proofs of the kind one expects in a scientific treatise. Yet the synthesis of fact and observation, the imaginative reach and bold exposition surely indicate that science is more than observation and experiment. There are occasions when a bold leap transcends long-accepted ideas and arrives at a conceptual plane that alters the course of investigation. Such is the gift of genius for which there is as yet no explanation.

The theory of psychosexual development has one foot in biology, the other in psychology. The biological basis of psychosexual development is that the sex drive is innate but varies in strength among individuals according to constitutional factors. For some individuals the drive is stronger than for others, and maturation proceeds along a different timetable. The strength of the drive accounts for differences in the onset of puberty and the variability in other stages of social development.

What has been said here concerning the biology of the sex drive and its variability among individuals could also be said about the aggressive drive, although it has not been studied as intensively, and the theory of aggression has not yet been clearly formulated. All that should be presumed at this stage of the discussion is that drives are in large measure a function of biological phenomena. Even if human drives cannot be observed directly in psychoanalytic practice, the biological hypothesis underlying the theory of instinctual drives cannot be dismissed or ignored.

As for the psychological aspects of psychosexual development, the presumption is that desire is a mental derivative of instinctual drives. Although the connections between instinct and desire are not clearly understood, the linkage permits observation of such mental derivatives as fantasy. These derivatives demonstrate some of the transformations that occur in mental structure and function as the result of the individual's efforts to deal with inner changes as well as his or her relation to the outside world.

Whereas the body of theory regarding psychosexual development rests on psychological formulations, the content of the theory depends upon the notion of changes in body zones of excitation from which derivative desires and fantasies emerge. The body zones central to sexual excitation at any given stage of development correlate with changes in attachments to others and the intermediate shifts in the relationship between fantasy and reality.

The understanding of psychosexual development best begins with Freud's *Three Essays on Sexuality*. The material that follows is an explication of this text, including clarifications, interpretations and questions.

FREUD'S THREE ESSAYS ON SEXUALITY

The first essay, "The Sexual Aberrations," attempts to solve several problems including:

(1) Defining sexuality beyond the conventional understanding of genital intercourse between members of the opposite sex;

(2) Within the definition, comparing differences in sexual aberrations according to the sexual aim and the sexual object;

(3) Relating the aberrations to so-called normal sexuality; and

(4) Establishing the critical connections between sexual aberrations and neuroses.

Conventional understanding of sexuality, that is, genital intercourse between adults of the opposite sex, does not exhaust the range and variety of sexual activity. In referring to behavior outside of this conventional definition, the terms "aberrations" or "deviant" behavior are often used.

Behavior outside the range of the conventional requires explanation and two obvious hypotheses come to mind. Either the behavior is innate or it is acquired. The explanation of the innate hypothesis indicates that deviant sexual behavior occurs in response to different biological demands. Individuals who engage in deviant practices therefore do so as a result of constitutional and inherited factors. For such an explanation to be convincing, it would be necessary to demonstrate what the innate factors are and how they function, both in individuals who prefer deviant practices and in those who prefer conventional modes of sexual behavior.

Such evidence is not available. Therefore the biological or constitutional explanation can be neither verified nor falsified, although the likelihood that deviant behavior will be fully resolved in biological terms is slim. Some individuals, for example, are not exclusive in their sexual preferences. In addition, conventional behavior sometimes gives way to deviant practices under unusual conditions, such as incarceration.

Before proceeding further with the problem of sexual aberrations, it would be well to distinguish the *object* or person, and *aim* of sexual activity. Variations in behavior may arise entirely from choice of object or of aim, but they also can involve both simultaneously.

When an individual selects a person of the same sex for sexual activity, this deviant choice of the object is called an "inversion." When the aim of the sexual instinct deviates from genital intercourse, the deviation is called a "perversion." Deviation as to gender of the person need not involve obvious alterations in gender characteristics: men who select other men for sexual pleasure may be as masculine in appearance and behavior as heterosexual men; similarly, women exclusively interested in sex with other women do not necessarily display outwardly marked masculine characteristics. However, the object or person chosen may display characteristics of the opposite sex. In addition, the objects chosen may include immature persons and even animals.

Although it is not clear whether sexual inversion is innate or acquired, the possibility that bisexuality is a constitutional trait must be considered. It may be that bisexuality is inherent in all individuals but that generally during the course of development, single-sex identity takes hold. If this is so, then it is possible that individuals who seek others of the same sex for sexual partners may have followed an unusual course of development. Constitutional factors may have caused them to acquire a sexual disposition the opposite of their physical make-up or developmental experiences may have established an aversion to heterosexuality. In the case of the male, for example, the fear of women could be a consequence of early development so that the longing for a person of the same sex arises from the need to avoid women. In any case, it seems clear that the sexual impulse does not link aim and object in a determined fashion. The same aim can be satisfied with heterosexual and homosexual persons.

Inversion of sexual objects can be habitual or transitory, depending upon circumstances such as temporary deprivation that may occur in the military and does occur in prisons. If an individual is disposed to homosexuality, one cannot judge the mental or moral quality of that individual. Throughout history some of the most extraordinary intellectual and cultural achievements have been those of individuals whose sexual preferences were for persons of the same sex. In some ancient cultures that were both highly developed and culturally advanced, homosexual practices were common and formed an important part of the life of the elite. Homosexuality cannot therefore be considered a form of degeneracy in which individuals are in some way mentally or culturally impaired. The explanation of sexual inversion requires that an examination of its origins go beyond constitutional factors. An examination of deviations regarding sexual aim may help clarify these origins.

The aim of sexual instincts, as with other basic appetites such as hunger, is the satiation of desire. Conventional ideas about the sex drive focus on it as a unitary force from which gratification occurs during genital intercourse with orgasm. But for genital intercourse to realize the aim of the sexual drive, intermediate activity, which involves caressing, kissing, looking, and other sensory experiences, increases the level of excitation to the stage where genital intercourse may be accomplished successfully. When the intermediate activities become the sole aim and when they displace genital intercourse, the sexual aim has become perverted and the practices are forms of perversion. The terms "perverse" and "perversion" refer strictly to the alteration of the *aim* of the sexual impulse, which is genital intercourse as the final pleasure of the sexual act.

One of the mechanisms limiting perverse activity (present to some degree in all sexual behavior) is through inhibitory affects such as shame and disgust. When these affects dominate, sexual pleasure may be entirely restricted. The relationship between genital intercourse and the intermediate activity suggests that the sexual drive, rather than being a unitary appetite, comprises components that can either accelerate the drive toward genital union or can become the primary aim.

Perversion of the sexual aim can take various forms. Oral pleasure, which is present as a matter of course in foreplay, can be extended to include oral-genital contact as the exclusive aim. Parts of the body other than the genitalia may become dominant in sexual pleasure as, for example, in fetishistic attachment to special parts of the body.

Securing sexual pleasure exclusively through inflicting pain (sadism), or enduring pain (masochism) deserves special attention. In both sadism and masochism, alteration occurs in the relation between sex and aggression. Conventional sexuality depends for its success on a strong measure of aggression, but the aggression is subordinate to the sex drive or is used in its service. The reverse seems to occur in sadism and masochism: aggression is dominant, and using it to inflict pain or enduring it to experience pain is primary.

Another way to approach sadism and masochism is to consider pain in its active and passive form. There is a tendency to establish a parallel between active and passive modes, on the one hand, and masculine and feminine, on the other. Active and passive modes exist side by side before development creates a bifurcation of the "masculine" and "feminine." Even after bifurcation occurs, both modes continue to coexist. In the extreme form, one is likely to find both sadism and masochism present in the individual who is definitely attached to pain as sexual pleasure.

The study of sexual aims indicates that the sexual drive is not unitary. Rather, it consists of components that come together in the form of pleasure through genital intercourse. Forepleasure represents a necessary and pervasive part of sexuality. It differs from perversions only in the matter of exclusivity of the aim. In sexual development, forepleasure must come to assume a transitory position toward the final aim. When the acts associated with forepleasure, or the heightening of sexual tension becomes dominant and exclusive, the components of the sexual drive fail to integrate or have become divided.

In studying the sexual preferences of people with psychoneurotic disturbances, one is likely to find the absence of overt perverse behavior. But close examination of these disturbances indicates no lack of representation of perverse sexuality in the fantasy life (usually unconscious) of the individual. These observations suggest that what one individual may do in expressing component sexual impulses in the form of perversions, another person may experience in the form of symptoms. Although sexual development has failed in both cases, the expression of this failure differs. In the case of a person with a psychoneurosis, the expression of the impulses is restricted by various mechanisms of the mind. This leads to compromises in the form of disabling symptoms. In the other case, the impulses lead to action and securing of sexual satisfaction through perverse behavior as the exclusive aim.

These considerations gave rise to Freud's formulation toward the conclusion of his first essay, "The Sexual Aberrations," that *neuroses are the negative of the perversions:* If there is something innate in the tendency toward sexual perversion, it is innate in all human beings. The innate quality of perverse sexuality can be observed in the development of the sex drive in children. This leads to the hypothesis that in the case of neurosis, the sex drive has remained fixated or has been brought back to some infantile state.

Infantile sexuality, which formed the subject of the second essay in Freud's *Three Essays on Sexuality,* is difficult to study because of aversions that arise from a variety of sources. Individual experience with infantile sexuality is forgotten as a result of the massive amnesia that overtakes early childhood—an amnesia encouraged by education. Parents seek to divert the child's attention from sexual activity by using shame, disgust, and moral aversion to overcome the child's feelings of delight, interest, and pleasure in the sensations associated with sexual excitation. In addition, it is in the interests of the individual and society to divert attention from sexual excitation during the early years. The sublimation of the sex drive shifts attention to "higher" aims by transmitting sexual curiosity and voyeuristic desire into the thirst for knowledge. However, despite all the efforts of educators, manifestations of sexual excitement will break through, and this permits opportunities for directly observing them.

The most common activity that reflects sexual excitation is thumbsucking. The pleasure gained from sucking one's thumb during the early years depends upon the earlier pleasure derived from sucking at the breast or bottle. These early oral activities serve the purpose of nutrition, but there can be no question that in thumbsucking the pleasurable activity has detached itself from the more elementary functions of feeding. The chief characteristic of thumbsucking as a sexual activity is that the orientation is inward toward part of one's own body and away from other people. Thumbsucking, along with later masturbation, consequently, should be classified as an autoerotic activity.

Autoerotic activity, in addition to its convenience, provides a measure of control not present when one is dependent upon another person for pleasure. The particular part of the body selected for sexual stimulation is one of a number of erogenous zones that are the centers of excitation. As indicated previously, during the early years particular zones, such as the mouth and the alimentary canal, are involved in other bodily functions. The discovery of erogenous zones may also occur by accident. But once discovered, the child returns to the particular zone and repeats the pleasurable activity.

The anus becomes an erogenous zone as a result of the regular activities of retention and elimination. The withholding of feces and their later elimination stimulate the mucous membrane of the anus with pleasurable sensations. As with the mouth, the anus assumes importance through the fantasies that occur simultaneously with the heightened excitement and the experience of pleasure. By withholding feces, the child expresses rebellion toward authority; by learning continence, the child expresses compliance. Feces associatively may also play a part in fantasies about one's body, about valuable materials, about gifts, and about babies and reproduction. One of the sexual theories of childhood is that babies are created by ingesting food through the mouth and delivering a baby through the anus. As with the oral zone, the anus may be stimulated in masturbatory activity.

The genital region of the body is a third erogenous zone. There is no lack of occasion for stimulation in this region, including bathing and the normal frictions that occur. Once stimulated, the genitalia are easily returned to as a source of pleasure. Before the genitalia become the main erogenous zone of adulthood, the prior experience with this region during infancy and childhood sets the stage for their primacy in puberty and adulthood.

The importance of the erogenous zones in sexual development arises first from other bodily functions such as feeding and elimination. But they may also be aroused by seductions. Conscious or unconscious seductions by older children, playmates, and even adults may occur during a child's early years.

It cannot be assumed that moral aversions to sexuality are either natural or innate. Shame and disgust, two affects that give force to reaction formation, are learned. But before they are learned, a natural interest in one's own body is easily converted into interest in bodies of other children and adults. Seductions stimulate this interest and even overcome the aversions of shame and disgust. Once stimulated through seduction, interest persists, and it may become more difficult to divert the child's interest from sexual stimulation and pleasure. But the influences of seduction should not be exaggerated nor their meaning restricted. Normal play activity is seductive, if one means that the stimulation occurring during games and wrestling is arousing. When parents play with their children, there may be arousal, and in this sense the parents are being seductive. But this form of seduction should not be confused with traumatic sexual assaults. In this connection, mention should be made of the effects of physical punishment such as spanking. While intended often as punishment in the service of educating the child, physical punishment may also be sexually arousing and form a predilection for masochism, the pleasure gained while enduring pain.

Children are curious about many things, including sex. This interest reaches a peak during childhood between the ages of three and five. Children want to know where babies come from, and the force of this "instinct for knowledge" is magnified by the unpleasant feelings they have when a baby is born and they lose the exclusive attention of the parents, particularly the mother. Questions cannot go unanswered nor be held in reserve to impart knowledge. Children construct their own theories by reference to their own experience with body sensations and functions and by observation. One of the answers that children provide to the "riddle of how babies are born" is that babies are taken from the breast, from the navel, or are expelled from the anus.

It is in connection with this theme of the search for knowledge and explanations that modern readers of *The Three Essays on Sexuality* encounter great difficulty. In the second essay, "Infantile Sexuality," in which Freud discussed children's curiosity about the anatomical differences between the sexes, he stated that boys are shocked to discover that not all people have a penis. Initially boys believe there is only one sexual organ. When the knowledge sinks in that there are two sexes, the need for explanation intensifies. One of the common theories is that both sexes once had a penis, but that for the girl it was taken away. This belief sets the stage for the "castration complex" in the boy, which is the urgent fear that he too is in danger of losing his penis. According to Freud,

> Little girls do not resort to denial of this kind when they see
> that boys' genitals are formed differently from their own. They
> are ready to recognize them [the differences] immediately and
> are overcome by envy for the penis—an envy culminating in
> the wish, which is so important in its consequences, to be boys
> themselves.[2]

Needless to say, this theory of penis envy and the unconscious wish to be male has been a target for much modern-day hostility toward psychoanalysis and a cause for rejecting its findings and theories. Freud's conclusions have also fueled many efforts of the revisionist theorists, who reject the significance attached to the theory of infantile sexuality and its foundation in libido theory.

Another theme of the second essay is that children make conjectures about sexual activity between adults. This curiosity and concern can arise from actual observation of sexual activity of parents, by hearing noises emanating from the parents' bedroom, or by observing animals copulating. One common conclusion children draw from observation and fantasy is that the sex act is violent, with one person, usually the male, inflicting harm on or subjugating the other, usually the female. This sadistic view of sexuality can create a tendency for either avoidance or for some cruelty. Whatever conclusions the child reaches about sexual intercourse and about how babies are made and delivered, they are bound to be the wrong ones. This is almost inevitable, given that the source of the conclusions is the child's own fantasies and the tendency to project his or her ideas onto the outer world. But there is little question that the need to know, which arises from observation and fantasy during the early years of childhood, accelerates the child's progress toward independence and separation from the adults upon whom he or she previously relied.

Freud concluded the second essay with a discussion of the phases of development of sexual organization and the sources of infantile sexuality. He divided the phases into two categories, the pregenital organization and the genital organization. During infancy, sexuality centers upon the child's own body parts and is therefore autoerotic. Sexual impulses, however, focus upon an object and away from one's self. The two monumental tasks of development—genital primacy and object love (love of another person)—must be successfully completed to transform infantile into adult sexuality.

The problems encountered in this development involve taming primitive affects associated with the component instincts, such as the desire to incorporate the object and the desire to control the object. The former is an integral aspect of the oral stage of development at infancy.

In searching for a sexual object at puberty, the love objects of infancy are taboo because they are incestuous. Lingering associations between sexual pleasure and the longing for the early objects can create difficulties in finding a love object and experiencing adult sexuality.

Infantile sexuality originates in the self-preservative functions such as nutrition and elimination. These sources of stimulation are reinforced by peripheral stimulation of the body zones, by passive stimulation through agitation of the body, and by muscular activity. Sexual arousal also occurs through affective stimulation such as fear, dread, and mental fatigue. Whatever the sources of sexual excitation, the pathways that originate from body zones can be traversed in two directions: toward integration, which takes the form of genital primacy, or backward to the original zones and the component instincts associated with them. While securing genital primacy is an outcome of the early stages of development, the original impulses may find their way into independent activities as a result of sublimation. Sublimations, however, may also traverse the path backward to their origins in pregenital sexuality.

The psychosexual development of infancy foreshadows the major developments of puberty and adolescence. The tasks of puberty are two-fold: to consolidate the phases of infantile sexuality into a secure stage of genital primacy; and to establish suitable relationships with others that permit genital sexuality as well as mature and satisfying human relationships.

Infantile sexuality, including both the pregenital and genital phases of development, is limited by the fact that it is not until puberty that the individual attains the capacity for genital intercourse. The male is then capable of ejaculation and the heightened pleasure this experience provides. The female develops heightened interest in sexual relationships and childbearing. Changes occur in both the male and female bodies to correspond to the new sexual capacities.

Achieving genital primacy calls for consideration of pregenital sexuality, forepleasure, and the climax of genital intercourse. The purpose of foreplay and the stimulation associated with body zones focused on during the pregenital period is to heighten sexual excitation as a means of encouraging the movement toward genital intercourse and orgasm. If the sexual excitement generated during foreplay becomes too intense, there may be little motivation to proceed further. If there is too little arousal and sexual tension, the result may be a loss of interest and lack of desire for genital intercourse. Fortunately the childhood stages of development prepare an individual for puberty in the sense that during the second stage of childhood (from age seven to puberty), usually referred to as the latency period, the genital region is subject to excitation, although of low intensity. The onset of puberty is therefore not detached from the earlier stages, although the term *latency* usually connotes the absence of sexual arousal. It would be more accurate to refer to latency as a period of lessened sexual tension, but with its focus on the genital region.

Although a thorough understanding of how human sexuality arrives at the stage of genital primacy must start with the biology and chemistry of sexuality, the major focus of psychoanalytic investigation is on the sphere of the psyche, or the mental representations of biological factors. In this pursuit, the crucial concept of libido is a purely psychological construct that neither negates nor overlooks the available biological knowledge to explain human sexuality.

Libido is the quantity of sexual energy that is available for attachment either to other people or to one's body as self-image. While Freud used the terms "object libido" and "narcissistic libido" to refer to the displaceable quality of sexual energy, this distinction suggests that two different kinds of libido exist. It is more useful, however, to conceive of one kind of libido that can be alternately attached to other persons or returned to self. In this context the use of the term "narcissism" refers, of course, to Narcissus of the Greek legend who looked into a pool of water and fell in love with his reflected image.

If one of the two main tasks of puberty leads to consolidation of the impulses into genital primacy as a precondition for a mature sexual relationship, the second task is to find a love object. What prevents finding a satisfying object is the continuing attachment to early love objects, which by necessity are incestuous. The mother, by virtue of her caretaking responsibilities, inevitably arouses the sexual impulses. Relinquishing the early incestuous love object is a cultural imperative upon which society relies for its perpetuation. The longing for the early object is reflected in fantasy. As this fantasized attachment dissolves, the parents concomitantly lose some measure of their authority, serving the aims of society in permitting the independence required to foster a new family. Individuals unable to achieve this independence reflect their continuing tie to incestuous objects by developing psychoneurotic symptoms. The shadow of these early objects appears of course in the content of unconscious fantasy and therefore remains inaccessible to the individual for alteration through rational thought.

The task of finding a love object is complicated further by the tendency to seek an object of the same sex, a tendency that arises from the early triangular relationship with parents. Some degree of hostility toward the parent of the same sex propels the individual toward an object of the opposite sex. The effects of this triangular relationship appear clearer in the case of the male as compared with the female. Freud's third essay contains some further suggestions on the differences between the sexes that contemporary readers find controversial if not objectionable. Despite the controversial aspects of Freud's views on the differences in sexual development and object relations for males and females, the content of his views should be understood.

Freud believed that before the distinction between male and female entered the rational sphere, the difference between active and passive aims more fundamentally affected the psychology of the individual. In dealing earlier with the anatomical differences between the sexes, Freud considered that for the child, the penis was the primary organ and that the active aim became associated with masculinity and the passive aim with femininity. This view seems to gain credence when considering the fact that genital primacy and the act of sexual intercourse required that the penis enter the vagina. By what steps or transitions in sexual development does the female permit and gain sexual pleasure from vaginal penetration?

Again, the transitions in female sexual development appear more complicated as compared with the male. For the male there is only one genital organ that acts as the center of sexual pleasure during intercourse and even during the later stages of childhood. For the woman, however, the earliest center of excitation in the genital region is the clitoris, which can be compared with the penis. Clitoral stimulation is the form of autoerotic activity for the female during the early years and continues as a zone of excitation. But, according to Freud, a shift of sexual pleasure must occur away from the clitoris to the vagina, lest sexual development fall under an anesthesia and impair relationships with men. This conclusion, or hypothesis, is the subject of much debate, one source being the studies of sexuality by Masters and Johnson.

Freud considered this problem in the context of the inherent nature of bisexuality, libido being "invariably and necessarily of a masculine nature, whether it occurs in men or in women and irrespectively of whether its object is a man or a woman."[3] The fact that in *The Three Essays* Freud established the basis of female sexuality as a derivative of masculine sexuality leaves much unexplained concerning female development and object relationships. In another context Freud admitted to some mystification on this subject, reserving for other investigators the task of reformulation and clarification.

PSYCHOSEXUAL DEVELOPMENT AND THE NUCLEAR CONFLICTS

At the conclusion of chapter 5, we considered three conditions within which nuclear conflicts of early development arise: (1) developmental deficit; (2) object loss; and (3) the oedipus complex.

From birth until about the age of one and a half years the infant is in its period of greatest dependency. The inability of mother and child to develop a nurturant activity that is rhythmic, regular, and mutually gratifying can establish a degree of dependency that is difficult to reverse in its adverse effects on personality. Some of the most severe pathologies stem from the deprivations of the oral stage of development. Oral deprivations can impair the child's capacity to make object ties, thus reinforcing the deep ambivalence toward other people that can be observed in cases of severe impairment in object relationships: The child comes to view people and the surrounding world in malevolent terms and is under the sway of rage. The fear of people coupled with intense dependency wishes create a "whipsaw" effect. On the one side, the dependency need establishes a wish to merge with the maternal figure. On the other side of the ambivalent reaction, the rage within becomes frightening because it appears consuming, fueling fantasies of destroying the loved object. Simultaneously the fear of being destroyed emerges from the tendency to project the hostility onto the object and the wish to merge becomes the fear of obliteration. Under these circumstances, primitive reactions appear in the form of disabling symptoms that include loss of interest in the real world, thought disorders, and deep depression.

One potential source of confusion in understanding development deficits is the question of how much gratification is necessary during the oral stage to permit safe progression through the succeeding stages of development. This question is difficult to answer because of the numerous variables that affect outcomes. Take for example the problem of "too much or too little." The failure to encourage separation of mother and infant can create a sense of confusion regarding self and object; the lack of secure and clear boundaries sets the stage for impaired object relationships. Conversely, the inability to nurture reinforces narcissism, resulting in feelings of emptiness, of deep longing for a nurturant figure, of grandiosity alongside diminished self-esteem.

For psychoanalysts the concept of "the average expectable environment" places nurturance in a human context. Mothers do not have to be superhuman to fulfill the necessary, though vague demands of the average expectable environment. Another way of putting this position is to recognize the resiliency of the infant. Parental anxiety about the capacity to nurture may do more harm than some deprivation because it interferes with a relaxed and easy ambience in which nurturance can unfold.

Object loss occurs during each of the three stages of infantile development. Each stage requires a resolution of the conflicts generated by the incremental loss of the object necessitated by maturation. During the oral stage of development, as we have indicated in discussing developmental deficits, the initial task is to secure a mutually gratifying condition of nurturance in which the infant is fed, kept warm and dry, and cuddled. The rhythm of gratification thus established encourages the first moves toward separation: the infant becomes a person separate from the mother who provided the gratification.

A second separation occurs toward the end of the oral stage of development when the breast or bottle is withdrawn. The weaning that occurs over a period of time is a form of deprivation experienced as object loss. The loss of the object is to some degree traumatic and may cause some regression in development. The tendency during this period of object loss is for the infant to turn inward, to increase autoerotic activity, and to develop a narcissistic reaction in the shift of interest from mother to the inner world. No one knows the content of the fantasies and other mental activity during this period of object loss, since it occurs prior to the capacity for putting thoughts into words. There is, however, some conjecture as to the content of the fantasies based upon observation of adults during various stages of psychological regression.

The critical question about these fantasies is how the love object (the mother) is represented within the psyche from infancy. Perhaps the object, as incorporated in some form of mental representation, appears malevolent as a result of the pain experienced during early alterations in the relationship with the mother. Simultaneously, the infant may experience enormous rage, which is attached to this malevolent image of the object as it has been internalized. The attachment of rage to some inner representation of the object may later in life motivate the need to project both the rage and the image of the malevolent object onto some object in the outer world.

Object loss during the latter part of the oral stage of development has three consequences: (1) libido turns inward; (2) diverse images of the object are incorporated within the psyche; and (3) rage intensifies in response to loss. These consequences of early childhood loss thus provide the foundation for paranoid reactions following perceived or real losses later in life. The tendency to project malevolent fantasies onto objects in the real world is powerful and is mitigated by the strength of a countervailing force inherent in the notion of basic trust. It should be emphasized here that no direct evidence exists to prove the occurrence of oral introjection of the good and nurturant object, on the one hand, and of the bad and depriving object, on the other. Again, these ideas are drawn from hypotheses about the oral stage of development and object loss while observing children and adults capable of verbal interchange. The observations that are particularly striking include paranoid reactions.

Paranoid reactions consist of fears that some harmful events will occur as the result of intentions and actions of other people. These fears, while using whatever reality can provide to feed them, are often exaggerated, if not totally groundless. The mechanism underlying paranoid reactions depends upon projection as a defense. The rage within is projected onto people or situations in the real world. The one doing the projection, in turn, becomes the victim.

Projection involves a reversal of subject and object as the source of the rage and hostility. In some sense, every experience with object loss requires the cathexis of, or investment in, fantasy. As a result, the object is not lost, since the cathexis inward is directed toward a representation of diverse images of the person who formerly commanded the emotional investments. But the images of the object tend to be fragmented—pieces of rather than a whole person. Fragmentation of the object leads to idealizations of the particular fragment of the object representation equated with all that is good, powerful, and giving. Such idealizations are also available for projection onto people in the real world. When what is real about another person falls short of these idealized images, secondary rage reactions occur, as though the individual is once again experiencing object loss patterned after the early loss of the object during the latter part of the oral stage of development.

Object loss during infancy is a form of psychological trauma not reserved solely for the oral stage of development. It occurs during the anal and phallic/oedipal stages as well. These later experiences of object loss differ from the earlier, however, in the effects of cumulative experiences with parents who meet and perhaps exceed what is required in "the average expectable environment." The infant has more psychological resources to enable the necessary transformation to occur in relation to parents. The resources available during the oral stage are relatively primitive. The infant is at the peak of narcissism. The boundaries between the inner and outer worlds are still tenuous. While the expected outcome of the oral stage is a favorable balance in the direction of basic trust, of optimism, and of the perception of the world as sustaining, it is only a balance. The opposing outcome of mistrust, pessimism, and hostility can have far-reaching effects on the psyche in later years.

The trauma of object loss during the second stage of infancy, the sadistic-anal stage, occurs in the context of increased physical capacity, the beginning of verbalization, and the "pull" that parents exert on the child toward greater independence. Toilet training occurs during this period, which covers the ages of two to four. Although there is no strong inclination for the child to learn continence, the mother exerts her influence in this direction through training and indications of approval and disapproval. The variations in training practices, including the severity of the training and the forms for expressing approval and disapproval, are in part culturally determined. But they are also in part determined by the residues of the mother's own early and repressed experience during this phase of development.

The erotic experience surrounding retention and elimination amplifies the experience of control, omnipotence, and the battle of wills in the relationship between the infant and the mother. This relationship is dyadic in nature because the mother is still the dominant object for the infant and the center of attention. It is a highly ambivalent relationship as it revolves around pleasing and being pleased by the object, controlling and being controlled by the object, and dominating or submitting to the object. Because of the conflict of wills, the image of the object, centered upon the infant's narcissism, is altered and consequently perceived as a fresh loss of that object. The loss is exaggerated if during this stage the mother gives birth to a baby and the child feels displaced as the person in control of the mother.

The rage felt in reaction to the experience of loss gains force in the normal increase in aggression, in muscular facility, and in the more elaborate fantasy life of the child. As with the oral stage of development, legacies of the sadistic-anal stage figure in later neuroses. For example, the symptoms of obsessional doubting, of alternating deep rebelliousness with submissiveness, and of exaggerating thinking at the expense of feeling appear as outcomes of this second stage of infancy. The positive legacies must also be acknowledged. Assuming the parent and child are able to reconstruct their relationship to accord with the growing capacities of the infant and the demands of reality, a sense of autonomy and important character traits take hold. The feeling of accomplishment that goes along with the ability to regulate one's own behavior increases self-esteem and prepares the child for new and more complicated relationships. The initial new relationship involves the shift from the dyadic relationship to the triangular relationship of the oedipal stage of development.

The oedipus complex can be viewed as another experience of object loss. However, because it is contained within a triangular relationship that surrounds the shift of eroticism from the anal to the genital region, it stands as a separate circumstance for both growth and neurosis.

One of the murky areas in the study of object relationships as a crucial aspect of development is the role of the father. By shifting terminology from mother to caretaker, it would seem that the parents could be interchangeable in the course of development during infancy. But without more knowledge, caution should be exercised that in this ready substitution of caretaker for mother the problem of development has not been obfuscated.

Freud argued that biology is destiny. What does this formulation mean? Only women can conceive and bear a child. If the capacity to bear children involves narcissistic advantages to women, these advantages do not manifest themselves solely in the act of conceiving and delivering a child. The infant must stand in some relation to these narcissistic advantages beyond the sheer physiology of childbirth. Just as the infant must separate from the mother, the mother must alter her attachments to the child to foster individuality and the sense of separateness. Presumably, the alteration takes time and cannot be completed upon the physical birth of the infant. It is possible that fathers can be intrusive in the intimacy of this narcissistic attachment and the work of separation. The successive phases of this intimacy have already been described as largely the progression from a unity or symbiosis to a dyadic structure in which both mother and infant are separate individuals, albeit with different positions of dependency.

In contrast to the notion that biology is destiny, consider an alternative: There is considerable flexibility in who ministers to the child. The functions of this ministration need to be completed, but in a way detached from the individual who performs them. The functions are therefore determined, but the roles are interchangeable. Crosscultural studies, including those of communal child care such as occurs in Israeli *kibbutzim,* would seem to provide material to judge whether biology or role performance is destiny. Such studies are inconclusive at this time. We are a long way from understanding the relative influences of biology, role performances, and cultural influences on the development of children.

The theory of the oedipus complex occupies a special position in psychoanalytic theory, and the "classical" neurosis best illustrates the relationship of symptoms, defenses, and conflicts that constitute it. The oedipus complex also exemplifies the tension between two types of approaches to psychoanalysis. The first is the "mechanistic" approach focusing on the interplay of psychological forces. The second approach is humanistic. Here the universal problem of existence is viewed as the need for individuals to relinquish objects, tame desires, and face reality under conditions that stimulate, if not force, growth and development.

The theory of the oedipus complex also bridges the areas of individual and group psychology. In detailing how character develops under the sway of oedipal conflicts, the theory accounts for much of human suffering as well as much that is heroic in the human condition. This duality, of suffering as a result of neurosis and heroism in the attempts at resolution of conflict, belongs to individual psychology. The universal theme of attraction and rivalry contained in the oedipal situation provides the locus of group psychology, at least the psychoanalytic view of group relationships. In considering group psychology, psychoanalysis further postulates certain ideas about society, morality, and responsibility and therefore examines the problem of individuality as well as collective relations.

The content of the theory follows the Greek myth of Oedipus' tragedy. Oedipus was cast out at birth and left to die because Laius, the King of Thebes, had a message from Apollo that a male child conceived by him and delivered by his wife Jocasta would someday kill him. Oedipus survived as a result of the compassion of a shepherd. True to the prophecy, he killed the king who, unbeknownst to Oedipus, was his father. Oedipus answered the riddle of the Sphinx and assumed the throne of Thebes. He then, innocently, married his mother, who was the Queen of Thebes. A plague fell upon the kingdom, and when Oedipus became aware that he, as the murderer of King Laius, was responsible for the misfortune, he blinded himself and wandered the earth in expiation of his guilt.

Following the pathways of psychoanalytic investigation, Freud gave the name "oedipal" both to a stage of development and to the psychoneurosis that results from limited or only partial resolution of the conflict. Between the ages of three and five, the child enters into a triangular relationship involving strong libidinal attachments to the parent of the opposite sex and rivalry with the parent of the same sex. Because the desire to possess the opposite-sex parent cannot be gratified, the child must relinquish these desires and reestablish ties to the parents with more realistic goals and with friendly attitudes toward them.

The engine driving the oedipal conflicts is libido and aggression. The term "phallic stage" of development, in which the oedipus complex unfolds, designates the shift in erogenous zones from the anus to the genitalia. In the case of the male child, the phallic zone is the penis and in the case of the female child, the clitoris.

An integral part of the theory of the oedipus complex concerns the motive for relinquishing the object attachment and the rivalry. In the case of the male child, the impetus is derived from the superior position of the father and the fear of punishment in the form of castration. In the case of the female child, the fear of castration becomes the attitude of acceptance in which the child acquiesces to the fact that she has no penis. This acquiescence becomes one of the foundations of feminine masochism, as it is supported by the unconscious conviction that she once had a penis but it was taken away or lost.

In defining the oedipus complex, we referred only to the positive version rather than the two versions described for both the male and female child. In the positive configuration, the attraction is to the parent of the opposite sex while the rivalry is with the parent of the same sex. In the negative version, which arises in reaction to the positive form, the parent of the same sex becomes the libidinal object while the parent of the opposite sex is the rival. The two versions alternate and then coexist during the height of the phallic phase of development.

Earlier discussion referred to the controversial aspects of female psychology and the still unclear position psychoanalysis takes with respect to feminine development. The problem of female psychology is more complicated than in the case of the male. In the positive oedipal stage the male child is returning to the mother, who is the original love object. For the female, the positive oedipal stage suggests the child is in a rivalrous and even hostile relationship to the mother, who is also the original love object for the girl. This hostility can be colored by a deep resentment characterized by penis envy and the unconscious idea that the mother is implicated in the "loss" of the penis. Therefore the desire for the father may involve a wish to incorporate and possess his penis as a way of restoring what she, in her unconscious conviction, believes she once had and then lost.

The turn away from the mother can itself be a traumatic loss for the girl, who because of earlier attachments, still desires closeness to her. According to the theory, the resolution for the female child involves substituting a wish for a baby instead of a penis and consequently the restoration of her attachment to the mother in the form of a strong feminine identification. The mother and infant are thus reunited in this identification without underlying guilt and diminished self-esteem. There is no longer need to feel inferior and it becomes possible to cultivate talents, to learn, and to achieve. Without some form of resolution, the girl may be burdened by continued envy and by ambivalent relationships to her parents. The negative side of this ambivalence is twofold: continued resentment toward the mother, as though she caused the felt deprivation, and toward her father for not giving her what she wants in the symbolic penis, a baby, and the special relationship that he reserves for the mother.

The male child's conviction about the danger of castration makes awareness of the physical differences between the sexes threatening. Upon observing sisters, female playmates, or his mother, the boy may become convinced that castration is a possibility as a consequence of the arrogance of his desires in the rivalry with his father.

Resolution during the oedipal stage for the boy requires that he relinquish his desires—a mental event propelled by the sense of his father's superior position as well as the fear of castration. The resolution can restore the boy's self-esteem if another mental event occurs in the form of identification with his father: "If I cannot overpower him, I can try to be like him." Without a favorable resolution, lingering doubts persist as to his adequacy, his capacity for independence, and his ability to negotiate the complex conditions presented in the real world. Conditions may also be established for the outbreak of neurotic symptoms later in life when the adult is unable to make commitments and to establish gratifying relationships with both women and men.

The reason for emphasis on the oedipus complex as the "classical" neurosis is that clinical experience demonstrates that oedipal conflicts in children of both sexes mark the point of closure in infantile development. Closure means the existence, although in latent form, of an independent ego that is supported by positive identifications or, in more popular terms, with "role models." The oedipal stage also results in an internalized moral capacity that is no longer totally dependent on parents. The sense of guilt leads to the formation of the superego in the form of conscience and ideals. The capacity for judging right or wrong and for self-control is a condition that can then exist within the personality of the child. Finally, the mechanism of self-control through signal anxiety is in place. Signal anxiety alerts the ego to the danger of acting on impulse without prior thought. A wish that cannot be gratified in the real world will not be acted upon because signal anxiety alerts the child, and later the adult, to the dangers in converting desire directly into action.

Unfortunately the superego and the mechanism of signal anxiety can, and usually do, operate disproportionately to the dangers of both desire and conditions in the real world. This lack of proportion, or "overkill," is the essence of neurotic conflict and leads to the formation of symptoms.

As far as anyone knows, a taboo against incest exists in all societies. No recorded society permits or tolerates incestuous behavior. The taboo does not mean that incestuous behavior does not occur. But universally, incest is viewed as a severe aberration and as a threat to the community. Oedipus could find no forgiveness in society with the claim of lack of awareness of his deed, nor could he justify himself with the initial malevolence of his father, who sought to destroy his rival at birth. Because children have incestuous wishes, society must find a way to force the repression of desire. The urgency of society in fostering repression of incestuous wishes thus leads to "overkill" and ultimately neurosis. Society's fear of incest is a major element in the struggle that must be renewed with each generation and cannot be won once and for all.

It is worth speculating at this point on the possibility of an inherited biological structure that leads to an aversion toward incestuous desire, just as the desires themselves may also be innate. Assuming two conflicting biological structures, the oedipal drama still remains intact. The impulses upon which the oedipal conflict secures its impetus are not erased as a result of some biological change. But here, too, society may be at an advantage. If the impasse of the oedipus complex furthers the transformation of desire by way of sublimations, then conceivably the gains of civilization involve certain costs in the presence of neurosis as a part of the human condition rather than simply as an illness.

Psychoanalytic revisionists and other students of human nature object to the tragic view of man that is integral to the theory of the oedipus complex. While, strictly speaking, the theory can neither be proven nor disproved by conventional scientific methods, the observable facts of neurotic disturbances and the varieties of social and political conflicts require explanation. Revisionist theories that are humanistic and optimistic, postulate an inherent goodness in man. Psychoanalysis adopts a tragic view of man in which individuals and society confront the sense of guilt as a legacy of the oedipus complex. Both views must face the test of observation and experience.

Endnotes—Chapter 6

1. Sigmund Freud, *Standard Edition*, Vol. VII
2. *Ibid*, 195.
3. *Ibid*, 219.

MECHANISMS OF DEFENSE

Louise Bentley, age twenty-five, made an appointment with a psychiatrist to help her decide if she should undergo psychoanalysis. Her chief complaint was an inability to sustain a lasting relationship with a man and her repetitive need to approach marriage only to break off the relationship at the last minute. She reported at least three such incidents in recent years and commented on how she was being pressed, currently, to marry an attractive and successful young business executive. She believed this relationship would go the way of the others because of her doubts and uncertainties which had spread from marriage to career. She commented, "Doubting is becoming a way of life."

During the evaluation interview, Louise described her family and her parents. She came from a large family. Her mother and she had the same temperament: affirmative, but not dogmatic; amicable and outgoing; intuitive; not overly affectionate, although not resistant to cuddling her children. Her mother left college short of a degree. She showed no particular joy in homemaking, but, she showed considerable interest in Louise's academic achievements and career. When Louise brought home a fiancee whom she planned to marry, her mother commented that "the boy was young and unsocial." According to her mother, he wasn't warm and open. His background was not the same as Louise's and she added, "he couldn't lead me."

Earlier, while a senior in college, Louise became engaged to a man in her class. According to Louise, her mother expressed the feeling that it was dangerous to get married, and that she should wait. Louise recalled this incident: "I remember that I was sitting at the breakfast table with my mother. I was nervous and I had developed a lump in my throat that wouldn't go away." The wedding was cancelled one month before the date set. Louise commented on how she had always tried to please her mother. She said that she and her mother were interdependent, like two sisters, leaning on each other. Louise thought she would eventually settle in the same town as her mother since she felt drawn to be near her permanently. The psychiatrist conducting this interview noted the impression that "more than the other children in the family, Louise feels she is mother's favorite, and that her mother has infused Louise with the feeling that she is very special and must have only a very special man."

As for her father, Louise described him as a complacent man who was a calming influence in the family. His attitude toward his children was "anything you want to do is fine." Louise wished he had voiced stronger opinions about her decisions in life, and would have stimulated her to think.

Louise currently was seeing two men. One, who wanted to marry her, was much like her father, but perhaps with more energy. He was serious, trod the straight and narrow, was organized, and successful. The other man she described as lighthearted, spontaneous, impulsive, and much more capable of emotional expression. She had had sexual relations with the latter (and not the former) but without satisfaction because she believed sex cannot be enjoyed outside of marriage. Summarizing her thoughts about herself, Louise said, "I'm trying not to depend on anyone and wanting always to be in control if that's possible." She concluded, "I'm always wanting something I can't have."

Louise began psychoanalysis and reported the following two dreams during the fourth week (the twentieth session):

I had two funny dreams. They were humorous and interesting. I dreamt them both last night. The most recent one had to do with my mother. She was pregnant—the dream took place early in her pregnancy. I found out about it because she was wearing something tight. The doctor told her she had to wear maternity clothes. She was in an exercise room. She was talking to an older woman, who reminded me of my older sister. I was concerned. The whole situation recalled an incident of how I discovered my youngest brother was on the way. My oldest sister and I were in the kitchen. Mother had on regular clothes and was bulging. I asked her, "Are you pregnant?" She said, "Yes," in a shameful way. My sister was 16 and I was 12. She was an older woman and she didn't want another child. There was the expense, and she had outgrown child-bearing. The dream paralleled the situation—she was wearing a dress for nonpregnant women. In both cases, she was embarrassed to talk about it and in the first case, I had to ask her. In the other case, the dream, it was a medical problem. The dream was in the present.

The other dream was displaced. I walked across town in New York toward the Metropolitan Museum. I was walking from 80th to 100th street. Should I take a cab? I was lost, and it was cold and windy. The next thing I found myself in some kind of deep hole, climbing something, ferreting out, doing research. There was one person above me, a bright graduate student just back from Germany, teaching. He has revised ideas about mathematical game theory, ideas of Von Neumann who has not been refuted since his original work with Morgenstern. He was there, and one other, I don't know who. He was holding on to something and toppling. We had to hold on. We were doing research, and we stepped down into another space. That outstanding thing was being on something that might have fallen—it was a great fright, we might have fallen. I woke up and went on my normal activity.

Louise's immediate association was the talk she had had with her roommate the night before. She told her roommate she was in analysis and she felt her roommate reacted with awe. Her roommate was curious about analysis, "Do you lie on the couch?" Louise continued, "Analysis is too precious. If I shared my thoughts, it would dilute it. It isn't such a selfish and precious activity although it's one time that's my own—you're here because of me." Louise then indicated her desire to let her roommate share her experience in analysis vicariously, and described the pleasant evening the two of them had talking, although she felt a little guilty over not working on her general exams.

Louise made no further references to the dream during this hour.

Personality structure will be examined further in this chapter.

Psychological development from infancy through the resolution of the oedipus complex forms personality structure. In his book, *Society of the Mind*, Marvin Minsky explains:

All people talk of goals and dreams, of personal priorities, of goods and bads, rights and wrongs, virtues and depravities. What makes our ethics and ideals develop in our children's minds?

In one of the theories of Sigmund Freud, an infant becomes enamored of one or both parents, and somehow this leads the baby into absorbing or, as Freud put it, "introjecting" the goals and values of those love-objects. Thenceforth, throughout later life, those parent-images persist inside the grown-up child's mind, to influence whatever thoughts and goals are considered worthy of pursuit. We are not compelled to agree with all of Freud's account, but we have to explain why children develop models of their parents' values at all. So far as the child's safety is concerned, it would suffice for attachment to keep the child in the parents' physical vicinity. What could be the biological and psychological functions of developing complicated self-ideals?

The answer seems quite clear to me. Consider that our models of ourselves are so complex that even adults can't explain them. How could a fragmentary infant mind know enough to build such a complicated thing—without some model upon which to base it? We aren't born with built-in Selves—but most of us are fortunate enough to be born with human caretakers. Then, our attachment mechanisms force us to focus on our parents' ways, and this leads us to build crude images of what those parents themselves are like. That way, the values and goals of a culture pass from one generation to the next. They are not learned the way skills are learned. We learn our earliest *values* under the influence of attachment-related signals that represent, not our own success or failure, but our parents' love or rejection. When we maintain our standards, we feel virtuous rather than merely successful. When we violate those standards, we feel shame and guilt rather than mere disappointment. This is not just a matter of words: those things are not the same; it is like the difference between ends and means.

How could coherence be imposed upon a multitude of mindless agencies? Freud may have been the first to see that this could emerge from the effects of infant attachment. It was several more decades before psychologists recognized that separating children from their attachments can have devastating effects on the growth of their personalities. Freud also observed that children frequently reject one parent in favor of the other, in a process that suggests the cross-exclusiveness of sexual jealousy; he called this the Oedipus complex. It seems plausible that something of this sort ought to happen regardless of any connection between attachment and sexuality. If a developing identity is based upon that of another person, it must become confusing to be attached to two dissimilar adult "models." This might lead a child to try to simplify the situation by rejecting or removing one of them from the scene.

Many people dislike the thought of being dominated from within by the image of a parent's wish. Yet, in exchange, that slavery is just what makes us relatively free (as compared with other animals) from being forced to obey so many other kinds of unlearned, built-in instinct-goals.[1]

While personality modifications occur throughout life, the nature of the changes depends upon the intact structure that emerges as a result of developmental conflicts from birth through the oedipal stage. Individuals are not free to reshape their personalities divorced from the elements set in place in early development. Personality changes slowly. The appearance of marked transformations attest less to the inherent resiliency of personality than to the morbid effects of trauma.

Let us consider how a person becomes a separate individual.

When a person is totally dependent on other persons for regulating behavior, he or she scarcely exists as a separate individual. Only when that person achieves autonomous control—or better yet, a balanced measure of autonomous control—can we accurately point to the existence of individuality. Autonomous control over behavior is not an "all or nothing" condition nor is it achieved once and for all. Yet the personality structure of the individual who has achieved autonomy is markedly distinct from the state of dependency on others during the stages of development preceding the oedipal phase.

DEPENDENCY AND AUTONOMY

The concepts of dependency and autonomy discussed here in the context of psychological development have a narrower construction than in their more general use. Here they refer to the degree of a person's need for others to regulate and control his or her behavior; the more need for others, the greater the dependency and the lesser the autonomy. Conversely, the more the individual is able to regulate responses to internal and external stimuli, the greater the degree of autonomy he or she has achieved. But what is the dynamic that shapes autonomy as the term is used here?

IMPULSE CONTROL

The control of impulse is the first element to consider in regard to individual autonomy. The capacity to delay motor action is an essential component of impulse control. This capacity for delay permits the ego to differentiate the sources of stimulation—to demarcate clearly the inner and outer realities. Suppose an individual perceives that danger exists in the form of some threatening event. Does the perception reflect accurately the source of danger? The perceptual functions of the ego must make this determination in advance of motor activity for rational behavior to occur. Assume that the perception of danger arises as a result of strong stimuli from within. When the individual feels the discomfort associated with arousal of some drive and is unable to gain satisfaction, it is imperative to tolerate the frustration in order to permit an accurate assessment of the situation. Responding to inner arousal as though the source of frustration existed in the outside world may lead to inappropriate action and continuing frustration.

One of the purposes served by the capacity to delay action is the opportunity to perceive accurately what is causing this frustration and to gauge the steps necessary to produce satisfaction. Delaying action, or the capacity to tolerate frustration of desire, arises from routine satisfaction in the past. Repetitively experiencing tension arising from need, followed by satisfaction, leads to a state of mind sometimes called basic trust.

The end result of the cycle of maturation, in which delay plays an important part, is to liberate the individual from the control of unsatisfied impulses. This liberation from impulses is a form of autonomy from within. In due course it must be matched by an appropriate degree of autonomy in relation to the environment. Individual actions, ideally speaking, have therefore achieved a vital measure of distance from the forces emanating from the psyche and from the environment, permitting a broad range of activity as compared with constricted and even automatic responses.

MORAL CAPACITY

Moral capacity is a second element in autonomy. Conceptually, that component of personality referred to as the superego represents the moral apparatus of the mind. The ability to distinguish right from wrong independent of the restrictions imposed by authority figures changes as the individual matures, but the basic moral structure must be in place within the psyche to permit development of a sophisticated moral capacity. Prior to the resolution of the oedipus complex, the moral capacity of the child resides largely in the parents who distinguish right from wrong and who present the standards of acceptable and desirable behavior. The parents also teach the need to avoid danger, not only in the form of punishment when transgressions of moral standards occur, but also in regard to actions necessary to avoid objective danger. Children must learn to look in both directions before they step into a street. This lesson can be taught gently by example and by hints. On occasion the lesson must be taught firmly with clear indications of the dangers present if the rule is not followed.

For autonomy to exist, moral codes must be absorbed and made part of the psyche apparatus. The moral codes are of two kinds: the prohibitions, or "thou shalt nots" that form the conscience, and the "musts" of behavior, which are integral to the person's ego ideal. Unlike conscience, which concerns what the individual should not do, the ego ideal establishes the goals and aims of behavior the individual should strive to achieve. Conscience and ego ideal go together to form the superego. Once it has been formed, the individual has the basic psychological and educational equipment to distinguish right from wrong and to guide behavior generally in the direction prescribed by the ego ideal.

As suggested in earlier chapters describing and explaining the neuroses, a substantial part of mental disturbances can be accounted for in the distortions that occur in the superego. Those unfortunate people who suffer depletions in their self-esteem, who are burdened by an unrealistic sense of guilt, and who must punish themselves to placate a bad conscience have distorted and overworked superegos: conscience assumes a disproportionately large role in governing behavior at the expense of the ego. Similarly, those individuals who function under the influence of grandiose ideals and ambitions run the risk of neurotic disturbance: what they achieve falls short of what they expect, and, therefore, leaves them feeling unfulfilled and angry.

These two kinds of distortion in the superego help explain what has become known popularly as the two pathologies of work and career: fear of failure and fear of success. While both of these syndromes are related to disturbances of the superego, they reflect different aspects of the problems of dependency and autonomy. The fear of failure, which probably should be portrayed more accurately as the expectation of failure, appears as inhibition of performance: the individual will not undertake or complete work because an overriding sense of guilt tells him he is not worthy and will (or should) fail. Note that this syndrome is really aimed at self-punishment. If the individual expects to fail and is inhibited in performance, he or she remains dissatisfied because few of the rewards that accompany performance and achievement will be enjoyed. One of the important measures of autonomy is the ability to secure pleasures and to enjoy them.

The fear of success is more closely related to the problems experienced by individuals who have grandiose ambitions. The term *grandiose ambition* suggests that goals arise from fantasy of a particularly infantile quality. It is one thing to play openly as a child at being king of the world; it is another to harbor secret wishes as an adult to control and dominate people and situations. If the underlying aim of ambition is to realize these secret wishes, then disappointment and frustration are inevitable consequences, despite appearances of objective success. When the fruits of one's labor appear as only the simple pleasures, and not the pleasures envisioned in the secret fantasies, the reaction is likely to be rage. All people probably are aware in some way that reality and fantasy occupy different places in their lives. The inability to accept a distinction leads to the disappointments associated with achievement, otherwise known as the fear of success.

COMPETENCE

A third aspect of autonomy is individual competence. The development of competencies, whether in relation to nature or to people, is acquired through learning. The individual must master some combination of abstract knowledge, technical skills, and social skills in order to take care of himself or herself and ultimately to look after other people.

There is obviously more to competence than being able to care for one's self and others. Competence begins with the discovery of one's own talents; abilities and talents can then be cultivated through training and craftsmanship. No one has formulated a satisfactory explanation of talent and it remains a mystery to this day, particularly in the case of exceptionally gifted people. But it seems consistent to observe that the more defined and unique the talents, the more dedication required to cultivate and use them. It also appears to be true that self-esteem has a direct link to the use of talents in gifted people. People with more ordinary abilities diversify their sources of self-esteem and are less single-minded than gifted people.

No matter now special or ordinary the individual's talents, competence requires a substantial capacity for self-regulation and the control of impulses. When children, or adults, are impulse ridden, they are frequently restless, hyperactive, and unable to concentrate. The consequent difficulty they encounter in learning severely limits their ability to acquire skills and master life tasks. This limitation leads to dependency and ultimately poor self-image.

A fourth condition of autonomy is the capacity for defense—the subject of this chapter. Conceptually, defense is a set of functions of the ego aimed at preserving the individual from disruptions occurring both within the psyche and in the outside world. The concept of defense is related more broadly to the importance of maintaining homeostasis—a steady state—as a precondition for effective functioning of the individual.

The concept of homeostasis in medicine goes back to Hippocrates, who observed that when all other conditions are equal, a sick person tends to get well. During illness, physiological processes begin in response to alterations that occur with the disruption of equilibrium, resulting from infection, trauma, and other noxious invasions of the organism. The organic processes activated in responses to disruptions of the steady state aim at restoring conditions that existed prior to the disruption.

A similar homeostatic principle applies to mental processes. A disturbance of the equilibrium of the mind implies that a stimulus is either unexpected or out of proportion to the individual's range of experience under similar external conditions. A nightmare is a good example of a disturbance of the psychological steady state. The sleeping individual will dream, but the protective mechanisms in censorship and distortion of the dream content will usually prevent disturbance of the sleep pattern. When a nightmare occurs, the protective mechanisms fail and the individual reacts as though a dangerous condition existed; the danger exists internally, in the impact of psychological material and not in external circumstances. Here the noxious invasion or intrusion in the mind consists of impulse arousal, in both quantity and quality, that is painful and consequently unacceptable to consciousness. The means by which mental equilibrium is restored is through the operation of the defenses of the ego.

The defenses of the ego attempt to maintain the steady state or the condition of equilibrium. In the broadest sense, the defenses can be defined as those functions of the ego that deal with painful stimuli within the psyche in order to maintain the psyche in a state approximating that which existed prior to the appearance of the painful stimuli. The discrepancy between the condition of the person after the painful arousal, compared with his or her condition prior to arousal, can be measured or described according to the psychological symptoms that appear for the first time or that have been present but are now exacerbated.

The defenses are part of the unconscious activity of the mind. They do not depend upon calculation or reasoning. Defensive responses are learned and consequently can be modified through maturation or through psychotherapeutic interventions. But modifications do not occur easily. Defenses are unconscious even though they function within the sphere of the ego.

What triggers the defensive process? A number of emotional actions automatically trigger defenses. The clearest and perhaps most general triggering effect occurs with anxiety, which is both an emotional and physical reaction to perceived danger. With regard to mental function, however, it is important once again to differentiate between danger present in the real world and danger perceived as a psychological event. Danger perceived in the real world leads to motor activity in the form of fight and flight in order to deal with the danger. When a psychological event is perceived from within as dangerous, however, there is nothing to fight in the objective sense and little one can run away from. The danger arises in excessive stimulation from impulses, which leads to the concomitant effort of unacceptable unconscious ideas to break through to consciousness. The unacceptable content of these ideas triggers the need to dispose of them in one way or another. The signal that alerts the ego to internal danger is the experience of anxiety, which is painful.

Affect or emotion that serves to mobilize the defenses to internal danger is not restricted to anxiety. Guilt, shame, the sense of dread, the feeling of loss and helplessness also are signals of danger. However, in the case of all of these affects as well as others, they probably are accompanied by some measure of anxiety. Once signalled, the ego defenses respond according to some learned pattern to reduce or do away with the internal danger.

THE MECHANISMS OF DEFENSE

This section will consider the hierarchy of defenses along a developmental continuum from the sophisticated to the primitive.

1. Intellectualization
The mechanism of defense called intellectualization describes a means of warding off anxiety and threatening ideas and feelings by abstract thinking.

> A young man was beset by problems of separating from his parents. He felt he had been cheated during his childhood and had few ways of dealing with his anger other than to become enmeshed in abstract ruminations on theories of how the universe

began. He was especially intrigued with the "big bang" theory which suggested that the origin of the universe was a huge explosion. One of the implications of this theory was that there would be another explosion that would destroy the universe as we know it today and the world would begin its slow evolution once again.

All defenses resemble symptoms in that they permit some degree of satisfaction of impulses while disguising the content of the impulses, the persons toward whom they are directed, and the nature of the danger perceived. The efficacy of intellectualization as a defense is determined by how far removed from the conflict it permits attention to roam while simultaneously providing ample material for the absorption of energy. One measure of the efficiency of a defense such as intellectualization is its power to ward off anxiety while permitting some useful work.

Intellectualization as a defense is prominent among bright and often gifted adolescents. The rapid changes occurring in their instinctual life and in their relationships to parents often require some way of removing themselves from direct confrontation with their conflicts: they are playing for time. One of the ways of buying time is to intellectualize; others are attachment to cults or becoming too quickly involved in deep intimacies. Both attachment to cults and premature intimacies tend to interfere more with the tasks of school and learning than does intellectualization.

2. Rationalization

The main difference between rationalization and intellectualization as mechanisms of defense lies in the degree of generality of each. Intellectualization is the more global defense in that it uses abstract thinking to overpower underlying conflicts and the anxiety derived from them. Rationalization is more specific in that it attempts to deal with a particular act or event that reflects underlying conflicts. For example, an individual may fail to complete a piece of work as promised, but may readily find reasons why the commitment could not be met. The motivation for this lapse in performance may entail unconscious wishes, such as the desire to make the boss look bad as an act of revenge for some insult or perceived injury. The defense of rationalization focuses attention on the stated reasons for the behavior. It directs attention away from the underlying conflict, of which the individual has no awareness, in order to minimize the pain connected to the conflictual ideas and feelings.

A humorous but telling example of rationalization is contained in the story of the man confronted by his neighbor for neglecting to return a pot he had allegedly borrowed. He replied: "First of all, I never borrowed the pot; second, I returned it, and third, it had a hole in it so it was no damned good and I had to throw it away." Obviously rationalization does not have to meet the test of rationality or logical consistency to serve its purposes.

3. Idealization

Idealization is a defense involving reactions to falling in love. It consists of an overestimation of the love object—an inclination to see the individual only in the most favorable and even grandiose light and consequently to ignore faults and human limitations. To illustrate:

> A middle-aged man falls in love with a woman considerably younger than himself. Married and with a family, he is naturally beset with pangs of conscience and cannot face the conditions that have led to his being overcome by desire and to his dissatisfaction with his marriage and his family life. Instead he places the highest value on his new love and overestimates her beauty and her intellectual and aesthetic qualities. He feels that only someone of superior qualities could justify his emotional reactions and the sense of guilt he feels.

In this situation, the act of falling in love might also entail the fantasy that he is her savior: she has hidden qualities of such rare beauty as to require his love as a means of allowing these qualities to flower. Idealization in this case goes beyond his lover and reflects on himself; he becomes her savior and redeemer—her ideal, or his notion of what her ideal would be.

The effects of idealization on the love object is worth some contemplation. Because one individual can seldom fulfill all the expectations contained in the idealization, the beloved is actually being burdened, perhaps even abused, in the service of defense. Rarely can a relationship survive such a burden. Deeper insight into idealization reveals that the individual who uses this defense is seeking through the love object to restore a desired relationship with a parent who also was once idealized. Idealization exemplifies the way the past maintains a hold on the present even though the participants are unaware of the meaning of the drama. The person least aware is the one who inflicts his idealizations onto others.

4. Identification

The key to understanding identification as a defense rests on the fact that life progresses from a state of helplessness and dependency to one of competence and independence. Prior to achieving independence, where do individuals acquire their ego strength? One way of acquiring ego strength is to identify with strong figures: in early childhood the parents provide the models with whom the child can identify; in later years, teachers and other authority figures provide models for identification. By identifying, the individual unconsciously assumes the strengths perceived in the person and therefore manages to allay anxiety and to overcome insecurities, even if only temporarily. When the individual, particularly in the case of parental identifications, manages to see the object in fuller perspective, residues of identification continue to influence the ego. Identifications may provide the building blocks out of which later individuality may flourish.

Identification as a defense plays an important part in group psychology and in the hold that leaders have over followers. Since a later chapter will be devoted to group psychology, we shall reserve fuller discussion of identification and group relations.

One aspect of identification that is important both as an individual mechanism of defense as well as in group psychology is identification with the aggressor. Anna Freud discussed this defense in her classic book, *The Ego and the Mechanisms of Defense.*[2] She demonstrated how this defense serves to allay anxiety in children regarding transgressions, real or imagined, and how it aims to avoid punishment. A child who fears punishment will imitate the person most likely to deal out the punishment and proceed to go on the offensive. Instead of being scolded, the child will do the scolding in the best imitation of the would-be aggressor. Miss Freud also cited the case of a young boy who was seen in consultation because of facial distortions that his teacher perceived as either a tic or misbehavior. The boy was actually imitating, unconsciously, the face of his teacher when the teacher became angry. Rather than succumbing to his fear of the teacher, the boy derived some strength from this identification.

Identification with the aggressor occurs with regularity in childhood. If it becomes a major defense, however, it leads to a dominating characteristic of personality signifying that the individual feels internal weakness and doubts his or her capacity for mastery. Identifying with a powerful figure, an actual or potential aggressor, becomes a means of borrowing strength. This loan is repaid with obedience and conformity. Overt aggression is reserved for those with lesser power and obedience for those with more power. The formula "kiss up and kick down" summarizes the effects of identification with the aggressor. Clearly this defense deserves more consideration in the formation of social and political movements, which will be explored in greater depth in the discussion of group psychology in relation to authoritarianism and the authoritarian personality.

5. Repression

Well before psychoanalysts understood the ubiquity of defense and the array of defenses used to allay anxiety, repression played a dominant part in understanding how individuals dealt with unacceptable impulses. In fact, repression and defense were once synonymous. Repression as a defense means that the individual forgets painful situations or unacceptable impulses, such as sexual attraction to the parent of the opposite sex. Much of the content of the oedipus complex, for example, is repressed. The evidence for its existence is the recurrence of oedipal desires, but in disguised forms. Repression forces the desires into channels that maintain the disguise, even though the end result may be the formation of symptoms. Repression also is at work in making it difficult to remember dreams. Far more dreaming occurs than an individual remembers after a night's sleep—a fact that has been verified in sleep laboratories and in research on dreaming.

Repression accounts for various mistakes, such as forgetting important engagements or dates and slips of the tongue. In forgetting an engagement, repression is fully successful. In the case of a slip of the tongue, repression is only partially successful in that the distortion of a sentence or the mispronunciation of a name contains both the effort to repress and the desire to put some impulse into action.

There is reason to believe that a great deal of what we find humorous represents the effects of repression. Because a joke gives expression to what in most of us is repressed, appearance of the repressed (and disguised) material produces laughter often out of proportion to the intrinsic value of the joke. Jokes at the expense of authority figures produce some of the best laughter because to some degree a measure of hostility toward authority exists in most of us. More accurately put, most people have ambivalent reactions to authority. While it is easy to give expression to the positive feelings, it is more difficult to express the negative feelings. Humor helps express the negatives, usually under conditions where recriminations will not follow.

Confusion often arises in distinguishing between repression and suppression. Repression as a mechanism of defense is the *unconscious* work of the ego whereas suppression is the *conscious* effort to withhold ideas and feelings for private purposes. Since the mechanisms of defense operate in the mind as unconscious ego functions, it is more accurate to consider suppression as a tactic used for purposes of avoiding unpleasant situations. It is not a result of unconscious motives, and the effects of suppression do not result in forgetting. For example, a subordinate may fail to report some unpleasant information to his boss because he recognizes the danger that "the messenger may be killed." But this suppression is a conscious device to protect oneself from a potentially dangerous situation.

Another distinction worth reflecting on is the difference between amnesia and repression. Amnesia is forgetting, but usually in a massive way and as a consequence of some major trauma. Repression is also forgetting, but its effects work over longer periods of time and are not sudden or massive. While amnesias may be reversible, perhaps as suddenly as they begin, repressions cannot be undone easily. The recovery of the memories of early childhood is no easy matter because the equilibrium of personality often depends upon continuing repressions.

6. Displacement

Displacement is familiar as one of the characteristics of primary process thinking—the form of irrational thinking that denotes the workings of the unconscious mind. Because the unconscious is not governed by rules of logic, it is therefore possible for one idea to stand in place of, or be substituted for, another, without a logical connection existing between the two. The psychological work of displacement is manifest as symbolism and is seen most clearly in dreams. Thus, a horse may stand for a masculine figure, a house for a maternal figure, and a subway for the unconscious mind itself. Displacement in dreams is defensive in that it disguises the content of painful ideas and feelings. For example, a man may have homosexual desires, but in his dreams the only figures who appear are women, in order to disguise his attraction to members of the same sex. A woman agitated by certain situations in her life may dream of quiet scenes to belie just how upset she feels.

The use of displacement is not restricted to dreaming. It applies to an overall method of disposing of painful ideas and feelings and of disguising the persons who may be involved in these painful associations. To illustrate:

> A group of people working on a book had a great deal of difficulty in criticizing one another's chapters. One of the senior collaborators, evidently not able to tolerate the absence of criticism, gave vent to his rage over the quality of one of the chapters, accusing a coworker of sloppy thinking and writing. Much

> to his chagrin, the critic learned that he had believed that the chapter had been written by one of the junior members of the research team when in fact it had been written by one of the senior members.

It seemed most unlikely that the critic had mistaken the identity of the author. Rather, he could not bring himself to criticize the author, who was his peer. His defense was to substitute or displace mentally a junior person for the senior and thus give vent to his rage. This displacement was not a devious move on the part of the critic; rather it was a manifestation of the unconscious side of the ego that conveniently allowed him to defend himself against hurting a friend while giving him the opportunity to express his negative feelings.

Displacement, although often a very convenient defense, can lead to bizarre situations:

> A commander of a military squad discovered a breach of discipline. The offender refused to acknowledge his act and the commander could not discover the real offender. To avoid losing face, the commander punished the entire squad. The need to punish overcame common sense, leading to a major breach in the relationship between the leader and those he led.

This example of displacement is reminiscent of Freud's story of the judge in a small village who was faced with trying the town's tailor for homicide. He decided to hang a cobbler for the crime because there were two cobblers but only one tailor to service the town's needs.

A final example will illustrate how displacement works as a defense, but this time in combination with the defense of identification with the aggressor. A small child has disobeyed his mother and is afraid of being punished. He begins to scold his pet dog for misbehaving. In this small drama, the child identifies with the parent who will do the punishing and displaces the blame from himself onto the dog.

7. Regression

Psychological regression involves the retreat from more advanced to more primitive function as a reaction to stress. An uncharacteristic outbreak of rage represents psychological regression. The individual loses control at his or her existing level of organization and reverts to some earlier form as the best solution available for dealing with a difficult life situation.

Regression is at work when individuals under stress become ravenously hungry and devour large quantities of food. Instead of becoming angry in conflictual situations, some individuals withdraw and need large amounts of time for sleep. In other cases, people are reduced to tears when they are unable to deal with situations facing them in their work or family life.

Regressions may occur episodically during periods of marked tension. They may be temporary lapses in self-control or they may reflect deeper disturbances in personality organization. Losses of function, such as the ability to concentrate, or exaggerated activity, such as overeating, may be early indications of the onset of deeper disturbances and may be a prelude to the outbreak of psychological symptoms. Under these circumstances, it is sometimes difficult to distinguish whether regression represents a mechanism of defense or a more general deterioration of personality. Even in the more serious instances of regression, the workings of the defensive functions of the ego are evident.

In general the individual under stress is searching unconsciously for a stabilizing level of organization. Whatever the new level of organization, it will be less than satisfactory, but in view of how far back into more primitive forms the regression can lead, the attempt is to ward off deeper regression while retreating from the stressful conditions. Once again, it is important to bear in mind that stressful conditions are present not only in one's relations with the real world but also in the workings of the inner mind, particularly the regulation of impulses. When an individual suffers a loss, particularly of a loved one, regression may emerge in two ways. First, it may occur in the face of the frustration one endures in the loss of gratification associated with the person lost. Second, the loss may produce instinctual arousal at new levels of intensity, placing added burdens on the individual for self-regulation and control.

8. Isolation

Isolation as a defense separates thinking and feeling. Thoughts are readily accessible but the feelings connected with them are repressed and remain unconscious. Two of the most important and prevalent types of feelings that most frequently lie buried are grief and anger. Although memories may be accessible that ordinarily would contain appropriate affect, such as the memory of some painful separation during early childhood, the individual literally does not experience the appropriate affect.

There is no clear reason why the separation of thinking and feeling occurs. If some painful experience or memory had to be disposed of to avoid anxiety and pain, then why not the total experience? Why should the ideas and events remain accessible to consciousness but the feelings inaccessible? There is no explanation for these questions, largely because there is no satisfactory answer to the question of why people become disturbed in the particular way that they do. Isolation as a defense is characteristic of obsessional neurosis. Those afflicted with obsessional problems characteristically keep thoughts and feelings on different tracks, with painful results in their relationships with other people. They have difficulty understanding other people and being understood in return because of their relative inability to gain access to their own and other people's feelings. It is possible that isolation as a defense occurs through learning in the family and identification with parents. What often is avoided through the defense of isolation is angry feelings, which in exaggerated form are connected with destructive fantasies. Socialization practices in many families stress the avoidance of anger. In the face of the possible loss of love and the protection of parents, the child, and later the adult, represses anger as a means of preserving the relationship that has been secured with the parents.

One of the common experiences in the family leading to anger is that of being displaced by a younger sibling. It is not uncommon for the displaced child to make threatening comments about the rival and even on occasion to make a physical gesture. Parents protect the most dependent child and will suppress, sometimes harshly, the would-be aggressor. Under the circumstances, the child will avoid carrying into action the desire to hurt the rival but, more importantly, will feel threatened by his or her own aggressive impulses, since attached to them is the fear of being abandoned, with no one to provide love. Although it may be impossible to repress all the associative material connected with fear of abandonment, the most economical means of dealing with the conflict is to repress the feeling but not the memory of the events, including the acts of hostility toward the rival.

The defense of isolation may gain further support in later socialization experiences. Certainly in school most authorities strive for discipline and control to proceed with the tasks at hand. The child who isolates feeling and elaborates thinking may do very well in school but may falter later in life when more complex situations demand some creativity and subtlety—qualities not easily available if isolation is a dominant defense.

9. Reaction Formation

A defense closely related to isolation in its tendency to manipulate feelings by the use of ideas is reaction formation—the attempt to transform a feeling into its opposite. If a child is angry at a younger sibling and wants to give vent to this anger, the child will exaggerate the opposite feeling and express love and solicitude for the rival. In adults it is not uncommon to see individuals who yearn to be helpers to other people, particularly those junior to them. Reaction formation is exposed when it becomes evident that the helping goes beyond what is needed and takes on characteristics of "killing with kindness." People generally find excessive solicitude smothering and often an interference with efforts to achieve independence and make contributions for which personal recognition is reasonable and expectable.

Reaction formation as a defense attempts to turn a threatening feeling into its opposite. It also can be used in avoidances. For example, an individual who is threatened by his or her own feelings of dependency may make exaggerated claims to independence and refuse to accept assistance and support from others even when appropriate and useful. Individuals who appear to be compulsively hard workers may be using reaction formation by converting dependent wishes and passive aims into activity that expresses independence. The "weekend neurosis" suggests a reaction to what drives people to exaggerate activity: at those times calling for relaxation and reflection, the individual may be beset by anxiety due to the pressure of unconscious fantasies that become difficult to contain during relatively quiescent periods. Such individuals can hardly wait to return to their work and to engage in activity as a means of dampening disturbing feelings and associated fantasies. The routines of work and the structure of relationships in organizations help buffer the content of their disturbing impulses.

Experiments in sensory deprivation suggest that activity controls fantasy. When deprived of routine and external stimuli, regression to primitive modes of thinking occurs. People who become overly fatigued in the course of their work, or who display evidence of regression in the face of stress, are often advised to take a vacation and to rest. While on the surface this advice seems sound, it can actually be harmful for individuals who rely on reaction formation as a major defense. For such individuals, activity is reactive to passive longings that are unacceptable to consciousness. Stripped of their accustomed routines, these individuals may find the resulting anxiety even more unbearable than the conditions that induced the fatigue.

10. Undoing

No society can work without an inbred morality transmitted from one generation to the next. An excess of morality, however, in the form of a deeply held conviction of sin, produces the need to defend against guilt connected with deeds committed in fantasy rather than in actuality. The defenses used to buffer painful feelings—displacement, isolation, and reaction formation—are often set in place as a result of an overworked conscience. Undoing as a mechanism of defense stands alongside these defenses that attempt to deal with a bad and overworked conscience.

In its extreme form, undoing, which is acting to reverse the imagined deeds derived from unacceptable impulses, leads to compulsions and rituals totally out of the individual's control. The clearest example of such rituals is the compulsive washing of hands and other acts of cleanliness that go well beyond necessary practice. In milder forms, undoing as a defense leads to the reversal of decisions. For example, executives who engage repetitively in changing formal organization structure are not infrequently utilizing the defense of undoing. By shifting authority relationships, they are unconsciously dealing with disturbing fantasies of hurting people. As a result, they are unable to permit an organizational structure to remain in place, to live with it, and to provide some measure of stability that coworkers have a right to expect within the framework of formal organizational relationships.

People who are inconsistent in their use of discipline are often involved in the defensive maneuver of undoing. At one extreme, an individual may be harsh and punitive with those people over whom he or she has some control. At the other extreme, actions may be oversolicitous and inappropriately generous. Others may at one moment be the target of opprobrium and in the next the beneficiary of lavish gifts and expressions of solicitude from such individuals. While on the surface confusing, oscillations in behavior are perfectly understandable as a defensive need in reaction to pangs of conscience. In these circumstances the individual's sense of guilt is no less operative in the corporate relationship than it is in intimate family relationships.

Discussion of doing and undoing leads to the interesting problem of ritual, which operates in both individual and group psychology. For purposes of understanding defenses, one needs only to relate undoing to the ritualistic forms of dealing with anxiety and guilt. The defense of undoing is the reversal of a fantasized (and sometimes real) action that results in the guilt and the conviction that one has sinned. Ritual carried out by an individual either separate from other people or as collective experience is a *compulsion*, such as excessive cleanliness. The more extreme the ritual, the more detached it appears from reality and, consequently, the easier it is to establish the defensive quality of the behavior. Although ritual in groups or other collectives bears many similarities to doing and undoing, to assuaging guilt, and to allaying the fears associated with impending danger or punishment, it has another quality that distinguishes it from a mechanism of defense. Group rituals also give expression to feelings of community and the desire of people to participate with their fellows in common enterprises.

The loneliness of individual defenses such as undoing further separates the individual from other people. Rather than drawing a person nearer to others, the defense sets him or her apart. In the long run it places greater demands on other mechanisms of defense to maintain the personal equilibrium under conditions of stress. The defenses used when ritualistic actions in undoing no longer serve the purpose of maintaining equilibrium usually result in tampering with reality in dangerous ways.

Undoing itself usually affects the real world and the individual's relation to it. But the more primitive defenses, which we shall now consider, all require major distortions of reality.

11. Denial

Among all of the mechanisms of defense, denial may be the most evident, requiring little by way of definition. A few examples will illustrate:

> A middle-aged man has been advised by his physician that he has a serious heart condition. Instead of recognizing the fact of his illness, he refuses to accept that it exists. He may follow his doctor's prescriptions, but he denies to himself and others that he is seriously ill. Because the potential injury he must endure to his self-image and sense of worth is too devastating, he simply dismisses the notion of physical impairment.

> A business consultant was asked to undertake consultation on management succession in a business that had enjoyed considerable success in its field. The active chief executive, a man in his early seventies, met the consultant at the airport and insisted on carrying the luggage despite their difference in years. During a long walk to the parking lot and the car, the elderly chief executive reported on his vitality and good health. He described in detail his routine which consisted of rising about 5 a.m. and going for a jog. He compared himself favorably with his younger subordinates, particularly the two men who were logical contenders for the chief executive position.

Although these actions seem relatively harmless, the chief executive was using the mechanism of denial in his behavior: he was avoiding the reality of his advancing years and the probabilities of, let alone the need for, management succession.

An amusing story was told during the last years of Konrad Adenauer's chancellorship of Germany. "*Der Alter*," as he was called, remained in office well into his eighties. The story goes that upon his eightieth birthday, his young grandson came to greet him and to wish him well on such an auspicious occasion. The grandfather asked his grandson what he hoped to become when he reached manhood. The boy stood erect and replied, "Grandfather, when I am a man, I will be Chancellor of Germany." Upon hearing this, Adenauer also stood erect and said, "But that's impossible, there can't be two of us!"

Compulsive gamblers, risk takers, and many entrepreneurs use denial as a defense. They cannot accept the prospects of bad results and therefore cannot plan their actions in the light of probabilities. They scorn as weaklings those who express caution. Herein lies the probable conflict underlying their defense. Some people have the greatest difficulty accepting the anatomical differences between the sexes. For some men, the notion that women have no penis is a truth that they have denied since early childhood. Their denial takes the form of action that symbolically rejects the reality of the differences between the sexes because they unconsciously feel their masculinity is threatened. The same situation may exist for women who may use situations and other people to deny the physical reality of their sexuality. Or, they may attach themselves to powerful men and in this way support their denial, largely by fusing their identity with that of their male counterparts.

That power plays a large part in the individual's use of denial should come as no surprise. When Henry Kissinger is supposed to have said that power is an aphrodisiac, he probably had in mind the deep sexual aura powerful people project. Kissinger might well have added that besides being an aphrodisiac, power is also therapeutic. Once in place, either directly or vicariously through some attachment, power serves to deny limitations that often are too painful to accept. The securing of power may also give some life to the full range of fantasies that have been used as the content for denial of painful realities, including personal limitations as well as disappointments. It is for these reasons that power is dangerous, not only to those who must respond to powerholders, but also to the powerholder. Lord Acton's cryptic comment, "Power tends to corrupt and absolute power corrupts absolutely," leaves open for consideration whether the corrupting influence of power is in the social structure or in the psyche of the powerholder. The observation of denial as a defense provides firm indications of the latter. Power may corrupt when the defensive mechanism of denial must confront reality and falls short as a defense, calling for the added support of defenses that are even more gross in their distortion of reality.

12. Splitting

The emotions most people experience about events, persons close to them, and themselves are mixed. The term given to describe the coexistence of polar feelings is ambivalence. An individual can feel both love and hate for one person; unlike the physical laws of nature, two contradictory feelings can occupy the same mental space at the same time, although it is usual that one of the opposed feelings will be unconscious while the other is elaborated and kept within consciousness.

Ambivalent reactions of an intensity likely to produce anxiety are subjected to control through the mechanism of defense called splitting. Most commonly, the splitting occurs in relation to valued persons. When a child encounters hostility toward, for example, a parent when the relationship had been close, nurturant, and mutually enhancing, two contradictory images of the parent are available for incorporation within the ego. Incorporation of these parental images may occur through identification. But the form of the incorporation involves mental activity of a more primitive nature than suggested by identification. This more primitive maneuver is known as introjection, which will be discussed separately as a mechanism of defense. The splitting that occurs as a result of incorporation of ambivalent images of a person leads to relationships that exaggerate characteristics of people to conform to the split images that have been internalized. The tendency toward splitting as a defense leads to a variety of bifurcations and polarizations of the real world in which people are perceived as either ideal or debased. Abstract thought can also fall under the sway of splitting so that good and evil, heaven and hell, clean and dirty, and moral and immoral can be placed in neat compartments. This compartmentalization may help establish an order in a person's life that, although rigid, serves to allay anxiety and to control impulses.

The tendency to use splitting as a defense is a costly way to deal with anxiety and the problem of instinctual control. The more an individual bifurcates the world, both internal and external, the greater the restriction of the ego, and the narrower the range of adaptive response. The tendency toward splitting as a defense is not easily relinquished. Since it is not too difficult to see in the real world all of the polarizations reflected in this defense, the tendency is also self-perpetuating. Learning from life experience and attempting to modify the defensive structure with splitting at its core are therefore difficult.

The human and social costs of splitting as a defense run high, given the propensity of individuals who use this defense to categorize people for immediate identification, in the manner of the old-fashioned western film where the good guys wore the white hats and the bad guys the black hats. To undo the defense of splitting, one must get at the root of the instinctual and interpersonal dilemmas that cause high levels of anxiety.

The defense of splitting seldom operates by itself; rather, it utilizes other defenses to secure the effects it seeks. While the agglomeration of defenses is usual, of particular note here is the tendency for splitting to rely on two more primitive defenses—projection and introjection.

13. Projection

Projection consists of placing in the external world unacceptable content belonging to one's inner world. Individuals often experience their impulses and the derivatives of instinctual life as oppressive and as an assault on their self-esteem. By placing this threatening unacceptable content onto the outside world through the defense mechanism called projection, the individual may feel *just as* threatened, but the danger has been objectified, albeit falsely, through its representation in the outside world. An individual conflicted by aggressive impulses may be able to deny these impulses by establishing would-be aggressors in the outside world.

Projection involves major distortions of reality and is the dynamic of paranoia, in which an individual feels beleaguered and under threat from hostile people in his or her world. In some instances, of course, external threats are real enough, but a real threat can be verified and, if proven, suitable action to ward off the threat may be available. However, where the underlying causes of the perceived threat arise through projection, it is extremely difficult to disprove the case. To tell an individual who feels a boss is hostile that the threat is in his or her mind will not work because the motivation from the perception arises defensively and is the work of projection.

The end result of projection may appear as an idiosyncratic problem: an individual feels someone in the real world intends to harm him or her in some way. But the dynamic of projection, perhaps in its milder forms, can attach hostility to groups, to malevolent forces that are depersonalized, and indeed can become the basis for forming groups and other associations. The political arena seems to be especially vulnerable to this mechanism.

The more subtle aspects of projection depend upon reversals to accomplish their defensive work, but again at some cost to one's relation to reality. Some evidence suggests that projection occurs after a reversal takes place within the psyche. An individual who has homoerotic feelings may reverse the affect, from love to hate, before the actual projection takes place. In this instance, a reversal from subject to object also occurs, so that the individual does not recognize his or her own instinctual involvement with others. Relationships consequently become highly distorted.

Occasionally attempts to assassinate public figures, which in recent times have become more frequent than we would care to admit, calls attention to the range of machinations involved in projection. John Hinckley's attempt on President Reagan's life is a case in point. Two manifest persons surrounded his preoccupations. One person, in the form of President Reagan, became the target of his aggression; the other, in the form of Jodie Foster, became the target of his erotic fantasies. While they held visibility for different reasons, both persons were remote in Hinckley's life. One hypothesis that would have to be investigated to understand Hinckley's motivation is that he had sexual longings toward a powerful masculine figure that he displaced onto Jodie Foster. Simultaneously, he reversed his love for a strong man into hatred and consequently attacked the President. Instead of being able to recognize the way he felt oppressed by his own impulses, Hinckley resorted to projection as a means of defense.

14. Introjection

Projection of unacceptable impulses onto the outside world is clearly implicated in an individual's interpersonal relations. The projection cannot occur without a prior psychic event called introjection, in which the mental representation of the valued person has become fixed in the psyche. This image or mental representation is then subject to the opposite event called projection. We are now dealing with psychological events that depend on theoretical formulations that are difficult to verify directly. Rather, they are based on inferences from the observation of pathological processes, particularly the psychoses and psychotic-like manifestations. These processes occur originally during early infancy and are largely preverbal. Direct observation therefore hardly provides the material either to falsify or to prove the explanations for primitive mental function and correlative defenses of projection and introjection. Data provided by clinical observation are sound. Questions mainly concern verification of the hypothesis that during early infancy, when the boundaries between inner and outer realities are fuzzy, the infant takes in, or introjects, images of what is pleasurable and painful, attaches them to mental representations of caretakers, and then projects the representations onto the outer world.

As a defense, introjection functions as a biological condition wherein the outer and inner worlds do not exist separately. And without introjection, projection cannot take place. If the only sensations and object representations introjected were pleasurable and benevolent, the psychological process would be easier to formulate and understand. Positing that a powerful drive toward self-preservation governs the mental apparatus seems to make sense as an extension of the biological theme explaining human behavior. Yet the evidence provided by the existence of masochism, of self-destructive behavior, raises doubts about self-preservation as the only overriding biological impulse. This line of argument, arising from the need to understand the workings of projection and introjection as mechanisms of defense, brings us to complicated issues concerning the existence in nature of death instincts analogous to questions of entropy in physics.

This chapter cannot deal with such complicated philosophical issues, but the problem does lead to other considerations concerning the concept of defense. These go beyond describing the variety of mechanisms of defense available to the ego. Broader questions ranging beyond description of the mechanisms of defense include: (1) What is the evidence for postulating a hierarchy of defenses? (2) Are there defensive positions of the ego that go beyond specific mechanisms of defense? (3) Are defenses pathological? (4) What is the link between the concepts of defense and modes of adaptation? These questions will be considered in the next four sections of this chapter.

HIERARCHY OF DEFENSES

The order in which the mechanisms of defense were described implies that a hierarchy of defenses exists, organized according to the appearance of defenses in the various stages of development. The three stages of development during infancy—the oral, anal, phallic—each present particular mechanisms of defense.

It is necessary to be very careful in attempting to make tight correlations between stages of development and mechanisms of defense. With this warning in mind, observations have nonetheless revealed links between particular stages and specific defenses. The observations come from the study of adults in the midst of significant neurotic disturbance and from observation of infants and children. Regression, itself a form of defense, reveals the pattern of defense available once psychological retreat occurs in the face of stress. All of this evidence taken together makes a strong case for suggesting that the defenses are arrayed in some consistent fashion that correlates with developmental stages.

The earliest forms of defense occur during the oral stage of development and include most prominently introjection and projection. In earthy or bodily terms, these defenses may be viewed as the equivalents of taking in and spitting out. Both of these oral modes symbolize the undifferentiated state of self and others in the infant's world. Oral incorporation is defensive in that it acts to fuse with what is comforting and sustaining, while oral rejection attempts to sever the connections with whatever appears painful and malevolent. Introjection and projection as dominant defensive patterns occur during severe mental disturbances. They, in effect, serve to reject the outside world and lead to withdrawal into fantasy as a means of gaining some comfort in the face of a highly insecure relationship to other people.

The defenses of the anal stage of development include isolation, reaction formation, and denial. These defenses are also referred to as obsessional since they are associated with neuroses that exaggerate thinking at the expense of feeling. In bodily terms, these defenses are involved with sphincter functions of retention and letting go. In purely psychological terms, they concern attempts to exert control over people, most frequently parents, in the child's world.

Defenses of the anal stage are often confusing because they are at the midpoint of infantile development. They may appear as the result of fixation in development or as a consequence of retreat from the phallic stage. Patients recovering from severe psychotic disturbance may stabilize with marked obsessional defenses, but the stability and attachment to reality of these patients is superior to their condition during psychotic episodes. On the other hand, the anal defenses involve certain costs as compared with the defenses of the phallic stage. These costs are mainly in limitations of the ego—in constrictions in relationships with people, and in the inability to gain pleasure from experiencing the full range of emotions. To think is not to feel, and thinking is not the only way of knowing.

Intellectualization and rationalization, two defenses characteristic of the phallic stage of development, may also seem to emphasize thinking over feeling. But compared with the anal defenses, intellectualization and rationalization are mild in that respect. They coexist with what may be a fairly rich emotional and fantasy life and do not necessarily interfere with the ability to work and to experience intimate human relationships.

In considering the hierarchical nature of defenses, it is easy to conclude that the concept of defense can be interpreted in at least two ways. The first is to see the mechanisms of defense in relation to a regulative function that is particularly valuable. The second is to see defenses in relation to how they limit and often distort the individual's relation to reality. Both ways of looking at the mechanisms of defense are valid and applicable. Clearly the balance tilts in the direction of distortions as one moves backward in time from the phallic to the oral stage of development. But even this correlation has shortcomings. How are we to understand, for example, talent and creativity, the expressions of which may run the whole gamut of defenses, including those defenses most closely associated with primitive mental activity?

Before exploring these questions and considerations, one link is necessary to complete the chain of ideas about defenses. We have restricted the discussion in this chapter to defense as a set of mechanisms available to the ego in dealing with anxiety and other painful affects that signal a disturbance in the individual's inner equilibrium. Within this framework the mechanisms of defense appear in response to signal anxiety and presumably recede once the period of danger has passed. But in considering how the individual maintains inner stability, and particularly how he or she maintains some constancy in relation to reality, examination must go farther than the concept of defense as mechanisms of the ego. The critical word is constancy and involves the idea of character.

CHARACTER AND DEFENSE

Character implies a moral judgment about an individual. A person who has a "good" character is trustworthy, fulfills responsibilities, and meets the standards of conduct expected in a community. A person of "bad" character has just the opposite qualities. Indeed, this connotation of character is not far from that used in discussing pathologies of behavior. People who are addicted to drugs or alcohol or who engage in criminal conduct are referred to in the lexicon of psychopathology as having "character disorders."

The term *character* is also used in the same way as "personality," particularly in connection with describing a person's attributes. Psychological tests can measure these personality attributes on a variety of scales that include ranges of introversion-extroversion, active-passive, dominant-submissive, and dependent-independent traits. These traits are commonly used to establish a profile of an individual and to compare one individual with another.

Traits, or attributes, of an individual describe what is constant in the way that individual appears to others. Someone is recognizable by the consistency of appearance and behavior. James Thurber's character, Walter Mitty, may enjoy the most heroic fantasies, but he is known to others as a diffident, mild mannered, and unassertive individual. He is known not by these individual traits alone, but by their total impression and by the unchanging and enduring effects in conveying to others the knowledge they have of him. Dr. Jekyll and Mr. Hyde are, for all practical purposes, not the same person!

There are obvious gains in being and appearing constant to others. People adjust to an individual's traits. Only when the individual does the unpredictable is there occasion to wonder just who that person is. From this standpoint the economy of constancy is also impressive. It is not simply that others know what to expect of an individual. He knows, reciprocally, what to expect from them in their behavior toward him. In addition, the individual also uses this image of himself or herself to good advantage in regulating relationships to people and the real world.

Anxiety causes apprehension of what is about to happen. The uncertainty of what is about to happen causes further anxiety. The more an individual appears recognizable to others as well as to himself, the more predictable is the behavior of others toward him and the range of responses he might be called upon to make. Character and recognizability might make for a dull existence, but it is important to recognize how crucial they are for an individual's psychological equilibrium: character is the individual's habitual mode of response and appearance that provides for recognizability from outside and the sense of constancy from within, all in the service of regulating relationships. This definition of character implies defense, if we choose to go beyond defense as mechanism of the ego and extend its definition to all those qualities of the individual that maintain an equilibrium within the psyche and in its relation to the outside world.

Character as a defense is the armor plate that protects the individual by providing for outer recognition and inner identity. Two questions arise in considering character as defensive armor. First, is character, and the traits that comprise it, part of the unconscious? Second, how does character form?

Individuals often have considerable awareness of their character, but they may be unconscious of its meaning. An individual may be cruel in relationships with other people, but may be unaware of the important part that sadism plays in his or her motivation. By being cruel, the person attempts to dominate and hurt parents who once dominated and hurt that person as a child. The sadistic individual may also need to keep people at a distance because of unconscious fears of closeness. There are also important sexual gratifications that perpetuate cruelty, but once again, the individual is usually unaware of the sexual significance of his or her behavior toward other people.

To be conscious of one's character, on the one hand, and unconscious concerning motivation on the other, are consistent in the defensive function of character. When people take courses or read self-help books on changing their characters, they may come away empty-handed. To be told one is unassertive and to be instructed in how to take charge leaves untouched the motivational aspects of character. Changes in character occur gradually and slowly. People should be skeptical of promises that one can change overnight by taking a seminar or reading a book. The euphoria that often accompanies seminars has little to do with change and more to do with the subtle way people are temporarily relieved of the effects of a bad conscience.

Character forms through the developmental stages. Each stage contributes certain traits. It is often obvious which of the stages have left precipitates that now dominate character. The famous triad of traits associated with the anal stage of development—stinginess, orderliness, and cleanliness—reflects the conflicts of retention and expulsion. They result from a combination of training, the desire to retain approval and love, and the gradual loss of interest in body waste as development moves forward and repression and reaction formation do their work in restraining impulses.

Character traits also take hold through the identifications children make with their parents, but later in life as well, with other people who are important to them. Anyone with power over another individual has the potential to influence that person's character. The way this influence takes hold is through unconscious identification. The clear example of identification with the aggressor showed how the motive of defense leads to taking over the attributes of the potential aggressor and using them almost preemptively. This example explains in part how and why individuals become "authoritarian personalities." But many other attributes, fortunately, help form character through identification. What parents value most they tend to transmit to their children. As identifications take hold, the values thus transmitted become firmly entrenched in character structure. Well before the individual has a reasoned understanding of codes of conduct and ideals, the foundations for moral conduct have been established in the life of the individual through identification.

ARE DEFENSES PATHOLOGICAL?

Defenses, both in the form of mechanisms and character, are present in all people; they are necessary to maintain psychological equilibrium. But intrinsic to defense is a play of forces that results in some compromise involving both the motives of desire and the motives of defense.

Psychological compromises that result from a psychodynamic

process inevitably involve costs as well as gains. The costs reside in the restrictions endured in the interests of allaying anxiety and guilt. The gains are represented in the total esteem enjoyed in meeting life's challenges. The idea of self-esteem probably refers to the accounting individuals make to themselves of how they think they are faring in dealing with challenge and conflict. At some point, individuals become aware that they are facing a depletion in self-esteem, that the costs they endure exceed the gains.

Looking beneath the surface of the experience of loss of self-esteem, we are probably going to find that defenses less benign and more pathological have begun to appear. The definition of what is pathological in defense is the degree to which distortions of reality are involved and the degree to which the defenses become alien to ego aims. At such a juncture the concepts of defense and symptom are alike. All symptoms of psychological conflict result from the compromise of forces within the psyche. The symptoms that appear are also defensive in the sense that they are attempts to halt regressions and to ward off further deterioration in mental function and stability. Hatred that exists within the mind, once projected outside one's self, results in symptoms of feeling persecuted by evil people. But the act of projection also attempts to block off further regression in which any hold on reality will be abandoned in the form of, for example, total investment in hallucinatory experience.

To cite another example of the connection between psychological symptoms and defense, people ward off depressions by engaging in frantic activity. Mania and depression are two very different states of mind, mood, and behavior. Yet the connection between the two states exists in the idea of defense. We should emphasize here that defense at this level of mental function is the process of seeking some equilibrium—a steady state in reaction to significant disturbance in thinking and feeling, in which the symptom is the defense.

The concepts of symptoms and defense become more alike as movement occurs down the hierarchy of defenses. The regression that occurs is not restricted to the array of defenses used to control anxiety. Parallel regression occurs in the organization of impulses and in various aspects of ego function, including the sense of self-worth. Consequently, in understanding the ways in which defenses are pathological, consideration should be given to the disturbances in psychological equilibrium that call forth a new and more costly pattern of defense.

DEFENSE AND ADAPTATION

The discussion of mechanisms of defense and the hierarchy of defenses omitted sublimation, which presumably should stand at the pinnacle of the defensive structure. To sublimate is to purify, to transform impulses unacceptable in their raw form into valuable and constructive activity. Just as valuable products, such as lubricants and gasoline, result from the distillation of crude oil, so beneficial products of human activity result from primitive desire and intrapsychic conflict.

How does sublimation work? Unfortunately we have no good answer to this question. Psychoanalytic observation focuses on mental conflict. Presumably, when sublimation is taking place, it is not possible to observe conflict. This fact has led some theorists to postulate a source of human energy which is "conflict free:" the energy needed to perform useful work has somehow been detached from psychological conflict and in its direction outward into work bears no resemblance in quality or content to neurotic struggles.

Take, for example, the case of a school-age child who cannot read. While the parents of this child gain considerable comfort in the diagnosis of "dyslexia," the probability of a neurological problem leading to the symptom is slim. Rather, the probability is high that the ego functions necessary for reading have become enmeshed in sexual and aggressive conflict. Expectable functions that fail as a result of psychological conflict often involve the "sexualization" of the activity, which is the opposite of sublimation. The nature of the disturbance takes the form of distortion, as in the case of reading problems, or inhibition, as in the case of children who refuse to go to school at all.

Sexualization and its counterpart, the attachment of aggressive desire onto ego functions and activities, are fundamentally issues both of quantity and quality. The quantitative aspect is the sheer magnitude of energy; because it is excessive it cannot be easily controlled within the defensive capacities of the individual. Consequently, the "best" solution available, although faulty, is the formation of a symptom such as a reading disturbance. The qualitative aspect has to do with the content of unconscious fantasies that become displaced onto otherwise neutral content through fundamentally irrational processes. As with dreaming, the innocent content of written material becomes the metaphor for the expression of unconscious fantasy. The activity of reading, which involves attention and the recognition of conventional symbols, has been taken over by the fantasies of neurotic conflict.

While it is not possible to observe how sublimation works in process, observation of the undoing of neurotic conflict and the appearance of capacity to perform provide retrospective data. It is not clear from such observation what proportion of the transformation results from the quantitative and what proportion from qualitative factors. Probably both sets of factors enter into the transformation of activity, although it is easier to describe the changes that occur on the qualitative side. By trying to find the words to express the conflict, the individual is able to understand the distortions imposed on activities and relationships. Meanings therefore change and activities can go forward.

Another way of making at least partial observations of sublimation is through the study of creative people. Fortunately, there are enough biographical and critical materials to allow for some speculations, if not constructions, about the place of psychological conflict in creative work. Artists, writers, and other gifted people not infrequently use the content of neurotic conflict as themes for their work. For many gifted people, conflicts are painfully accessible. They may have little choice but to organize, reveal, and hence objectify or transform them.

The accessibility of these conflicts is sometimes a major impediment to creative work. The novelist who works productively and then falls into a depression after his work has been published may not be reacting only to the critical reviews. The attachment to the novel may have become symbolically associated with earlier persons so that letting go is a renewed failure to separate from parents.

We should be careful in discussing creative work to avoid reducing the activity to neurotic struggles. There is much more to creativity than we understand. But, clearly, the element of personal conflict enters into the thrust of exceptional work. The special acuities that gifted people have for words, sounds, color, abstractions, and thought patterns derive some of their power from the transformations of conflict. When the real world becomes too painful, we all try to reconstruct a better one in the inner world of fantasy. But something must occur to allow for the distillation of fantasy into a universal expression of human drama.

The creative experience, whether through sublimation or some other event, is present in many endeavors other than artistic activity. For most people, however, performing work is an ordinary experience. They simply do what they have to do without the need to detach themselves from routines to examine more reflectively the demands their psyches make on their work. While sublimation is necessary in ordinary work, it does not require special efforts to keep it in place. To witness such ordinary work would easily lead to the conclusion that rationality underlies most human behavior, and that people adapt easily to the circumstances confronting them. This appearance is real enough, but adaptation, beyond creativity, implies a two way street: the real world is made to fit human requirements whereas the individual conditions himself or herself to fit into the real world.

Another important difference between ordinary and creative work is in the involvement with external structure. The more creative the activity, the less it occurs within group structures. It is not that creative work is necessarily solitary, but rather that it requires fewer consciously constructed structures to coordinate effort. The absence of external structure in creative work further places greater demands on successful sublimation. One of the functions group structures perform is to provide for auxiliary defenses. Creative people tend to be on their own in defense and adaptation, whereas members of groups can rely on the protective devices that groups regularly offer.

The psychology of group formation will be the subject of the next chapter. Clearly the initial question it must answer concerns the relationship between individual and group psychology. Are there two psychologies, one for individuals and the other for groups, or is one derivative of the other?

Endnotes—Chapter 7

1. Marvin Minsky, *Society of the Mind* (New York: Simon and Schuster, 1985, 1986), 181.

2. Anna Freud, *The Ego and the Mechanisms of Defense* (London: Hogarth Press, 1937).

Group Psychology

One of the oldest debates in the social sciences concerns the position of the individual, the group, and society in the explanation of behavior. For sociologists, whose work focuses on groups and society, there is a powerful commitment to explain behavior that can be described apart from the people performing the action. Take, for example, patterns of interaction in a group. These data can be described quantitatively without reference to specific individuals. Sociologists claim that there are social facts dealing with groups and other collective structures that follow laws of behavior distinct from those that apply to individuals and their personalities. Clear examples of social facts consist of population movements, crime rates, marriage, divorce, and other family statistics, occupational mobility, and other behavioral trends within a society.

Even an act that seems completely individual may be considered a social fact. Suicide is a case in point. Comparing rates of suicide among different strata of a population, or among populations reveals differences that presumably can be explained by the presence, real or assumed, of certain characteristics of the society. Even at a microscopic level, the individual act may be a function of some condition in the society. Here the argument is that the social facts cause individual behavior. The suicides that occurred after the stock market crash of 1929 were presumably a reaction to the loss of economic and social position.

The meaning of suicide may differ among societies. In Japan, for example, suicide is a ritualistic act to undo or expiate some harm, grievous error, or dishonor in a failed obligation to society. In contrast, in a Western society, suicide may appear as an act of individual psychopathology resulting from severe depression. But even in this case, the so-

CHAPTER

8

ciologist can claim that depression is also a social fact reflective of a condition of *anomie,* the alienation of the individual from society or the absence of primary group relationships. According to this explanation, self-esteem depends upon a person's position in a social structure, which is the main source of recognition and respect. People who lack a position in a well-defined structure are without resources to establish an identity and concomitant feelings that they are worthy of respect.

Powerful arguments support the position that social facts—phenomena apart from an individual—exist and should be explained by reference to other social facts or theories. Nevertheless it is difficult to pursue explanation of social facts without recourse to motives, and the most direct way to study motivation is to inquire what goes on within the individual in the form of desires, thoughts, and fantasies.

Studies conducted during World War II on the American soldiers presented interesting findings on problems of morale.[1] The investigators found that promotion rates varied according to the branch of service and subdivisions within the services. Rates of promotion were highest in the Air Corps and lowest in the military police. Yet in studying survey results on satisfaction with promotion, members of the Air Corps were least satisfied with their advancement in rank while the military police in all branches were most satisfied. As a purely social fact, this finding made no sense. Presumably the branch of service providing the greatest opportunity for advancement should also show the greatest satisfaction with mobility among its members.

The explanation offered suggested that an intervening variable exerted a powerful effect on satisfaction. The intervening variable between the actual promotion opportunity and satisfaction was the individual's expectation. Rates of advancement affected expectation so that branches of service that offered more opportunity also increased the desire for advancement. The problem of satisfaction therefore became one of responding to rising expectations as well as actual mobility. People who expect less in any given situation will be more satisfied with what they get than people who expect more.

This phenomenon of rising expectation or aspiration also affects responses to social programs. People who are economically deprived will be passive under a conservative regime that promises little by way of improvement. Under a liberal administration that promises much, unrest will be more likely to appear even if people are better off. They are responding to changes in their rising expectations, which have concomitantly affected their motivation and desires.

Social scientists have also conducted studies to determine who reads automobile advertisements and who retains the message. Two groups of people were in the study: One group consisted of people who had just bought a car, the second group of people who were thinking about buying a car. Before going further, it would be valuable for the reader to predict which of the two groups would be inclined to read automobile ads and retain the message. Are people who want to buy a car more inclined to read ads and remember what they have read?

Common sense would seem to lead to a "yes" answer to this question. It makes sense to believe that people who are about to make a decision would want information so that they could weigh alternatives whereas those who have already acted would no longer need information and would therefore ignore the automobile ads.

The results of the study showed just the opposite to be true. People who had recently bought cars appeared to be more attentive to advertisements and retained the message to a greater degree than those who were contemplating purchase of a car.

Buying behavior can be viewed as an action that depends upon utilitarian considerations such as the age of the car one is driving, the money available for spending, and the alternatives for using the disposable income. Decisions to buy are also influenced by taste, preferences, and habits that develop as a consequence of belonging to groups and living in a defined social stratum of society. The result of a decision to buy a product involving considerable sums of money is not only product satisfaction, but also support in group membership. The support can come from peers directly or from access to information that suggests peer approval in buying one product and not another. Failure to make the correct decision can lead to considerable anxiety and fear of loss of position and support in groups that the individual uses as a point of reference in defining his or her status and identity. It therefore becomes more important to relieve the anxiety that occurs after taking action rather than before the decision is irrevocable.

The question of what is social fact and what is individual motive does not lend itself to a clear-cut answer. There is little doubt that groups influence people's thinking and that motives take shape under social influences. At the same time, the factors that influence the structure and function of groups depend upon what people need. Social structures serve human needs. Not the least of these needs is the relief of anxiety under conditions of tension and stress.

To understand what happens in groups requires reference to the state of mind of the people in it. Social structures take form and develop content in response to the changing state of mind of the people who claim membership in them. When groups fail to be responsive to individuals, they can lay little claim on their emotional investments, particularly where people have alternative ways of satisfying their desires.

Evidently one of the motives for group membership is to receive confirmation of beliefs and actions. The support received in a group can go a long way to assure confidence in one's self. A theory that generated considerable interest a few years ago dealt with the problem of stability in beliefs and actions. Suppose that people hold certain ideas important to them and are subsequently exposed to information that contradicts what they believe to be true. Or, suppose an individual enjoys a close friendship with another person in which the friends share many of the same ideas. Let us assume, for example, that the friends share liberal convictions about social and economic problems. What happens if information appears that questions whether the friends really share common political convictions? Suppose one friend makes the decision to vote for Bush for president despite that person's liberal beliefs. The situation described is in a state of imbalance because of dissonant information. The friendship will either dissolve because other "facts" will conform to the new image of the friend or it will remain intact by means of a parallel change in the beliefs of the other friend to conform, in the interests of maintaining the relationship. It is even possible through mechanisms of repression and rationalization to eliminate the dissonance without a corresponding change in thinking on the part of either of the friends.

The theories of cognitive dissonance and balanced states in social relations illustrate the uses of motivational ideas to explain social and group phenomena. In this case the motivational concepts belong to perceptual and cognitive psychology, which do not assume the presence of unconscious motivation. When dealing with social facts, there seems to be a drift from purely sociological to psychological explanation. It is difficult to escape this tendency because of the limitations in explaining situations apart from the motives of the actors.

Another distinction in addition to that of social fact and individual motive will help understand the perspective that links psychoanalytic ideas and group psychology. The behavior that interests students of social behavior can occur in two kinds of contexts. The first context is a *site* and the second is a *situation*. The difference between these two contexts lies in the meaning people ascribe to them and the significance they have for people's thoughts and emotions.

A site is a collection station for aggregating people. In the mental health field the collection unit is called a "catchment," since it defines a geographic area for, and delineates the clinical settings within, that area that have responsibility in the treatment of mental illness. Sites can be described according to the attributes of the people who populate them. Once the demographics have been described a good actuary can make predictions about the events that are going to occur with stated levels of probability. The predictions will indicate that so many people will have heart attacks, so many will die, and so many marriages and divorces will occur. Such predictions have little to do with the individual in the context. They are simply reflections of experience and make no assumptions that the events have some relationship to the context.

When does a site become a situation? A situation, with people acting in it, almost always exists in fact. Take a collection of 500 people who appear at a theatre at the same time. Is this a site or a situation? The people do not know each other and are transients to the site. Yet the theatre is a situation that depends on the capacity of the actors to create a group out of an audience and to convert a site into a situation. For the performance to work, the audience must identify with the actors and the plot. Once the identifications occur, the group is cohesive and the members are linked psychologically to one another.

It is hard to imagine a case where people come together over time and fail to create a situation in which relationships and expectations develop. Once a situation is intact it will affect people's state of mind and conditions will alter depending upon how people think and feel. The idea of a situation, as contrasted with a site, requires a conceptual shift that places the individual in a context in which motives exist and consequences follow in human relationships.

For purposes of this chapter, a group is a situation. Rather than attempting to define a group according to the number of people in it, we shall consider a group to be any aggregation in which identifications have been made so that, consciously or unconsciously, the ego of the individual undergoes some modification as a result of his or her membership.

A primary group is small enough in number to permit interaction among all the members. The family is the prototype of all primary groups and, indeed, a case can be made that the patterns of behavior that occur in small groups follow the elementary forms of behavior learned in the family. Groups that form spontaneously, such as street corner gangs, are primary groups. Such a primary group is psychologically a situation that often will play an important part in the experience and acculturation of its members.

One spontaneous group that has been long celebrated in the social sciences is the Norton Street gang, a street corner group formed in an Italian neighborhood in Boston. The group had no purpose other than to provide satisfaction for its members and it was not accountable, except through law and convention. The evidence showed that despite the absence of purpose, the Nortons evolved an intricate structure in which members invested considerable emotional attachment. Efforts to change the structure, particularly the ranking of members in the group, met with considerable resistance. The Nortons regularly had bowling matches, and performance in the matches correlated well with the prestige of the group's members. This correlation was not simply because competence in bowling determined rank in the group. Rank in the group also determined, to some extent, competence in bowling. For example, when a lower-ranking member threatened to defeat a higher-ranking member, the group would resort to heckling and would so unnerve the contender that he would miss his throws and lose the match.

Rank order in a group is one of the dimensions that describes the social structure of a group. This dimension, along with other descriptions of group structure, is a social fact. It characterizes the group and not its individuals as such. It is possible to correlate measures of individual prestige with other variables such as rates of interaction and prestige in the group. Similarly a high-ranking member has more opportunity to initiate an activity successfully than a low-ranking member.

There is no dearth of social facts to describe groups. However, it is very difficult to try to explain these social facts without resorting to psychological hypotheses and theories. The deeper one delves into explanation, the more one calls upon psychology for ideas. The reason for this drift toward psychology is simple: groups do not think and act; only people do. Why should rank in a group and the structure that results from ranking become so important that people will resort to crude tactics to thwart others from improving their position?

Stability in group structure meets important individual needs. Suppose one individual in the group seeks to improve his or her position in the structure, to gain more power and prestige. This desire can create a period of intense rivalry. While attractive to those who expect to improve their position, others will feel threatened, will fear a loss of position, and, ordinarily, will fight hard to maintain the status quo. Even for those members of the group who experience a lesser position in its ranking, the status quo may be more desirable than fluidity and rivalry for position. However meager one's rewards under an existing structure, the possibility of even lesser rewards is always present: better to accept what one has than to risk a deprivation. Individuals in the middle-rankings of the group are peculiarly sensitive to the prospect of change. Perhaps they feel they have the most to lose in any reordering. As a subgroup, the middle-ranking members might feel that the improved position of one or a few of their subgroup hardly makes it worthwhile for others to risk a loss in position.

Obviously groups provide rewards and satisfactions for their members. Groups, therefore, arouse motives both of desire and of defense. While it is probably true that if members of a group work well together they stand a decent chance of increasing the amount of reward available for distribution to members at any given time, more often than not, a group is a situation analogous to a zero-sum game. The gains of one member of a subgroup result in a loss to another member or subgroup. Gains and losses can be calculated in absolute or in relative terms. While no one may experience a real or absolute loss, the proportions change. These changing proportions stimulate aggression, and a cycle consisting of aroused motives, heightened anxiety, and defense begins. To illustrate:

> A partnership formed for the purpose of providing services to the engineering industry prospered and grew. As the founding partners added members and expanded the number of participants who were full partners, discontents began to appear. Everybody was making more money year after year, but the younger partners began to feel that they were bringing in proportionately more income than they were drawing, while a few senior partners were drawing proportionately more than they were bringing in. To ease the discontents, the partnership managed to institute a complicated compensation program to give recognition to the differences in performance, regardless of age or length of service to the firm. While this satisfied the younger group, at least temporarily, it angered some of the senior members who felt that the group failed to recognize the special status and contribution of the founding members. Eventually the partnership dissolved because the level of strife and the displacement of conflicts became intolerable.

Nothing discussed so far in this chapter attempts to distinguish between conscious and unconscious motives in the evolution of group structure and dynamics. The motives and experiences described involve conscious and preconscious ideas and feelings with the exception, perhaps, of defenses such as rationalization and displacement. Because so much of what goes on in groups is visible and can be described qualitatively in ordinary language and even quantitatively according to patterns of interaction, it would seem on the surface that the psychology of groups would not provide a fertile field of psychoanalytic psychology. Apart from Freud's seminal paper on group psychology, there was little interest in the subject by psychoanalysts primarily because their base of observation involved the individual patient and the doctor-patient relationship. Work with children, however, placed greater emphasis on the family as a group. Experiments with group therapy during World War II also began to focus attention on group dynamics and the unconscious determinants of group structure and interaction. Group therapy in military hospitals was an invention out of necessity since it was almost impossible to deal with the number of patients in psychiatric wards using a one-to-one therapeutic model. With regard to transference (the tendency to recreate in the present, relationships of the past), psychiatrists conducting group therapy began to observe the effects of multiple transferences that occur in groups.

Another trend also accounts for the increasing interest in a psychoanalytic model of group psychology. Shortly before World War II a trend developed toward applying principles of treatment in mental hospitals that were at once more humane and psychologically sophisticated. Psychoanalytic theory played a large part in this development because it provided the tools for understanding the irrational communications of hospital patients. Many leaders in hospital psychiatry, particularly after World War II, were trained in psychoanalysis. They helped to expand the frame of psychoanalytic observation from the neurotic patient to those suffering from psychoses, and from the couch to the community, albeit the special community of the psychiatric hospital.

Awareness of the role of the unconscious in group life confirmed Freud's central hypothesis in his study of group psychology. This hypothesis indicates that the evolution of group psychology involves the attachment of individuals to the leader. This attachment is largely part of unconscious mental life and becomes the basis of group structure. Experiments from another direction after World War II also gave impetus to a group psychology, although it was not its intention.

A German psychologist, Kurt Lewin, came to the United States as a refugee from Nazi Germany. He founded in his adopted country the group dynamics movement for the purpose of training people to work more effectively in democratic groups. The initial target of the group dynamics movement was community leaders, such as members of school boards and volunteer groups in the community. Lewin's theories were based conceptually on field theory and ideologically on the precepts of democracy and participation. His framework did not include psychoanalytic psychology, but the group dynamics movement began to attract professionals with some exposure to psychoanalysis. The interaction of therapeutically minded and community minded people resulted in a shift in orientation of the group dynamics movement toward the aims of individual change rather than group change.

People working in this field began to pay particular attention to the nature of defenses in groups and the uses of group structures in the service of defense. Sometimes the effects were bizarre because without conscious awareness, the professionals conducting such groups (trainers) took over certain superego controls, and without necessarily realizing what they were doing, they permitted the acting out of sexual and aggressive impulses. In some cases, the degree to which these groups could strip away defenses left some fragile members in a highly vulnerable position. Reports began to appear of psychotic episodes in groups, of depressive reactions, and even occasionally of suicides. In effect, the workers in group dynamics had opened a Pandora's box which, inadvertently, confirmed the importance of unconscious mental life in group activity and relationships.

In detailing how psychoanalytic ideas came to the fore in understanding groups, we should not exclude the effects of large-scale social trauma such as war, the Nazi holocaust, revolution and ritualistic crimes such as the Sharon Tate murder by the Manson group, and the mass suicide of the Jones cult in Guyana. All of these phenomena cannot be explained without some insight into the way a leader can gain control of the psyche of small groups of people and of the masses and thereby unleash primitive forces that are grim reminders of the thin veneer that separates civilization and barbarism. It reminds us also that people who aspire to leadership positions take on an enormous responsibility. They had better know about the unconscious and understand fully what it means to become an important object for other individuals and the collectives to which they belong.

Obviously groups can exert powerful influence on individuals. But this power can be exerted only under conditions wherein the individual makes a considerable emotional investment in the group. This investment does not occur in all groups. Most work groups with which we are familiar do not require deep attachments or strong emotional bonds among its members. In fact, work groups would become unmanageable in the face of such strong investments on the part of its members. Indeed, this fact presents one of the more remarkable paradoxes in organizational life, particularly in the American culture.

Studies of productivity in groups very frequently urge greater participation and involvement on the part of members as a route to higher productivity. Comparisons drawn between Japanese and American work groups support conclusions noting the high correlation between work group involvement and productivity, although the descriptions of group life in Japan and the culture of work are so superficial as to leave one wondering about the base of evidence on which sweeping conclusions are presented.

In the final analysis, it may not be so much the effects of emotional involvement and participation as the willingness of people to comply with the directives and desires of authority. The effects of group life exert pressures in this direction with material benefits to productivity. Compliance can arise from a variety of sources depending upon the culture and expectations of individuals. In one culture, compliance may arise from authoritarian beliefs. In another culture, compliance may arise out of a sense of justice and reciprocity in contractual relations that people judge to be fair. In either case, the emotional commitments may be low-keyed and the degree of influence the group exerts on the individual's psyche may be restricted.

A conclusion easily drawn from studies of group behavior in American workplaces is that the underlying aim of group practices is to maintain a steady state—to avoid conflict and thereby to sustain a contractual relation in which emotions are kept at a relatively low level of intensity. But group structure evolves around ritualistic practices and a look beneath the surfaces of these rituals suggests that wherever potential for conflict exists, forms arise that preconsciously restrain the expression of conflict. Take, for example, groups with diverse ethnic representations, which may be perceived as a potential source of conflict within the group. Rituals in the form of competitive games, joking, and helping relationships give some acknowledgement to the potential for conflict among the ethnic groups, but by ceremony, ritualized communication, and even a reasonably equitable distribution of power, the conflict is contained. Heightened emotional investments would surely test the capacity of the rituals to keep behavior and conflict under control. Is this control a mystical "wisdom of the group," or is it in fact a result of past experience and of socialization that teaches people how to "live and let live" under circumstances fraught with dangerous possibilities?

Groups are conservative in practice and mentality. Pressures to conform to group codes exist and can be felt when deviant behavior appears. Perhaps it is the awareness of what exists under the veneer of ritual, conformity, and cooperation that leads to tight controls in the avoidance of conflict. The forces that exist beneath the surface are inherent in the make-up of people. Given limitations in the expression of impulses, the tendency is to accept control rather than risk the effects of passions unleashed and conflict acted out.

It is toward a better understanding of how group structure evolves, how communication occurs, and how groups control behavior that a psychoanalytic group psychology can make a significant contribution. As the reader will discover, all of the building blocks for this group psychology are in place through the exposition of the theory of conflict and defense in individual psychology. The concepts presented in this chapter are derived from the psychoanalytic theory of the individual.

GROUP STRUCTURE

Groups form and develop within a set of boundaries. A streetcorner gang establishes an identity through defining its physical space and giving itself a name to set it off from other groups. A family obviously secures its physical boundaries and who is in or who is out of the group is clearly established. Work groups also have boundaries, defined by external authority and the wider culture. Whatever the lines of demarcation, boundaries cannot exist as a powerful influence in the formation of group structures without the members first having accepted as part of their thinking the existence of the group and their membership in it. This acceptance occurs through identification and internalization. An idea or symbol that represents the group is incorporated within the thoughts, both conscious and unconscious, of the group members.

A cohesive group structure exists in proportion to the distinctive identity of the group and the strength of the internalizations that each member establishes within his or her psyche. The motive for identification is derived from the capacity of the group to provide satisfactions for its members. The more diverse the satisfactions and the greater the degree to which motives can be gratified, the more the individual will identify with the group. The negative side of satisfaction is potential deprivation, which also acts as a powerful motive for identification and group cohesion. People who have few alternative ways of securing satisfactions will tend to invest more highly in those situations with the potential for providing satisfactions. Under conditions where alternatives are limited, the capacity of a group to deprive its members makes membership in that group more valuable and tends to strengthen the identifications within individual psyches.

The power groups have over individuals can best be seen in cases of extreme conditions of isolation and separation. Studies of Chinese brainwashing of American prisoners during the Korean War indicated that the prisoners' ideas began to change as a result of primary group pressures. Because of the psychological hardships of the extreme isolation experienced by prisoners, a group was viewed as valuable when an individual was taken into it. The group then proceeded systematically to demolish that individual's sense of self-worth. The route toward restoration of self-esteem was acceptance into the group, and the price of acceptance was belief in the new ideas espoused by the group. Any totalitarian structure in which the individual is dependent for his satisfaction upon a single group has the capacity to reduce self-judgment and other individualistic capacities to a low level.

Most work groups are limited in their capacity to require powerful identifications on the part of individuals. Consequently they exert minimum leverage on the person and depend instead upon rational exchanges to accomplish the purpose of the group. People belong to work groups primarily to exchange their services for money. Studies of work groups during the past fifty years or more demonstrate that even under the most limited psychological circumstances, a fairly elaborate social structure develops quite apart from the requirements of group purpose. This observation has led to the formulation that two kinds of organizations exist simultaneously in work groups. The first is the formal organization. Here roles are defined, work flows established, and authority put in place—all to meet the needs of the task-focused goal of the group. Details of the formal organization of groups are built around technological requirements, all of which exist before the group is established. Sometimes these preestablished conditions of a group are called the "givens" around which group structure forms.

The second type of organization that develops within the "givens" of group structure is the informal organization. The primary characteristic of the informal organization is the rankings that establish the position of individuals within the group. The basis of the rankings derive initially from the power inherent in the roles allocated to group members. Beyond the initial power base, groups rank members according to the degree to which they represent the values of the group. These values vary according to the cultural background of the members and their position in the life cycle.

In one study of a factory work group, investigators found that the informal structure of the group formed around the values of the dominant ethnic culture, in this case Irish Catholic. Most Irish Catholic members were first generation born in the United States. Most of them had experienced relatively severe deprivations during childhood. The importance of a secure and protective atmosphere was the underlying value that established the ranking in the group. An individual's rank varied according to his or her ability to contribute to providing for security, but all were entitled to the protection of the group. Accordingly, few high-ranking members were older. Women occupied a special position compared with men. In fact, the informal leaders of the group were women because they were accustomed to and prepared for the special requirements of the protective role. Men on the other hand, were expected to be carefree, playful, and mischievous, if not occasionally irresponsible. The formation of sub-groups within the total group represented the values of the group and fostered activities characteristic of people of their age and sex. Allowances were made for members of ethnic groups other than Irish Catholic. As long as these "deviant" members conformed to the requirements of the ranking structure, they could secure for themselves a position in the group, albeit one subordinate in the hierarchy. Measures of individual productivity correlated well with position in the structure. Members of the "in-group" were average producers while those with lower prestige managed to keep their production rates below the "regulars." The few high producers were isolated in the group. They did not identify with the group or its values since most of them felt superior to the dominant group culture and unlike the low producers, had no aspirations to gain prestige or to improve their rank in the group.

The roles that individuals play in groups, seen most clearly in the informal organization of a group, resemble family patterns. The way these roles shape an interlocking structure into a constellation also resembles patterns that appear in the family. Two dominant figures in a group may unconsciously pattern themselves as mother and father figures, with other group members relating to this role constellation as children and siblings. By identifying with the parental aspect of the structure, the group may function as a cohesive unit until such time as sibling rivalries or parental favoritism erodes the identifications and hence the cohesion.

In a study of the top management group in a hospital, three key executives established a role constellation that became the dominant structure for them as well as their subordinates. The superintendent of the hospital, the chief executive officer, was clearly the father figure, and he acted out this role in all of its classical forms; he was dominant, aggressive, and controlling. He was also gifted in his handling of external relations and crises; if they had been handled badly, serious insecurities for the staff of the hospital would have resulted. The clinical director was a mother figure, much beloved by the staff for his warmth, his gifts as a clinician, and his ability to hone in on the main emotional problems of both patients and staff. The third executive in the role constellation was an avuncular figure, who as director of research was almost totally neutral in his emotional approach to his job and other people. He was egalitarian in his style and he neither supported with warmth nor punished with aggression as did his two colleagues in the executive structure. All three of these men were unaware of the roles they played or of the way their positions meshed in a coherent emotional structure. Their subordinates, however, acutely perceived this role specialization and began to use it for their own purposes. In this way, subordinates reified the structure, making it more palpable—an entity to which the key executives were expected to conform. This reification tended to prevent the superintendent from expressing warmth and affection, the clinical director from asserting himself and initiating tasks and procedures, and the director of research from positioning himself for appropriate emotional responses, the only aggression open for him being passive in form, within a neutral emotional tone.

Emotions in groups derive from the types of activities people engage in as well as from their personalities. Two emotional currents appear necessary within a structure. The first is the aggressive current; the second is the nurturant-supportive current. These currents, in turn, parallel the activities that appear necessary if a group is to get any work done and if it is to maintain its cohesiveness over a sustained period. Work tends to be divisive, and also competitive. These characteristics of work are difficult to observe in groups that perform routine tasks and that have imposed structures, technologies, and divisions of labor. They are more easily seen in loosely organized groups with an agenda and set of purposes over which the group exercises considerable discretion. Obviously the different groups at the extremes of this continuum are factory groups at one end and therapy groups at the other with executive groups standing in between, but closer to the "free-floating" than the routine ends of the continuum.

Periods of hard work heighten tension in a group and stress for individuals who inevitably feel judged in the interplay of ideas. With clearly defined leadership, members of the group become concerned about their standing in the eyes of the leader and of their peers. If such tensions continue unabated, the group atmosphere may become intolerable for its members. A phase of tension reduction and harmony needs to be established to rebuild the cohesion of the group. Obviously if this period of harmony and reduced tension persisted work would suffer. Task-related activities must then be reinstituted, and a renewed experience with aggression, competition, and possibly injuries to some people's sense of self-worth begins.

Personality factors appear to predispose individuals to engage in one or the other of these two phases of group activity. Groups tend to have task leaders and social leaders, with the task leaders operating reasonably well with aggression and the social leaders with tension reduction activities.

This bifurcation of group leadership, however, goes beyond the personalities of group members, particularly those who are inclined to take leadership. Bifurcation is also a characteristic of groups at work and the way people sort out roles and establish relationships with others. If members of a group are asked to name the persons in a group who contribute most to tasks and the persons they like best, they seldom will name the same individual for both roles. People who are good at work are also often threatening; another group member will be sought for support and this individual will be designated as liked most.

Putting the issue another way, anyone who exerts control over others and has power to affect what they do and how they react will not enjoy the affection of other people. In short, "love flees authority," a maxim of grief for powerholders who need to be liked. If the two types of role specialists in a group work well together and avoid the rivalries that tend to erupt when one becomes jealous of the other, then a stable as well as effective group structure is in place. Between the social leader and the task leader, the former is in an insecure position, particularly if the task leader also holds formal authority, which is not always the case. The insecurity of the social leader stems from many sources. This individual is displaceable more readily than the task leader. The social leader also tends to be conservative and resistant to change. When change becomes urgent, the social leader is often swept aside and gets lost in the currents of aggressiveness that attend innovative activity. To illustrate:

An entrepreneur had built a successful business in consumer products and, in collaboration with his executive vice president, had developed a formidable organization. The innovative chief executive made a series of bold decisions that placed the company in high technology fields which provided raw materials for his main business. But the diversification into high technology required substantial changes in his organization, including adding a research and development department and bringing into the company new types of people with advanced degrees and specialized talents. His executive vice president, who played a maternal role in the company, resisted the changes and managed to make life so uncomfortable for the new people that they came and left with alarming frequency. The company was never able to adapt to the changed requirements and eventually was sold to a large conglomerate.

As in this example, role structures can operate around certain collusive purposes. Collusions are unconsciously formed structures that serve neurotic needs as well as defenses. Two people in a group can initiate the collusion by forming a pairing the aim of which is to express certain impulses but in a way that from their purview, is amply defended.

The rest of the group may find that the only way it can avoid instability is to support the pairing without disrupting the defenses that keep the two individuals unaware of what they are doing.

In a family, for example, a father and daughter may be involved in a sexual attraction that is unconscious. This incestuous pairing may be surrounded by the rest of the family whose covert purpose is to permit the attraction, short of its being either acted out or revealed. The mother in this family unit may derive some gains from the existence of this pairing in that it permits her to reexperience, with protective defenses, her attraction to her own father. When the defenses in a collusion are weak or not supported by the group, anxiety can arise to undermine the group equilibrium.

> A female supervisor in a work group made up entirely of women developed a sexual attraction to one of her new employees. The motive for this pairing was not sufficiently disguised and the group was unable to cover it up by some displacement of aim, such as idealizing one or both figures in the pairing. The medical department of the company in which this group worked reported an outbreak of anxiety attacks among members of the group, including an upsurge in apparent psychosomatic complaints.

Collusions in groups take on many forms and purposes. One that unfortunately is not uncommon is the cohesive group that escalates aggression and channels its uses.

> A chief executive officer of a company isolated himself and his top management under the guise of enhancing loyalty in the group to ward off attacks from outside groups and potential sabotage from within the organization. This group developed a "fortress mentality" that ultimately resulted in the discharge of the chief executive officer because it became blatantly pathological.

People in power, who by their nature are suspicious of others and relatively uncomfortable in relationships, are especially prone to instigating collusive structures in groups. The best example of this tendency is the Watergate collusion carried out during Richard Nixon's presidency. From the start, it would appear that there was a lot of free-floating anger, as well as grandiosity, in Nixon's personality which got out of control and led both to the break-in and the subsequent cover-up. Like most collusions built to express the fortress mentality, it collapsed under the weight of its pathological purposes.

The group structure that forms as a collusive relationship to express a fortress mentality gives play to aggression. Whoever joins the collusion finds the usual superego restraints against aggression in abeyance. Another type of collusion can form to suppress aggression and to avoid the outbreak of overt hostility among members.

> In one group made up of two generations, those in the younger generation avoided rivalries among members in their age group. The underlying power problem lay in the impending management succession that could not be avoided. The pressure of this problem led to a collusion of cohesion among age peers in the younger generation. This subgroup refused to allow for differentiation in power and roles among those of their generation. Rather, members of this subgroup lived a rather depressed and boring existence and attempted to cover up differences in ability and motivation. The acceptable target of aggression was the older generation, whose members were accused of withholding power. In reality, the younger generation encouraged the older to hold on and not to institute the long overdue succession of power and leadership in the group.

Dependency problems frequently become the motives for the formation of collusive structures in groups. In work groups oriented to routine and repetitive tasks, the dependencies of members may be easily contained within the group structure and its rituals. Members can ask for help under the guise of exchanging information. People vulnerable to pressures to produce may be placed in less visible positions in the group or given tasks that cannot measure easily what any one individual contributes to output.

Obviously, a group must be highly cohesive to permit the expression and satisfaction of dependencies. In the example of the partnership that dissolved over dissatisfactions in how rewards were being distributed, the central problem was the unacceptability of dependency problems. For the older founding members of the partnership, their expectations of being able to rely on younger people and of being elder statesmen free of daily operating pressures were unacceptable to the consensus of the group.

Young people sometimes find dependencies intolerable because they have not yet reached a satisfactory resolution of their desire to rely on others, to be looked after by a good parental figure. Repressed dependencies usually appear in the opposite form: as hyperactivity and the ability to go it alone. When younger people are still struggling with angry feelings toward one or both parents because they feel they have been let down in their own dependency desires, it becomes especially difficult to provide for the needs of others. It is for such reasons that young fathers experience, much to their consternation, periods of jealousy toward their own children and resentment that the children's demands will get mother's attention. A group of ambitious individuals struggling with dependency desires and conflicts easily form structures that aim at undermining others who express more directly their desires to lean on others.

Groups form structures, both coalitions and collusive arrangements to solve problems in relation to authority figures. A formal leader of a group with strong neurotic problems will inevitably use the group to act out conflicts or to defend against the anxiety connected with them. In contrast, a formal leader who is relatively free of neurotic disturbances will be more ready to form coalitions that serve the multiple purposes of the group and its members. Just as pathologies in families derive from the unconscious conflicts of their parental leaders, so work groups tend to organize their structures in response to the needs and problems of the leader.

The crucial position of the leader in group formations can be demonstrated experimentally. In fact, one basic tenet of group psychotherapy and of training groups using therapeutic models is to create initially a leadership vacuum that then permits regressions to occur. When studying the forms these regressions take and their consequences in interpersonal relations, it becomes clear that power and leadership in groups are the major forces for the formation of structures. The purposes of the group become embodied in the person of the leader, and covert group purposes characteristic of collusions can easily swamp whatever rational objectives led to the formation of the group in the first place.

The terms *leader* and *leadership* are so often used to connote positive functions and purposes that it may be helpful, in considering the organizing force in groups, to refer to the "central person" rather than the "leader." The central person is the individual who embodies the group's purpose and identity and as a result is the figure with whom others identify. The central person need not be the same as the formal leader of the group.

One of the problems encountered in work groups occurs when the formal leader abdicates his or her position and responsibility. The individual who then emerges as the *de facto* leader of the group may be totally unaware of the position he or she holds. The assumption of leadership may result from the methods the group uses to deal with anxiety generated in response to the leadership vacuum. If the group takes flight from reality, for example, the central figure, selected through unconscious methods, may be the individual most capable of acting out fantasy. Group members, for example, may be resentful of the leader who has abdicated and may feel abandoned. The central figure who emerges as the *de facto* leader may lead the group in acting out a rebellion against all authority. In work groups, the wildcat strike is an example of the forms such rebellion can take.

In the case of the abdication of the formal leader, the assumption of *de facto* power by another person need not be a result solely of unconscious forces. Staff people are often in a unique position to grasp power directly in front of the chief executive who, while retaining title and formal authority, in fact abdicates his power. The staff person may act to forestall the harmful effects of the power vacuum or, in service of his or her own aggrandizement, foment or encourage them. In either case, who assumes power is not an accident. It depends in large measure on position, which sometimes presents to a staff person a unique opportunity to exercise power well beyond the scope of his or her own job. Alexander Haig in effect ran the executive branch of the U.S. government when Richard Nixon collapsed under the pressures of the Watergate cover-up. When Woodrow Wilson suffered a stroke and became disabled, his wife Edith Galt Wilson exercised, *de facto,* many of the powers of the presidency.

In exploring the problem of group structure, it is often tempting to construct a "life cycle" comparable in certain respects to the life cycle of individuals. Such constructions can be fanciful attempts to attribute to, if not impose upon, groups a quality or spirit in order to create a human entity called "the group." It then becomes relatively easy to speak of the group's "mind" or "mentality," or to refer to the group as having feelings.

Another way of stating the nature of a group is to suggest that a group totality is something greater than the sum of its parts. There may be ideological, as well as scientific reasons for the analogy between a group and an individual. For some social scientists, the group may appear as a device for rendering otherwise unruly tendencies in people human and democratic. Searching for better forms for conducting human activities, groups may hold the appeal of blunting the narcissistic tendencies found in talented people and of buffering the desires to dominate and control other people. Why groups should have these capacities is unclear, but the hope persists.

Putting aside the possibilities and problems attendant upon

the anthropomorphizing of groups, there may be a way of considering changes that occur in group structure apart from assuming a life cycle or natural history. Freud's central concept in his *Group Psychology and the Analysis of the Ego* (as well as in his earlier work, *Totem and Taboo*) provides some opportunity in this direction. Freud suggested that the prototype of all groups is the primal horde, in which a powerful figure (male) dominates the members of the group, and group cohesion or solidarity derives from the common identification members make with the leader. The individuals incorporate the image of the leader in the form of an introject, which forms a shadow on the individual ego. With such a common introject, the psychology of the group emerges around the emotions of love, fear, and idealization of the "central figure"—the leader with whom the group members identify.

Freud relates to this primitive group structure a myth concerning the death of the father/leader. The myth is that a hero emerged in the group, a figure who appeared least likely to overcome and displace the father. The myth continues that this hero, who could have been the equivalent of the youngest son, killed the father and because he became idealized, the group took him for the new leader. The idea that the destruction of the leader came about through an individualistic and heroic act is a myth arising from the improbability that a single individual could have accomplished this patricide. Rather, it grew out of the collusion of the members who, because of their guilt, had to repress the act. But once accomplished, the patricide provided a new possibility for group formation. Rather than creating a hero in the form of the youngest son who killed the father single-handedly, the group substitutes a totem for the slain father. By the common attachment to the totem, group cohesion is preserved—but in an egalitarian form, as compared with the autocratic form of the primal horde. This new group formation is called the "band of brothers" to suggest the equality of the members, all of whom are subservient to the inanimate object, as represented in the group totem.

Presumably group formations can then vary. Groups can form around a hierarchy with status and role ascribed. Or they can form as a bureaucratic structure with status and role achieved, but only according to the system or rules and procedures central to the psychology of the bureaucratic group. We need not stop with the notion of bureaucracy. Groups can be "psychologized" into an idealistic community based on the concept of need and dependency. But in this case, the ideals serve as the integrating function of the group and its durability is dependent upon individual identification with the codes and ideology of the group.

In the final analysis, the interpretation of group structure and its durability depends upon the state of individual needs and their satisfaction. If groups act to repress desire, they will be no more durable than the primal group with the autocratic father who ruled by fear and would not permit instinctual gratification. While the totemistic, ritualistic, bureaucratic, and psychologized groups may allow a measure of sexual gratification, they stumble upon two rocks. The first is the rock of aggression, which in the end may be far more hazardous to groups than sexuality. The second is the rock of purpose. If groups fail to create surpluses in the economic sense, they have nothing to offer their members and ultimately lose the hold that identification establishes on the psyches of the individuals who comprise the group. Once again, it could be argued, the reality principle dominates—even though groups may serve the defensive needs of the individuals. But if this service is at the expense of the surpluses that must be generated to reward members, then the groups exist in impoverished situations. The extent to which groups produce surpluses may depend a great deal on their capacity to release, channel, and utilize the aggressive energies of their members.

With these speculative reflections on changes in group structure, we may now turn to the second problem of the psychology of groups—that of communication. What occurs in the interactions of group members? What are the pathways along which members interpret what happens? How do group members derive meaning from the transactions that take place? These are questions of special concern to executives and managers at all levels.

COMMUNICATION

Structure in a group arises from the continuity of actions and intentions on the part of members. The essence of this continuity is found in the communications that take place as members go about their tasks, relate to one another, and fulfill expectations.

Communication, of course, is both verbal and nonverbal. Its aim is to extend to others one's understanding about the group and to convey where one fits into the total structure. To be able to fulfill the requirements of communication presumes a great deal about the stability of a particular situation and the capacity of group members to portray a commonly held definition of it. Miscommunications imply that a member does not know what the group is about or is uncertain about his or her position in its structure. Such miscommunications arise because the situation is poorly defined in the minds of the members, because the unconscious meaning of the group is inconsistent with the conscious or stated purposes of the group, or because of the dominance of certain neurotic patterns. In any case the failure of communication is a condition fraught with anxiety that members will try to alleviate with all of the tools at their command. Nothing is more uncomfortable than to go to the theatre and to listen to an actor fumble as he tries to remember his lines. Similarly, in a group, discomfort heightens while watching someone do what he or she is not supposed to do, or doing things that had best be left to others.

Meeting expectations, which is the essence of communication in groups, is not restricted to saying and doing the right things. It also consists of exhibiting the appropriate affect to accompany the understanding of the situation. Much of social learning is directed to meeting expectations, including feeling the way one is supposed to feel in the context of the moment. One does not laugh during a wedding ceremony but instead reserves hilarity for the party that follows the ritual. The job of conveying the right and expected thing to do is not left for each individual in the group. The group task at any given moment is to make sure that everyone knows what is expected and to exert the correct amount of pressure to assure correct performance. Usually this aspect of communication is not difficult to convey since it is in everyone's best interests to maintain the definition of the situation in order to get the work done and to provide an appropriate level of comfort for all the participants. If there were no preconscious region of the mind to permit people to gauge how they are supposed to behave in a given situation without the expenditure of much mental energy, it would have to be invented.

Some of the richest materials on what occurs in the face of failed communication in a group comes from the study of families in which one or more members are disturbed and in the midst of a treatment situation. In particular, the information available from studies of the families of schizophrenic patients throws into bold relief what results from poor definitions of the situation or the dominance of a collusive structure at the expense of a rational structure. Instead of expectations being fulfilled and roles being played out according to a commonly held definition of the situation, the schizophrenic family is constantly engaged in undercutting the efforts of those most dependent and least able to take care of themselves. The underlying aim, of course, is to undermine the ego rather than strengthen it.

Very rich case illustrations of defective communication in the schizophrenic family are provided in *Schizophrenia and the Family*. Take the case of the N family, for example:

Mr. and Mrs. N had had a stormy marriage almost from its start. Mr. N had been strongly attached to his older brother, whom he regarded as a father and who supported him. Mr. N's brother and father-in-law entered business together. Following reverses in this business, Mr. N's father-in-law committed suicide and his wife's family blamed Mr. N's brother and of course, indirectly, Mr. N. His wife seemed to side with members of her family against Mr. N's older brother, with the result that he felt she was disloyal to him. Furthermore, Mr. N felt totally excluded from his wife's family which appeared closely knit. Mr. and Mrs. N grew cold and distant in their relationship. Mrs. N would not accompany him on social engagements essential to his career and used her violent temper to avoid feeling dominated by him. For his part, Mr. N felt depreciated, unwanted, and unloved. To retaliate, Mr. N stayed away from home and fostered the impression that he was having affairs. The couple would not speak to each other for weeks at a time. As a result of their estranged and hostile relationship, along with other unconscious conflicts, Mrs. N turned to her son while Mr. N became seductive in his attachment to his daughter. It was the daughter who became manifestly psychotic and who entered a psychiatric hospital for treatment. (The case report, including the interactions in the family came from the hospital staff who worked with the N's daughter and the family.)

A hospital social worker accompanied the N's daughter on her first visit home since entering the hospital. The way the Ns talked and interacted with the social worker provided a clear picture of the family structure and the collusive enterprise maintained by this structure. Mr. N wanted to amuse the social worker. He began telling her off-color, sexually provocative jokes. For communication to occur to meet Mr. N's expectations and needs, as he defined the situation, the social worker would have had to laugh at the jokes and appear amused and entertained. If the social worker had responded in this way, she would have angered Mrs. N and the patient, who were displaying stony silence during Mr. N's performance. Not laughing would have placated Mrs. N but would have been damaging to Mr. N's fragile ego. The unconscious meaning of the situation facing the social worker and, incidentally, the schizophrenic daughter, was the question of whose side to take in a battle between the two "group leaders," Mr. and Mrs. N. The struggle for dominance involved important sexual and aggressive desires, serious defensive needs, and an almost life-or-death conflict of fragile egos. In this struggle into which the social worker was unwittingly but revealingly involved, communication deteriorated as a result of regressions and entered a delusionary realm in which the struggle could continue but in even more disguised forms.

A picture of this delusionary communication resulting from stress and regression became apparent during an interview in the hospital. The social worker informed the parents that it was necessary to cancel the following week's interview because the social worker had to be out of town. Mr. and Mrs. N assumed the social worker was going on vacation. Mr. N insisted that the social worker planned to take her vacation in Florida; Mrs. N responded that Florida was a dreadful place. Then Mr. N said that he was going to Florida soon for professional meetings, with sexual overtones that he and the social worker would have a liaison—unstated but nevertheless clearly implied. Mrs. N became angry and she glowered. Suddenly Mr. N began with a new scenario. The social worker planned to take her vacation in the city where the N family lived (not in Florida). Mrs. N agreed with this scenario. It continued; the social worker would stay in the N's apartment and sleep in their daughter's bed. Mr. N said that the social worker could go to the theatre every night. Hearing this, Mrs. N became angry again and said that he never took *her* to the theatre.[2]

From this delusional interchange, the social worker learned a great deal about the daughter's problem of maintaining her hold on reality. While it is not clear that this communication "knot" is the cause of schizophrenia in the victim of the family conflict (indeed there is much evidence to point to biological factors in the etiology of this illness), the families of schizophrenic patients often display the movement from reality to delusion under the sway of stress and in the search for a defensive position that will work.

The mode of communication illustrated in the case of the N family is called a "double-bind" pattern. In the popular vein, the double-bind and "Catch 22" are about the same. The victim of the double-bind is given a negative injunction: Do not engage in sexual activity. This injunction immediately creates a paradox because sexual arousal is a normal function and one can do little to avoid it (even if one wanted to). A second aspect of the double-bind is that the provocateur stimulates the victim into doing what was prohibited: The provocateur is sexually seductive. The paradox deepens since the one who established the negative injunction is now the agent for inducing the behavior which has already been prohibited. Of course, implicit in the prohibition is the fear of punishment. The third element in the double-bind is the inability of the victim to redefine the situation either by talking about it or by escaping the field in which the paradox has been established and is perpetuated. If the victim confronts the provocateur with the paradoxes that have been set in place, they will be vehemently denied and turned back on the victim. Thus one learns to live in this world of paradoxes by the only escape route possible—delusional ideas.

A patient in a mental hospital rushes to greet his mother who has come to visit him. He throws his arms around her. She automatically stiffens her body. The patient withdraws. The mother then says, "What's the matter son, afraid to show affection to your mother?" The double-bind has been reinforced.

The normal communication in groups is that which meets expectations. The premium is to present oneself as though one has full knowledge about what is expected and to emit information to indicate how the actor expects others to perceive and react to him or her. Much communication is suppressed in the process to avoid overloading the group with information that cannot be used. Even though it is impossible to restrict communications about one's self because of the derivatives of the unconscious, social convention requires that others ignore this information, aided by the work of selective perception. There are situations however, in which communication proceeds by consciously contriving ways of presenting multiple messages without the actor assuming responsibility for the meaning or the consequences.

The mode of conscious use of indirect information is called signalling. It is prevalent in the world of power where conflict is the agenda, whether overt or covert. Fresh attention to signalling as a form of communication grew out of the studies of game theorists and defense strategists. In game theory, there is rarely an optimal solution to a problem that can bypass communication and ultimately bargaining. The difficulty in these games, as in many life situations, is that communication often cannot take place directly: either the actors do not know how, the situation does not permit direct communications because of the risks of undermining one's own position in bargaining, or the threat of humiliation is so great that any one individual must approach the situation with the greatest of care. To say categorically that people should be open and trusting is naive. As in O. Henry's "The Gift of the Magi," two people who do not know how to communicate but are totally trusting can make poor decisions and, ultimately, the relationship suffers.

The purpose of signalling is to express intention and motivation as well as a course of action. In the famous game called "The Battle of the Sexes," in which husband and wife must decide on whether to go to the fight or the ballet on a Friday night, with the wife strongly preferring the ballet and her husband the fight, one or the other of the couple can try a preemptive signal. The husband says, "I'm going to the fight no matter!" and to prove he means what he says, he whips out a ticket for the fight. If he wants to indicate that he also values his wife's company and really wants her to go, he will probably whip out two tickets. The signals are plain as are the risks: to act preemptively runs the risks attendant upon one person feeling dominated and subdued in a relationship that is supposed to be equal. But preemptive signals may work only when there is no ambiguity about the actor's intentions or motivations. The story goes that two trucks going in the opposite direction occupy the same lane: who will give way? One of the drivers rips off his steering wheel and makes certain the other driver knows it. It is certain under the circumstances that the action is not a bargaining ploy. The signal is clear.

Ambiguity and conflicting signals appear when an individual or a group attempts to deal with constituencies with different interests at the same time. In *Bureaucratic Politics and Foreign Policy*, political scientist Morton Halperin describes how Defense Secretary Robert S. McNamara delivered a speech on deployment of an antiballistic missile (ABM) system.[3] The speech appeared to be an appeal to stop the nuclear madness and to end the race wherein in the U.S. and the USSR each made bids to protect their military power, only to be cancelled out by an action taken by the other side. "It is futile," McNamara said, "for each of us to spend $4 billion, $40 billion, or $400 billion—and at the end of all the effort to be relatively at the same point of balance on the security scale that we are now in." From this statement and others like it, the audience expected to hear a dramatic announcement such as a unilateral freeze on weapons deployment and the decision to forgo the ABM. Instead, the speech went on to announce the deployment of an ABM system, but now to protect us against the Chinese and not the Russians. The deployment step involved made no distinction between Russia or China as the "enemy."

According to Halperin, among the many audiences for this communication, McNamara's boss, President Lyndon B. Johnson, was the primary target. President Johnson was uncommitted concerning the arms race and McNamara was trying to get him to see the dangers of stimulating it. Instead of saying this directly by refusing to support deployment at all, McNamara chose to suggest on lesser grounds, a move that would placate the supporters and avoid placing President Johnson under severe pressure. The presumption was that with less immediate pressure from advocates of the system, the President would be in a better position to hear the main message McNamara wanted to convey: the dangers of the escalating arms race.

This example of the use of indirect methods of communicating, which depend heavily on regulating the performance one engages in, brings us to the third problem in group psychology: the control of behavior. The problem of control involves the attempt to influence other people as well as to regulate one's own performances.

Groups could not survive for long if members refused to accept and abide by codes of behavior. Social scientists have studied intensively the means by which groups reinforce codes of conduct and invariably focus on the equivalents of reward and punishment. In the family, the community, at work, and even at play, minimal levels of conformity maintain stability in group relations.

The more an individual prizes membership in a group, the greater the likelihood of conformity to group norms. It is both rewarding to conform, and potentially painful to suffer rejection for lack of conformity. The capacity to anticipate the pains of rejection tends to inhibit behavior that others find objectionable. Therefore, the ultimate locus of control is the intrapsychic region in which identification, along with the power of the superego, regulates the individual's conduct in group relations.

This same intrapsychic region leads to difficulties in controlling behavior. The so-called nonconformists, or deviates, may flout group standards with assists from their superego, maintaining a sense of superiority for the individual over the group. The more group members try to bring behavior into conformity, the more the individual finds it internally necessary to resist. Eventually groups give up and isolate the deviate.

The processes of control, within group dynamics and individual psyches, are aspects of preconscious and unconscious mental life. With some help, group members can put into words the expectations and standards that guide behavior. They often can provide interesting rationalizations for these group codes. For example, in explaining why work groups in factories restrict output by imposing a norm of production, group members will state that it's bad to produce above the group's norm because it will make some people look bad in the eyes of management and threaten their job security. Or, they might say that producing too much will result in layoffs.

At a deeper level, group norms operate to ameliorate external threats, usually involving authority figures. This deeper level of control persists because of underlying myths, not necessarily without foundation in reality, of the malevolence and capriciousness of authority. Group cohesion develops through negative identification with authority.

Much as the modern consciousness tries to eradicate history, and to govern as though there were no past, organizations are the conduits of history in group psychology. Organizations present a screen for projecting conceptions of authority, which grow out of personal and class histories. But this latent function of organizations occurs within a broad frame in which the "real world" of markets, competition, technology, and financial investments is one axis, the infrastructure of the organization is the second, and the images of authority, power, and dependency form the third axis.

Endnotes—Chapter 8

1. S.A. Stauffer et al., *The American Soldier*, vol. 1, *Adjustment During Army Life* (Princeton, N.J.: Princeton University Press, 1949).

2. Theodore Lidz, Stephen Fleck, and Alice R. Cornelison, *Schizophrenia and the Family* (New York: International Universities Press, 1965), 91-92.

3. Morton Halperin, *Bureaucratic Politics and Foreign Policy* (Washington, D.C.: Brookings Institution, 1974), 1-3.

ORGANIZATIONS

Organizations are instruments for accomplishing purposes. Their continuity depends upon creating economic value through defining objectives, and implementing goals in a marketplace. Chief executive officers must build an infrastructure to assure that all employees do their part in achieving goals.

This logic of purposes and coordination differentiates formal organizations such as the business corporation and autonomous groups such as the family. Previous attempts to apply psychoanalysis to organizations have relied much more on empirical observation of therapy groups than on the observation of formal organizations. Therefore, some preliminary observations need to be made on previous psychoanalytic findings and their limitations in understanding organizations.

Most therapy groups are made up of individuals with the problem of anxiety or other emotional disorders. Through the workings of transference, and also group pressure, painful affects seek expression in the attachments individuals form to the leader. These attachments are largely determined by individual conflicts. Besides the painful emotions that surface in group experience, interpersonal defenses against anxiety dominate the scope of observation in therapy groups. The concept of structure in such groups follows Freud's consideration of leadership and group cohesion. As discussed in chapter 8, the bases of structure are the patterns of defense that individuals construct, sometimes openly, sometimes collusively, to ward off painful affects and their underlying psychodynamic conflicts. But there is an important difference in the concept of defense applied to group psychology as compared with individual psychology. In the case of groups, the defenses observed are collective and

CHAPTER

9

interpersonal. In the case of individual psychology, defenses are intrapsychic mechanisms that become activated in response to signal anxiety. Obviously, the two types of defenses are closely related.

The "anxiety-defense" dynamic that dominates the observation of group life is a useful therapeutic tool. Indeed, this type of material is exactly what these groups are supposed to elicit. Formal organizations are designed for the exact opposite effect. The presence of shifting defensive patterns that arise in response to fresh waves of anxiety, which in turn stem from various sexual and aggressive impulses, usually interfere with the purposes of formal organizations. Therefore, without conscious intent the norms of behavior suppress emotional expression. Formal organizations aid, and in fact coerce, individuals to suppress intrapsychic conflict, to channel and limit the dramatization of interpersonal conflict. Such phenomena usually detract from purposive activity of organizations and waste resources.

This distinction between formal organizations and therapy groups also applies to the family as an autonomous group. The family occupies such an important position in the psychoanalytic theory of development that for very valid scientific reasons it weighs heavily in group psychology. In applying psychoanalysis to organization theory, the extension of family analogies to formal organizations creates more burdens than benefits.

The family is of interest to psychoanalysis because of the importance of the infantile neurosis and the consequent effect of parental images on adult psychic structure. Here again the important features of the family as a group bear on regressive phenomena, which organization structure tries to block.

Of course all formal organizations experience regressive episodes. Often these episodes result from the effects neurotic individuals have on others, particularly when such individuals are powerful. Under such stresses, there may be massive regressions with consequent alterations in organization structure and dynamics. Unless and until these episodes are played out and their effects diminished, the organization remains impaired. Therefore, responsible executives attempt to use their power to offset the impact of individual pathology and group regressions.

But this is a side issue for us here. The type of evidence such regressive phenomena yield may contribute more to our understanding of psychodynamics than to the structure and function of formal organizations. This yield of evidence is very important for psychoanalysis. It provides observations on interpersonal defensive structures and on the nature of acting out in situations beyond the couch. But considerable caution has to be exercised in using such data as a base upon which to build a solid bridge between psychoanalysis and organization theory.

The application of psychoanalysis to organization theory should begin with the observations and theories of social scientists who function usually without regard for the kinds of material and theoretical concerns that interest psychoanalysts.

One such theory is the mathematics of games. With its concern for optimal decisions, game theory appears to have widespread application to executive behavior. Game theory is a normative logic for maximizing gains and minimizing costs. The basic premise of game theory is that competition exists in all decision events, either among adversaries for end results, or among advocates for the distribution and utilization of scarce resources. The basic conclusions of game theory follow:

1. Decisions in which it is possible to apply a theoretical solution to the problem of maximizing yields are relatively rare.

2. Despite the absence of conditions that permit pure solutions, the logic of game theory enables decision makers to devise strategies for making decisions that increase gains and reduce losses.

3. The strategies involve problems of communication with adversaries and advocates where it may be crucial to convey, and sometimes disguise, meanings and intentions.

4. These strategies are most needed in cases where limited rationality on the part of adversaries and advocates may in the end prove to be destructive behavior.

In game theory, methods must be developed and implemented to go beyond a narrow logic of self and group interest. But these methods, call them communication under conditions of uncertain trust, must be based upon pragmatic approaches rather than ideological or emotional appeals.

This problem of the limits of rational decision structures in game theory leads in the same direction as functional analysis of decision events. Functional analysis interprets action by first describing the social structure in which events occur, and secondly portraying the subjective meanings of the events when viewed from different perspectives within the social structure. Rational behavior from one perspective may appear irrational from another. The effects of multiple meanings of action point to the dilemma of formal organizations: that the solution to a problem made at one level in a structure may initiate a set of problems for actors at another level in the structure. Another way to describe this approach is to consider the unanticipated consequences of action in the analysis of decision events.

An organization, for example, may decide to decentralize decision making and grant increased local autonomy to units in the field. Simultaneously, the organization introduces a financial incentive program to encourage field managers to achieve and even surpass the goals established in their projected budgets. The unanticipated consequences of such a program may include encouraging field managers to emphasize activities that will enhance the performance of their individual units while inadvertently detracting from activity that proves to be of larger benefit to the organization as a whole. Note here that the original aim of decentralization may be attained in the short run, while through the workings of the unanticipated consequences the goals may be subverted in the long run. Attention must therefore be focused on the various regulatory mechanisms that arise in organizations over time that simultaneously resist change, but also block the harmful effects of the unintended consequences of action. This brings us close to the analysis of bureaucratic organizations (used nonpejoratively), which consist of clearly defined subunits with independent power bases and goals.

Bureaucracies operate with manifest and latent purposes. The manifest purposes of organizations (referring both to the total organization and its subunits) can be measured and defined (usually quantitatively) in market frameworks. The latent purposes concern the conservation of power by groups and individuals. Much of the behavior in organizations that appears irrational from the point of view of the logic of purpose suddenly appears quite rational when viewed from the perspective of the uses and conservation of power.

As presented in chapter 8, when then Secretary of Defense, Robert McNamara, delivered a speech on deployment of the anti-ballistic missile, he appeared contradictory, if not irrational, in relating interpretation to recommended action. In his speech, McNamara emphasized the futility of Russia and the United States making moves and countermoves in building weapon systems, including the anti-ballistic missile. Heavy deployment by the United States would be countered by the U.S.S.R. with added offensive missiles to restore the balance of terror in the two nations' armaments. Yet Secretary McNamara concluded with the recommendation that we deploy "lightly" as defense against the possibility that China would develop an offensive missile capability, a conclusion "out of the blue" as it were. However, this decision effectively allowed other interested parties, within the bureaucracies, the executive, and the legislative branches, to compete openly for whatever point of view they espoused, including the original decision to deploy heavily the anti-ballistic missile.

McNamara's position and recommendation, while inconsistent on the surface, represent an outcome of decision making in a culture of consensus politics. The fact that multiple power centers exist in organizations, despite the presence of a chief executive officer, creates the basic structural condition of consensus politics. Here, groups within organizations become advocates of special positions on all major policy decisions. The results of decisions affect relative distributions of power and the capacity to influence decisions in subsequent policy matters. Therefore, the dynamics underlying the formation of coalitions and the achievement of consensus are essential objects of study for organizational analysis.

What position can psychoanalysis occupy in this multidisciplinary problem of organizational analysis? This brief review of the contributions and perspectives of the various disciplines now at work in the study of organizations suggests another perspective in analysis, that of the latent content of decision events. The problem begins with psychic control, the suppression of affects, and the direction of behavior toward coalition formation as a means of consolidating power and arriving at consensus decisions. All of these mental activities take place within a specific culture. Individuals internalize this culture, while the organization's norms pressure individuals to adapt. Thus, the basis of organization structure is not necessarily the internalization of the leader imago, or identification with the leader, but rather the internalization of the organization as a culture. In effect, individuals become oriented, perhaps programmed is too strong a word, to a customary way of life. This way of life defines the range of emotions that one is permitted to display. It guides the individual in conducting himself or herself in conditions of conflict. It even determines the range of problems one considers along with the alternatives available in solving these problems. Under this conception of an organization, one of its *latent* purposes is to acculturate individuals to the organization while its *manifest* purposes are defined in external goals, costs and benefits, and in the maximization of profit.

These manifest and latent purposes often operate at cross-purposes. To aid, or coerce, people to adapt to the organization, may in the end perpetuate a culture that is ill-suited to survive in a competitive environment. From a psychoanalytic perspective, this "illness of adaptation" occurs when the culture values the organization's equilibrium over its ability to compete in the long run. For example, mature industries such as steel and automobiles in the United States are in economic decline, and specific organizations such as the Curtis Publishing Company and the mass retailer, W.T. Grant, no longer exist. What blinds organizations and their chief executives from the trends in the market economy? Why do they fail to take action to anticipate and overcome the adverse effects of these trends?

The idea of failed adaptation suggests that organizations, in arriving at consensus structures and equilibrium in the distribution and uses of power among contending groups, use internalization of the ideals of their culture to suppress conflict. Conflict may be the essential means for examining policy and questioning existing modes of adaptation. But because attachment to ideals not only determines purpose, but assures the preservation of power among interested groups that participate in the culture's consensus, there is little immediate incentive to open the organization to conflict. Not all executives understand that conflict can be useful. And of those who do understand, not all act as if they do.

Only when the signs of the failure resulting from limited adaptation appear does the need for change become evident. Then it may be too late. At this point, the authority structure may be unable to act rationally given the inability of the organization to detach itself from its commitment to internalized ideals. When action occurs, without relinquishing the hold the culture exerts on individuals through the authority structure, magical thinking may dominate the basis of action. The latent function of this action and of the magical thinking is to preserve the attachment to ideals and the culture while appearing to change and alter positions in the marketplace. The changed positions are usually false and misleading.

Ordinarily, it is difficult to distinguish between individual and organizational pathology. There is often a strong causal connection, especially when the pathology resides in the organization's leader. But careful observation will show that the difference depends upon distinguishing between sites and situations on the one hand, and accidents and events on the other. As indicated in chapter 8, a site can be any location where individual pathology becomes manifest apart from conditions in the particular site. A situation contains the forces that enter causally into the appearance of symptoms of pathology. Thus, an *accident* is the happenstance of a person predisposed to fall ill encountering a precipitating cause, which is as likely to occur in one or another place. A *situation* contains the forces that cause troubles not likely to occur in any other place. Here is an illustration of an organization acting as a site for the occurrence of an emotional accident.

> Bill Ryan, vice president of a medium-sized company in the computer industry kept an appointment with his boss, the company founder and chief executive. The ostensible purpose of

this meeting was the routine review of financial information. Much to the CEO's astonishment, Bill opened the meeting announcing he had fallen in love with the chief's daughter and that he wanted to marry her. He continued, "I know this is going to be a problem for you because we have different religious backgrounds."

Part of the CEO's astonishment derived from the fact that he expected a business meeting and instead found himself facing a personal issue. In addition, the CEO knew that Bill and his daughter had met only casually in the office, and he was not aware that his daughter had any interest in Bill. But instead of confronting Bill with these anomalies, the CEO said to Bill that religious differences don't amount to much these days, and he then turned to the business at hand.

Meeting for lunch later in the day with other executives for the purpose of reviewing purchasing practices, Bill once again repeated his wish to marry the CEO's daughter adding that he thought religious differences would stand in the way of fulfilling his wish. The CEO repeated his reassurance that religious differences don't matter this day and age and turned immediately to the subject of purchasing.

On consulting with other executives later in the day, the CEO discovered that Bill Riley had been acting strangely in the office. He would sit at his desk staring into space, responding to other people only with difficulty. The CEO then called Bill's mother, with whom he lived, and learned that Bill had been behaving strangely at home. He had become uncommunicative and would take her out for a drive only to scare her out of her wits with reckless driving. Through various intermediaries, Bill sought psychiatric consultation. He entered a hospital for treatment of depression.

To the professional and lay person alike, Bill Riley's experience presents a vexing question: To what extent is the disability a result of conditions in the organization that strain the individual's capacity to maintain personal equilibrium? Conversely, is the disability purely a personal reaction, only marginally related to the organization?

Arguing from the obvious with the statement that it is probably both situational and personal begs the question. How do organizations affect the mental and emotional life of their employees? How do individuals use the content and relationships of organizations both to maintain their equilibrium and to play out the various personal themes that reflect the continuities in their development?

Returning to Bill Riley, these general questions focus on the causes of depression and the origins of the delusional idea that came to dominate his psyche. Investigation beyond the CEO's straightforward report of the incidents that led him to intervene on behalf of his valued employee's well-being revealed a probable precipitating cause of the depression and the delusional idea that he wanted to marry his boss's daughter.

For some months before the strange events reported in this case, Bill Riley had been engaged in managing a corporate crisis. The company had expanded rapidly and was on the verge of running out of cash. To meet this crisis, the CEO and Bill worked together closely in preparing materials for lenders and in securing loans to tide the company over its embarrassing cash-flow problem. The CEO found in Bill a stalwart supporter. Indeed Bill displayed leadership in deciding what information to collect for the lenders, in preparing and conducting presentations, and in finally convincing the lenders to help the company through the crisis. The lenders agreed to support the proposal. In due course the crisis abated. Life in the company returned to normal, with only intermittent contact between the CEO and Bill Riley.

The work situation had created for Bill transient gratification in having his boss dependent on him instead of Bill feeling dependent on his boss. Bill wanted a close relationship with a male authority figure, something he either missed or failed to gain in his relationship with his father. But as is often the case with a wish that is embedded in unconscious mental life, Bill could not accept his wish on its own terms. The corporate crisis gave him what he wanted (a close relationship with a male authority figure) but it also provided him with an idea in the form of a negation that allowed him to remain unaware of what he wanted. The idea was simply that it was not he who needed his boss, but his boss who needed him.

While it may strain credulity, the dependency wish was complicated by an erotic component that made any close relationship between Bill and a male figure who represented power a cause for considerable anxiety. Bill therefore faced two hidden psychological tasks necessary to reestablish his equilibrium upon losing a fortuitous situation which allowed him, so to speak, to have his cake and eat it too. The first task was to reestablish the tie to his boss without revealing to himself (let alone his boss) the true nature of his longing. The solution was the wish ungrounded in reality to marry his boss's daughter. With this wish, Bill could preserve a closeness he badly needed, but rarely experienced, while maintaining the aim and object of his wish without his conscious complicity. The depression both preceded and followed this complicated structure of ideas. It preceded the wish in response to the genuine loss Bill experienced when the CEO no longer saw as much of him as he had during the crisis, and no longer allowed the illusion that it was really the CEO who needed Bill rather than the reverse.

In the context of these observations and interpretations, it is plausible to suppose that the existence of this organization, the respective roles of the CEO and vice president had little causal significance in determining Bill's illness. While real enough, the case is similar in structure to a Georges Simenon novel. The protagonist has an accident, the aftermath of which is to change Bill forever. While it may provoke mystical delight, the idea that Bill's change will in turn change his relationships and the organization is remote and unlikely. We have a pure case in which an individual lives with a time bomb that will explode given sufficient provocation in the form of some accident that symbolically reproduces a loss endured psychologically in some remote time in the past. For this individual, and countless thousands of others, psychological accidents occur in sites that have little causal significance in the unfolding of their psychological destiny. This psychological realm is probably identical to the kind of genetic accidents that lead to the variable physical illnesses that afflict mankind.

Let us turn to psychoanalytic theory for guidance in understanding the difference between site and a situation. A choice immediately presents itself as represented in two of Freud's works, "Group Psychology and the Analysis of the Ego" and "Psychoanalytic Notes on an Autobiographical Account of a Case of Paranoia" or as it is more popularly known, the "Schreber Case." These two studies illustrate the difference between the psychopathology of groups and organizations, on the one hand, and individual psychopathology, on the other hand.

In "Group Psychology and the Analysis of the Ego," Freud suggests that the basis of cohesion in a group is the common identifications subordinates make with their leader. What prevents people from falling ill in a "primal" group is perceived equality in the eyes of their powerful leader. If a leader breaks this equidistance and favors one or another of the subordinates, the identification breaks down. The group and its members fall victim to regressive phenomena that arise in defense against sexual and aggressive arousal. If there is no common identification with a leader, a group may not exist. If it does exist, its structure depends on some foundation other than a common identification with an authority figure. When an individual regresses, the condition probably belongs to his psyche rather than to beliefs or attachments that are attributes of the organization's culture. From the point of view of this condition, the organization is nothing more than a site, a collection station where people gather. The population profile, once known, should make it possible to predict the frequency with which conditions such as physical and emotional illness, accidents and other related phenomena will appear.

To illustrate, let's look at the "Schreber Case." Dr. Schreber, a highly respected judge, suffered from delusional ideas in which he had been transformed into a woman for the purpose of redeeming the world through his special sexual relationship to God. The delusional ideas were revisions of his persecutory belief that he was a victim of attack by his doctor. The doctor had assumed the position in Schreber's psyche once held by his father whom Schreber had lost and for whom mourning had not been successfully accomplished. Whatever real objects existed in Schreber's world were distorted by the significance of his lost father. In this sense the real objects were innocent bystanders to an internal tragedy. Schreber's doctor no more caused his illness than the president caused Bill Riley's illness in the specimen case reported earlier. Two innocent bystanders existed in a context that lacked meaning as a situation. An organization as a situation implies that forces operating within a culture, which are partially determined by the members of that culture, affect individual and group responses. The events to be described and interpreted no longer depend solely on an individual's pathology, although the way in which individual members are predisposed toward illness may affect their contribution to the culture.

To clarify further the distinction between an organization as a site and as a situation let us examine a second specimen that involves a group acting out symbolically an episode of patricide.

> The chairman of the board of a company asked for consultation regarding his impending decision to discharge a newly appointed president. The chairman had assumed the position of chief executive officer of the company when his father died in an automobile accident. The CEO was in his early thirties and appeared to be heading a successful business which he had developed well beyond the size and scope of his father's firm. The young chairman and CEO had gained control of the business when he induced his brother to sell him his inherited shares. With the support of his mother, he then controlled well over 50 percent of the outstanding stock of the business.
>
> In describing his problems with the president, who was chief operating officer, the chairman recounted the following

story. The president had been with a company for some time as a successful head of marketing and sales. He was 25 or more years older than the chairman and he had assumed the presidency when the chief executive officer decided to separate himself from the problems of running the business in order to concentrate on long-range planning and possible acquisitions of new businesses. As part of the change the chief executive officer moved into a separate suite of offices in a splendid building and left his newly designated president to direct affairs at the old offices and plants.

The CEO reported that he had felt uncomfortable about this change almost immediately. He took advantage of meetings to elicit reports from subordinates of the new president on various company affairs. The new president left for Europe on a vacation trip and while he was away the chairman moved back into the old offices and began to make radical changes in personnel and product lines. He even reversed course on a previously agreed-upon plant expansion. He drafted a long letter to the president and sent it to his home to await his return from vacation. In the letter he detailed all the alleged inadequacies he had found in the operations since the change and all but suggested that the president was a failure and should resign. He based the charges in the letter on information he had gained in conversations with younger executives who reported to the president. In making his inquiries, the chairman had revealed his discontent with the president to these younger executives. Clearly he had established a climate in which he was urging people to give him ammunition against their immediate superior. These subordinates, who were close to the chairman in age, eagerly engaged in such reporting and presented him with situations and alleged facts of which he himself had no prior knowledge.

Later events indicated that at the time he appointed the new president, the chairman was aware, if only dimly, of impending developments in his industry. These developments ultimately led to a disastrous reversal in the fortunes of the business. After a period of struggle, the company finally declared itself insolvent and went out of business.

One might easily speculate that the engine driving the action in this specific case was fueled by the continued effects of a burning and unresolved oedipus complex in the young chairman-chief executive officer. In supporting this interpretation one could refer to the speed with which he assumed ownership control of the business after his father's death, the alacrity with which he excluded his brother from both ownership and participation, and the determination he displayed in forming an alliance with his mother in which he assumed the position of "father" and head of the business. She now depended upon him in place of her husband.

While this interpretation appears convincing it may be incomplete. Elements in the story are just too transparent to give the sense of conviction that arises from achieving a satisfactory interpretation. It is similar to that sense of incompleteness which is conveyed by an obsessive neurotic who details the symptoms, causes and consequences of his illness without the least ability to use this material to change his life.

A more complete interpretation would require a description of how people become aware of the signs of danger arising from changes in the environment; of how once they become aware, a collusion forms to disregard this information and deny its significance. The oedipal drama would then appear perhaps more nearly for what it may have been: a diversionary tactic to keep conscious attention directed toward internal struggles and rivalries. The fullness of this situation would appear in understanding the function of this collective denial. As in warfare, a strategic error can produce disaster for an organization. The fate of the army appears clear, but for the general command, perhaps with an eye to history, the main preoccupation may be to absolve oneself from blame, to relieve the sense of guilt. Another way of stating the case is that people collectively facing danger will sometimes create substitute anxiety dramas which they feel they can control. This sense of control is of course false and even harmful in dealing with the real danger. Nevertheless, under the sway of regressive forces, displacements occur which serve as a defensive position, albeit a weak and costly one.

The British psychoanalyst W.R. Bion made some pertinent observations on groups and organizations, particularly in his book, *Experiences in Groups.*[1] Bion's conflict-defense theory of group behavior is based upon the conflict-defense model of individual psychopathology. The difference between the group and individual model lies in the substitution of regressive interactional patterns and emotional states for symptoms or characterological disturbances. Neurotic symptoms arise as compromises between instinctual demands, inner prohibitions and reality. Furthermore, symptoms inhibit action. In the case of a group, instinctual derivatives appear in response to a group's problems with its leader, problems that arise from certain qualities of the leader or from the conflicting desires individuals attach to their leader. These desires prevent groups from engaging in what Bion calls a work modality, or activity related to the group's purpose. Because a leader cannot satisfy these desires, the group regresses in order to deal with anxiety, depression, and guilt. Bion describes these group regressions ("basic assumption" vs. "work" modalities) in terms of the group's structure and dynamics: flight, fight, dependency and pairing. While the basic assumption modalities can be observed in the group's interactions, their symbolic significance, or meaning, lies in the attachment to the leader defined by the nature of the instinctual conflict (dominantly sexual or aggressive) and the displacement of the conflict from the leader onto the group.

Bion's theory of group psychology provides an important lever for prying the rock of individual psychopathology away from the position of obscuring a genuine psychological event that occurs in a situation. But this theory has important limitations. Before considering these limitations, consider one other specimen to clarify further the distinctions between site/situation and accident/event.

> An air traffic controller in his early fifties slipped on the icy metal stairs of a control tower. He fell and injured his back. The accident had major effects on this man's life. He became depressed, isolated and paranoid, and had to be placed on medical retirement.

Many facts about the organization and his life in it played a part in his illness. The specter of technological change frightened this man who had been concerned about his ability to keep up and also about the uncertainties of retirement. The accident caused him to let go, to give in to his fears and to fuse his past dependency problems with his present physical injuries. The organization became the focus of his discontent and angry feelings. There was indeed considerable evidence to suggest that he was treated incompetently by supervisors, doctors, and lawyers, but an attempt to erect an organizational event out of this accident would be of little help in understanding the dynamics of organizations. It would only lead to a kind of mythology of bureaucracy involving the weak and the strong, the anonymous little man against the behemoth organization. Such mythology should not divert attention away from the real task of observation, description, and interpretation of events in situations. We will look at this specimen again in chapter 10.

Most of the literature on large-scale and bureaucratic organizations has been the product of sociologists who have been influenced by Max Weber, Emile Durkheim, Talcott Parsons, Robert Merton, and the schools of anthropology that deal with structure and function. In dealing with pathology, sociologists attend to such forms of maladaptation in large organizations as the phenomenon of "trained incapacity," the situation that arises when individuals are so thoroughly trained to do a job that they lose sight of the context of their action. In performing their jobs strictly in accordance with their training, they actually, even though innocently, harm the organization and its constituents. Similarly, when sociologists refer to "the displacement of goals," they are describing the effects of shifting attention from substance to procedure. Over the long run, such shifts calcify and even destroy organizations.

Another important problem raised in sociological studies of organizations is the matter of rational and irrational behavior. One of the most valuable contributions to this discussion comes from Michel Crozier, the French sociologist, in his book, *The Bureaucratic Phenomenon.*[2] Crozier argues that rationality has to be considered within the framework of the actor, whether individual or group, using the principle of conservation of power as an imperative for action. What may appear as irrational and nonlogical behavior from the position of one powerholder is quite rational for the actor who is concerned with preserving or enhancing his power base. The phenomenon of resistance to change becomes far more comprehensible when the analysis proceeds along the line of power relations. These sociological interpretations of large-scale organizations take us back to some of the original work in this field, especially to Harold Lasswell's pioneering study, *Psychopathology and Politics,* first published in 1930.[3]

Lasswell connected individual pathology and organizations by means of his hypothesis that powerholders displace "private" conflicts onto "public" issues. Although the locus of the private conflict is in the individual, according to Lasswell, it originates in the conditions of power. With Lord Acton, Lasswell believes that "power tends to corrupt, absolute power corrupts absolutely." Power is therefore a noxious stimulus that causes previously repressed or even neutralized conflicts to erupt. Notice the argument and how it differs from the view that a preexisting neurosis determines the distorted behavior. Instead it is the securing of power that triggers intrapsychic disturbances to the detriment of individual function and organization purpose. Obviously the challenge of these ideas widens the investigation of the nature of power relations, the function of leadership, and the genesis of stress in organizations.

Several years ago I published a study of stress in a large bureaucracy. The title of the paper, which appeared in *Behavioral Sciences,* is "Stress Reactions in Organizations: Symptoms, Causes and Consequences."[4] Although the investigation used survey research and statistical analysis rather than clinical methods, the ideas guiding the study relied heavily on psychoanalytic hypotheses and theories.

This study originated in the concern of the top management of the Canadian Broadcasting Corporation over the appearance of unusual indications of adverse reactions to stress. These indications included depression, alcoholism and suicide. CBC was a large, semi-public company that was charged with the development of radio and television broadcasting throughout Canada.

To carry out its mission, CBC relied on the talents of gifted people for its product and for its technical dissemination. CBC was in a highly sensitive position in Canadian society as a result of the changing and highly volatile political and cultural scene in Canada. As a public agency whose budget and other oversight functions followed a direct line to governmental and parliamentary agencies, executives were alert to government and media criticism. The population targeted for the study consisted of 3,000 people in three occupational groups: management, staff and operations. The management supervised work groups at all levels in the organization. The staff people provided expert services in engineering, accounting, legal, and personnel functions. The operations people did the work, often of a creative nature, in providing product and services.

Statistical analysis revealed the presence of five relatively independent stress syndromes: (1) emotional distress of a depressive quality; (2) medication use without specific illnesses suggesting hypochondriasis; (3) cardiovascular illness; (4) gastrointestinal disturbances; and (5) allergy-respiratory illness. The study originally predicted that the incidence of these various stress illnesses would be related to work location of the affected individuals in addition to personality and personal history profiles. The reason for the "location" prediction was the expectation that certain defects in supervision would result in a toxic atmosphere for individuals. Once identified, these locations could be studied in detail, identifying the forces in the situation which produced the disturbances. On the basis of such study, remedial action could be recommended. On the personality and personal history side, the study viewed the incidence of illness apart from location phenomena to be representative of "site" effects. Once those predisposed to stress illnesses were identified, two lines of action could be developed. The first could aim at selection and the second at providing channels for therapeutic intervention. The study was not prepared to suggest that the organization exclude stress-prone individuals since these individuals also tend to be very talented and capable of making a substantial contribution to the organization.

To tease out the information needed to test the original hypotheses meant using statistical controls, which by themselves revealed some very interesting information. For example, when French-Canadians became ill they tended to show symptoms of depression and other emotional distress while the English-Canadians had physical symptoms such as gastrointestinal disorders. These two illness patterns seemed related to two very different styles of response to stress. The first involves sensitizing the response, which means generating, and being painfully aware of emotional reactions; the second involves repressing the response resulting in adverse physical reactions. Statistical analysis showed that younger people and women tended to be sensitizers, along with being French-Canadian, and that older people and men tended to be repressors, along with being members of the English-Canadian ethnic group. With one possible exception, location appeared irrelevant to the distribution of illness. However, membership in occupational groups proved to be quite important. Managers were relatively unaffected by stress symptoms. Staff people were overrepresented in the gastrointestinal category while operations people tended strongly toward emotional distress.

This finding triggered a new line of investigation in which competing hypotheses were tested against the data. Although the study could in no way be viewed as conclusive, it did suggest new pathways for considering the relationship between organizational and individual phenomena. The view that this organization functioned as a site for the eruption of individual illnesses and that through the aggregation of people it served merely as the locus for psychic accidents did not appear to be tenable in the light of the information produced. *How* an individual succumbed to stress was more or less predetermined by cultural, personality, and personal history factors. *Where* the illness tended to occur resulted from organizational events which, played out over time, produced sufficient stress to cause unfortunate developments in the form of symptoms.

Before undertaking the stress study for this organization, top management had studied carefully CBC's organization structure. With advice from consultants, top management changed the organization structure with the aim of moving from concentrated centralization of power at the top to greater decentralization. The purpose: to develop coherent and effective divisions within the total organization. The top management group was relatively new in office. It had replaced one that had taken a defensive posture which can be described best as a "fortress mentality."

For many years, CBC had been extremely vulnerable to political events in Canada. It was especially affected by the highly charged, tendentious relationship between French and English Canada and the separatist movement in the province of Quebec. The government had published several commission and white paper reports on the problems of organization and management in the corporation; journalists had written newspaper articles, editorials, and one or more books about the shifting position of the company in Canadian affairs. The fact that the company had been under fire for some time contributed in no small measure to the formation of a "fortress mentality" in the former top management and, indeed, had led to the change in leadership that brought about the moves toward decentralization. The enlightened quality of this new management produced the stress study. Its purpose was to find means of improving the quality of work life in order to increase satisfaction and productivity.

Conventional wisdom suggested that managers as a group should show the greatest susceptibility to stress reactions. They were the main target of attack, and were especially vulnerable to the effects of changes in the distribution of authority. This proved not to be the case, calling to mind a similar finding in a study undertaken at various Bell System companies on the incidence of coronary disease. Here the investigators found that managers were less vulnerable to heart disease as compared with other, generally lower status, employees. Are powerholders in bureaucratic organizations simply better constituted to endure the stresses of authority and responsibility, or are they, after all, operating in a less stressful environment than individuals with less power? The second explanation appears the more plausible. Far from being noxious, power in a bureaucracy acts as a buffer against such illnesses. Executives well placed in the power structure enjoy a protected position as a result of their clear and unconscious involvement in the organization's mythology. In the face of adversity this mythology supports the self-esteem of those who belong to the organization. If individuals can rationalize their position in an organization and are protected from the chaos and arbitrariness that seem so often to dominate the life of members of organizations, then no matter what forms pressures take, self-esteem tends to be preserved.

Modern large-scale organizations may differ from organizations of the past whose latent purpose included protecting individuals by wide inclusiveness in their mythological structure. It is no accident that Freud used the examples of the Church and the Military to explicate his theory of group psychology. These organizations and others like them, including universities, perpetuate a set of beliefs and ideals that speak to the conditions that cause anxiety and the sense of dread. Contemporary economic organizations lack such protective mythological structures for all of their members except those who realize considerable power in them. For those individuals outside the mythological structure but who still are members of the organization, there tends to be a subliminal awareness of something missing in their lives. If it were simply a matter of an organized mythology to provide for dependency needs, the problem would be less significant than it turns out to be. It is the presence of the mythology that often causes organizations to go awry and become highly maladaptive to their circumstances. When this occurs, members of these organizations, regardless of their position with respect to the mythological structure, become vulnerable to the real dangers of economic dislocation and privation.

Endnotes—Chapter 9

1. W.L. Bion, *Experiences in Groups* (New York: Basic Books, 1961).

2. Michel Crozier, *The Bureaucratic Phenomenon* (Chicago: University of Chicago Press, 1964).

3. Harold Lasswell, *Psychopathology and Politics* (Chicago: University of Chicago Press, 1977).

4. Abraham Zaleznik et al., "Stress Reactions in Organizations: Symptoms, Causes and Consequences," *Behavioral Sciences*, Vol. 22, 1977, 151-162.

LEADERSHIP AND CORPORATE MYTHOLOGY

Anthropology teaches us that myths are used to confront a problem and provide one or more solutions that allay anxiety, put fears and uncertainty to rest, and above all, assure the individual's integration into society. Assuming individuality counts, a trade-off occurs. At the cost of conformity, the person submerges himself into the group to gain relief from anxiety and fears of the unknown.

Science generally is unconcerned with anxiety. Primordial fears, however, are with us all. They center on the individual's sense of detachment, loneliness, and isolation. Such fears can easily persist until some commonly held beliefs, expressed in myths, renew our sense of belonging and the communality of life. The common solution myths offer us is to trust one's family, clan, or society, to follow its norms, and to maintain the solidarity of the group. The ultimate protection from anxiety is to belong to a strong, cohesive group.

Modern corporations have well-developed mythologies despite the effort made to promote efficiency, rationality, and contractual relations between the corporation and its employees. Indeed, the contradictory nature of corporate life often stems from the coexistence of rational and irrational elements in its structure and function. A corporation's logic and mythology derive from the influence of its leadership. This can cause problems.

The irrational aspects of corporate life produce two distinct disabilities. The first, discussed in chapter 9, is the limited inclusion in the system of myths. Unlike the military and the Catholic Church, which Freud used to illustrate his hypothesis that cohesion results when members in common identify with their leaders, or some representation of leaders, in the form of ideals, there is an exclusionary principle at work in modern corporations. Life for the corporate elite is fundamentally different than for the underlings. For the elite, clinging to corporate mythology produces some pernicious effects resulting often in insecurity and withdrawal on the part of the excluded.

The second disability arises from the false sense of security the elite feels in its comfortable attachment to corporate myths. This security has its own price tag. It dulls the capacity to observe, analyze, and behave in relation to the competitive marketplace in which success and failure are measured. Men and women who become CEOs of corporations dominated by a system of myths, assuming they are free from its grip, sooner or later come to realize that they must destroy the mythology in order to shape effective strategy and provide an environment in which "real work" can be accomplished. That is, energy must be directed toward products, markets, and customers, and be buttressed by technology, know-how, and common sense. Indeed, an advantage of the modern corporate raider is precisely that freedom of thinking, that detachment from the target's mythology. It is far more difficult for those on the inside to break the commitments implicit in belonging to an organization and believing in its prevailing mythology. For leaders to function well, they must have available aggression to support their objectivity. Yet they must not lose their compassion and capacity for empathy with those who depend upon them.

In the American corporate culture, mythology elaborates the theme of teamwork: While Americans admire the hero, the individual who has the "right stuff," they worry about his or her recklessness, his or her willingness to take risks that endanger others. Frequently the "hero" is suppressed in favor of the team player who values the performance of the group over individual recognition. That person often rises to the top.

This social development was the basis for William Whyte's argument in the 1950s that corporate life had created the "organization man," the conformist who suppressed his individuality to support a corporate team. The rise of this phenomenon can be seen in the development of the U.S. automotive industry (particularly in the rise of General Motors), where chaos reigned following World War I.

William Durant put General Motors together by acquiring numerous businesses. In this process, he built a mammoth corporation whose survival was not at all assured. He then hired Alfred Sloan who, in bringing order out of the existing chaos, equated success with managerial teamwork within the top corporate group. By the 1950s, this group had developed a close and all-encompassing social network. They lived in the same Detroit suburbs, joined the same clubs, and attended the same parties, galas, and celebrations. The company created a way of life.

Sloan has justifiably been credited with consolidating the modern concept of management during his tenure as head of GM. Sloan's management system included decentralized operations with centralized financial controls, market segmentation between and within operating divisions, and committees to coordinate activities (e.g., purchasing, R&D) that divisions held in common. In place of the mercurial and entrepreneurial Durant, he created a system through which organization and teamwork displaced charismatic leadership.

His legacy, however, was not solely the design of a rational body of thought on how to organize and manage a large corporation. Because the social system he created was a closed one, providing its members with a secure life plan, his ideals also became a mythology—a structure of beliefs that established, in the eyes of its own corporate elite, the image of GM's invincibility. Implicit in this system was the belief that by adhering to Sloan's principles, GM could withstand competition and thus remain invincible in the corporate world.

But this mythology applied only to those in the corporate elite, those team members who rose in the hierarchy and were extraordinarily well compensated through the liberal bonus program established as part of the system. First-line supervisors (who seldom expected to rise within the hierarchy) and blue collar workers were excluded from the managerial/mythological structure. Indeed, Sloan's major management system failure was its inability to overcome hostile relations with its unionized work force.

The public became aware of GM's mythology when, during the Eisenhower administration, Charles Wilson, the head of the company, was being confirmed as secretary of defense. At his congressional hearing, he uttered the famous words, "What is good for General Motors is good for America." Possibly, he meant that since the business of America is business, the policies that benefit corporations benefit society as a whole. But what the press and the public heard was something different: the belief in GM's (and America's) invincibility. Whether or not it was his intention, Wilson found words to express the dominant mythology of his corporation.

The existence of this mythology helps explain why GM and other domestic automobile producers, each with their own mythologies, failed to meet Japanese competition in the 1970s. Focused on the inner life of the corporation, the automobile companies lost touch with changes in the marketplace. The success of the Volkswagen in the 1960s was an early sign that Detroit's emphasis on styling changes rather than function might not match new consumer preferences for efficiency and reliability. Detroit's continued emphasis on styling well into the seventies testifies to the belief in their own invincibility and their contempt for the consumer. Just as the corporate myth excluded workers and supervisors, so did it preclude real consideration of consumer preferences and needs. This story is well chronicled in David Halberstam's *The Reckoning*, which attests to the collective dysfunctions that occur when managers cling to their corporate mythologies.[1] Too often managers appear impervious to the fact that the competitive marketplace evaluates the corporation and its products from a different frame of reference than that experienced from within.

Why do mythological structures persist, especially since no corporation or society is invincible and no products rationally deserve loyalty or attachment in an impersonal marketplace? This question requires two answers. The first considers the part leaders play in the rise of a mythological structure. The second examines how the structure persists beyond the lifetime of the power figures who personify the mythology.

In the minds of their constituents, business leaders are larger-than-life figures. As charismatic creators of new products, builders of businesses, and accumulators of massive wealth, fantasies of omnipotence are projected onto them. The first Henry Ford is a good example. With the development of the Model T, he personified a vision of America that went beyond Horatio Alger. A tinkerer off the farm, Ford changed the pattern of living and working in this country by producing a popularly priced car every farmer and worker could eventually own. By introducing a five-dollar-a-day-wage, he dramatized the benefits of mass production and became a national hero. There was talk of his becoming President of the United States.

The mythological structure of the Ford Motor Company centered on Henry Ford's belief in the perfection and permanence of the Model T, which competitors eventually destroyed. His vision and conviction, in turn, were products of his own attachment to his parents and his attempts to rewrite his personal history.

Facing trouble as his commitment to the Model T sustained an increasingly antiquated organization and product line, Ford refused to listen to his educated and sensitive son Edsel, who had sensible ideas for modernizing the company. Upon his return from a vacation, Edsel and a group of engineers brought him into a room to see a mock-up of a new car that could replace the Model T. Ford walked around, inspecting it, and then tore it apart with his own hands. Attached to the Model T as a symbol of his own perfection, Ford distanced himself from Edsel and instead, drew close to Harry Bennett, the head of his "goon squad." Bennett's shady background and access to gangsters and thugs only reinforced Ford's paranoia and rigidity.

Let's look at this in psychoanalytic terms.

Ford's life history suggests that his obstinate commitment to the Model T was rooted partly in a private psychodrama, which he projected onto his role as leader and entrepreneur. Idealizing his mother and hating his father, Ford used an overvalued Bennett as the symbolic repository of his ability to take "revenge" while his son Edsel became the symbol of the boy "in need" whose hurt could be denied by being devalued. Ford's private struggles to overcome his unresolved attachment to his parents by creating the perfect car and by proving his independence also nearly cost Ford his business. The public myth of the Model T was undermined by its private and psychodynamic foundation.

The interplay of public drama and private struggle can have a strong impact on subordinates. The power-holder's compulsion to act out these conflicts draws other executives into a corporate psychodrama, which reveals the underlying mythology. The following vignette takes us through the dynamics of such a psychodrama.

The directors of an advertising agency appointed as the new chief executive officer one of its account executives who had a reputation for being a conciliator rather than a strong marketer. He could mediate disputes within his client organizations as well as his own agency. The directors chose him because he was the least controversial candidate and they were reluctant to appoint the most dynamic, aggressive, account executive who dealt with the largest account in the agency. This account alone brought in the largest proportion of revenues among all the accounts in the agency's roster.

The new head exercised little choice in how he ran the agency. The role of conciliator was deeply embedded in his character. Typically, at the opening of each account group meeting, he would find some good news to report and some complimentary remark about one or another of the agency's staff, usually a person of lesser rank and "clout." At his encouragement, lower ranking staff from the so-called creative departments conducted a fining ritual. Anyone arriving late for a meeting had to pay a fine. The cash accumulated through this ritual paid for a spring party. Observation of who paid fines showed that the highest ranking members of the agency's account executives tended to be fined, including the CEO.

For the most part, the CEO confined his substantive contributions to gentle questions about market research findings. He became most active and aggressive in presenting ideas when the most powerful account executive was absent from meetings. The lesson the CEO perpetuated through his behavior was that aggression is bad and ideas should not be attacked in or out of the account group meetings. The agency was propelled under the momentum of its past relationships with clients, but under the ominous threat that the lead account executive would depart and take his clients with him, or that the low-keyed, benign atmosphere would weaken the agency's marketing and advertising abilities. Abundant evidence appeared to suggest that the agency was losing its marketing edge because of the leader's low tolerance for aggression as amplified in the ritualistic behavior during the account group meetings.

Leaders who have difficulty with aggression often encounter problems with ambitious subordinates. The overt forms these rivalries take, and their consequences, are illustrated in the following case study.

On Feb. 11, 1983, Charles Warner, the chairman and chief executive officer of the Brandon Corporation, met with his president and chief operating officer, Frank Reynolds. The meeting took place late in the day and at Reynolds' request. Mr. Warner had had some prior indication that Mr. Reynolds was upset because Reynolds did not attend a product development meeting that Warner had convened earlier in the day. Before starting the product development meeting, Warner asked the sales vice president, who reported to Reynolds, where he was. The sales vice president replied that Mr. Reynolds would not be attending the meeting.

Reynolds was visibly upset and angry during his meeting with Warner late on Friday afternoon. He threatened to resign and showed Warner a list he had prepared that detailed, in writing, the ways Warner had broken the chain of command and, according to Reynolds, damaged his authority and standing in relation to his subordinates. The list cited the fact that Warner had called a product development meeting including as participants all of the people who reported to Reynolds. As a further indication to Reynolds that his authority had been subverted, he angrily reminded Warner that the chairman had negotiated a new arrangement with one of the Brandon Corporation's key licensees in Europe without Reynolds attending the negotiations, or reviewing and approving the terms of the new arrangement. Reynolds felt that the chairman had acted arbitrarily, without regard for the integrity of the chain of command, and in a manner that had diminished Reynolds' capacity to continue as president and chief operating officer.

While this meeting was not the first time Warner had confronted anger in his president and chief operating officer, nor the first time that Reynolds had threatened to resign, the anger appeared to Warner as both more intense and sustained so that the prospect of having to deal with a resignation appeared more real than on previous occasions. Mr. Warner had decided while listening to the complaints of his chief operating officer that he would ask Reynolds to hold in abeyance any decision to change his relationship with the Brandon Corporation until both he and Warner could discuss further and in more detail their relationship and the difficulties Reynolds experienced in working with Warner. He asked Reynolds to adjourn the meeting and to use the weekend for reflection on what had occurred recently to disturb Reynolds and what they should do next to improve the situation. Warner said that he planned to think long and hard about how he had upset Reynolds and how he might go about avoiding such situations that involved Reynolds' authority and his working relationship with subordinates. Warner further proposed a meeting for an early hour on the following Monday morning.

Reynolds responded favorably to Warner's suggestion and indicated that he would not reach a firm conclusion as to what he would do, which Warner took to mean that Reynolds would hold in abeyance his decision to resign. They both agreed to meet Monday morning and shook hands and left for their respective weekends. Upon arriving home, Mr. Warner called Mr. Reynolds to restate their commitment to a "cooling off" period. Reynolds had not yet arrived home, but Warner continued calling until he reached Reynolds who reassured the chairman that he intended to reflect, that he would delay any decision on resignation, and that he would be at the Monday morning meeting with Warner.

The Brandon Corporation was a medium-sized manufacturing company that designed, produced and sold a line of specialty electrical products. The products, mainly control devices, were used in the assembly of large pieces of equipment. Brandon's customers designed and manufactured the equipment, which usually specified the Brandon products as subassemblies or parts. There was only one major competitor in Brandon's business. Because of design innovations, which resulted from Mr. Warner's initiatives and expertise, the company had improved significantly its market share at the expense of its competitor and had enjoyed a number of years of success in its markets. The company's balance sheet was exceptionally strong. As a result of its improved market share, the company's profits and cash flow had increased and the balance sheet showed extraordinary liquidity and a very low debt-to-equity ratio.

A significant change had occurred in the fall of 1982, when Brandon's main competitor started a price war with the obvious aim of recapturing the market share it had lost to Brandon over the past five years. While Mr. Warner fully intended to meet the price competition, he had no idea how long the price war would last and how deeply the competition would cut into the company's profits and cash flow. It was in response to the price war that Mr. Warner had grasped an opportunity to make a favorable deal with his European licensee and had called the product development meeting. The night before he had called the meeting, Warner thought of a number of possible product innovations which he was eager to present to his executives in marketing and engineering. Warner felt strongly that the company's long-term success in the price war depended upon its ability to present new and improved products even though in the short run it had to meet its competitor's prices. He could hardly restrain his enthusiasm and therefore had hurriedly called the product development meeting without first consulting Reynolds. Exhibit 1 presents an organization chart that shows job function and lines of authority for the top management of the Brandon Corporation. The organization chart also gives each executive's age.

Besides dealing with the intense competitive problems through pricing and product improvement, Mr. Warner had undertaken in conjunction with his chief financial officer and an outside investment banker, investigation of opportunities for acquiring companies. The Brandon Corporation was owned privately with all the corporation's share in the hands of Warner and his immediate family. Warner believed that the company should expand by buying other privately held concerns in businesses that either related to or complemented Brandon's activi-

Exhibit 1

BRANDON CORPORATION

<u>Executive Organization Chart</u>

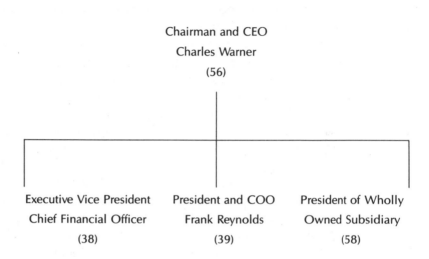

Chairman and CEO

Charles Warner

(56)

Executive Vice President	President and COO	President of Wholly
Chief Financial Officer	Frank Reynolds	Owned Subsidiary
(38)	(39)	(58)

ties. At age 56, Mr. Warner had no intention of selling out to another company, nor of retiring. He spent many hours discussing the company's future with his chief financial officer and the two of them had hired the investment banker after conducting interviews to decide which of several leading investment bankers would be in the best position to help the Brandon Corporation. This work entailed considerable travel for the two executives, extensive research work on the part of the chief financial officer and many hours during which Warner and the chief financial officer met to discuss the long-range plans for Brandon. Mr. Warner expected Reynolds to devote himself to managing the company day-to-day while he in turn would concentrate on ideas for product innovation in existing markets, and the problem of acquisitions.

Mr. Warner was aware of how difficult it can be to recruit, develop, and motivate key executives in a privately held company. He felt that if executives met his standards for ability and performance that they would constantly be tempted to leave and join a publicly held corporation where scope of responsibility and financial incentives might be considerably greater, including participation in stock option plans. To meet this problem, Mr. Warner had consciously and carefully arranged a compensation package for key executives that he believed would enable the Brandon Corporation to keep talented executives despite the drawbacks of working for a privately held corporation. The compensation package consisted first of salary and bonus that together represented at least 40 percent more money than these executives could reasonably expect to realize working for another company, either publicly or privately owned. In addition, there were the usual perquisites alongside a deferred compensation plan that raised the compensation value beyond the 40 percent premium to perhaps 75 percent or 100 percent above the market. The deferred compensation plan became fully vested after seven years and the plan was in its first year in early 1983. The only executives who participated in this compensation program were the president, the chief financial officer and the president of Brandon's wholly owned subsidiary. This subsidiary manufactured and sold a product that was totally independent of the corporation's main lines and therefore operated apart from Brandon. Mr. Warner had complete confidence in the president of this subsidiary and viewed him, along with president and the chief financial officer of Brandon, as his key executives for whom he had developed the special compensation package.

Charles Warner joined his father's business in 1949 when he graduated from college with a bachelor's degree in business administration. His father had founded the business, and at the time Warner joined it, the company was very small as measured in sales, profits, number of employees and product lines. It specialized in one product line which provided the family with a good income, but with little prospects for growth in sales or profits.

In 1957, Charles Warner formed a new company called the Brandon Corporation. Warner decided to establish this company so that he could pursue new market and product opportunities that went beyond the scope of his father's business. Charles Warner and his father each owned 50 percent of Brandon. The elder Warner received his 50 percent share in exchange for his willingness to countersign a note for $25,000 held by a bank that had loaned Brandon the money necessary to start the business.

By 1961, the Brandon Corporation was barely surviving. Despite the problems, Charles Warner decided that he wanted complete ownership of the business. His father balked at the suggestion that he should turn over his 50 percent of the Brandon shares to his son. Nevertheless, he transferred his shares to Charles who immediately put his father on the Brandon payroll where he remained until his death.

Reflecting on his desire to own 100 percent of the Brandon shares, Charles Warner said, "Brandon was my idea. I founded the company, and I couldn't live with the division that way and getting my sister and her family involved in the company." Warner had been conscious of the fact that should his father retain the 50 percent ownership, his estate might become burdened with taxes upon his father's death. In addition, Charles Warner faced the prospect of having his sister own shares in Brandon which she would inherit when the elder Warner died.

In 1973, Charles Warner suggested to his father that he consolidate his business in the Brandon Corporation. According to Charles Warner, his father was by that time sympathetic to the activities of the Brandon Corporation and felt that by merging his company with Brandon, his business would continue. Charles Warner said, "Father realized I would take care of him in a dignified way and as a result he became enthusiastic. He came into the office every day and saw young people. This kept him in good health. The last two years of his life, I insisted that he not drive his car. I had one of our employees who lived near Father pick him up in the morning and drive him home from work at the end of the day." The elder Warner died in 1981 at the age of 92. After his father died, Charles Warner realized that he would be the last member of his family who would run a business. His children had made definitive career plans which excluded the possibility of their ever coming into the Brandon Corporation and succeeding their father.

During the 1970s, the company was successful in expanding its product line and in opening new markets. However, it experienced severe difficulties in controlling quality and manufacturing costs and it appeared threatened by a number of years of unprofitable operations. Charles Warner recognized that he needed help in running the company. He sought advice from the president of his wholly owned subsidiary who recommended that Warner hire as president and chief operating officer an individual who had once worked for the president of the subsidiary. Warner accepted this advice and hired the man who remained for a couple of years but then decided to resign and go into business for himself. Warner once again sought the advice of the president of his subsidiary who recommended another executive from his industry. Mr. Warner hired this man who stayed with the company several years. This president brought to the company rich experience in the technical aspects of Brandon's product and made many changes which worked to the advantage of the corporation. However, he also displayed bizarre behavior in his relationships with women and was totally indiscreet, making no secret of the fact that he enjoyed extramarital affairs and that he encouraged his subordinates to do the same. Warner, after an extreme display of poor taste on the part of his president, decided to discharge him and at that point elevated Frank Reynolds from the position of vice president of sales to president and chief operating officer.

Frank Reynolds joined the Brandon Corporation in the early 1970s. He had graduated with a degree in engineering, but had worked in a large corporation in its marketing department, utilizing his technical background to master his understanding of product design and applications as a salesman. He advanced in his work and joined the Brandon Corporation on the advice of the president of its subsidiary for whom Reynolds had worked in the large corporation. Reynolds soon received promotions and he became vice president of sales two years after he joined the company. Reynolds performed well in this capacity but he became dissatisfied working for the president who was later asked to resign because of indiscreet behavior. His dissatisfaction reached the point where Reynolds tendered his resignation to Charles Warner, indicating that he was willing to stay on long enough for the company to find a successor to the position of vice president of sales. Warner was very reluctant to see Reynolds leave the company and decided to offer him the position of president and chief operating officer in order to keep him in the company. Reynolds accepted, whereupon Warner asked for and received the resignation from the incumbent.

In the position of president and chief operating officer, Reynolds recognized a number of opportunities for improving the company's performance. Costs and product quality were out of control and the company was losing money at an alarming rate. Reynolds acted decisively in making personnel changes, and in instituting procedures which improved considerably product quality and costs of manufacturing and distribution. The company became profitable and entered an aggressive program in which product innovations and marketing programs increased the company's market share and enabled it to accumulate cash and equivalent liquid assets for its future program of acquisitions.

Warner and his other two key executives recognized Reynolds' contribution and attributed his competence as an executive to certain personality characteristics. In their eyes, for example, Reynolds was an extremely well-organized individual who identified a problem, figured out how to solve it and then without deviating from his course implemented the solution. He was openly aggressive in his style, and was quick to display his anger at subordinates and even Warner should events appear to interfere with his program for action. Reynolds himself in commenting on how he worked in comparison with Warner said, "Charles is an idea man and I implement. He comes up with a lot of ideas and then I have to talk him out of his bad ones after figuring out which ones are good."

Frank Reynolds was born in a rural community the second of four children. His older brother was a machinist who had dropped out of college and gone into machine shop work. His sister, younger by three years, taught school and was unmarried. The youngest brother worked for the Brandon Corporation in the sales department. This brother dropped out of college and Frank arranged to get him a job in a Brandon manufacturing plant. When the younger brother applied for a promotion, Frank Reynolds rejected the application on the grounds that his brother was unqualified for the job. Reynolds took this occasion to tell his brother that he should leave work, go back to school and complete his college degree and then go to work. Reynolds also offered to support his brother through the completion of college, an offer the brother accepted. The younger brother completed college and came to work once again for the Brandon Corporation, but this time in the marketing field following the career path of his older brother Frank.

Frank Reynolds enjoyed a close relationship with his parents, especially his father. By a program of careful savings and investments, Reynolds had accumulated a substantial equity. He bought two farms in partnership with his father. His parents lived on one farm which the father managed in his retirement.

The father had been a teacher and football coach in high school and upon his retirement had the farm for his work and living. Frank Reynolds and his family, which consisted of his wife and two children, visited the farm at least once a month for a weekend and for holidays and in this way maintained a close relationship with his parents. Managing the farms and other investments required Frank and his father to confer during these monthly visits and on other occasions. The older brother was somewhat estranged from his parents, although he too was married and had children. Frank commenting on his brother's relationship with their father said, "They are too much alike in their personality to get along."

In reflecting upon his recent angry interchange with Charles Warner, Reynolds felt that he had been successful in running the company. At age 39, he believed he had to make a decision about his career, particularly in meeting his desire to own and manage his own business. Reynolds regarded his acumen in saving and investing with considerable satisfaction. He was proud of the equity he had accumulated through his investments and believed he had the assets to strike out on his own. He also believed that it was in Charles Warner's best interests to sell the business and realize cash from the equity represented in it. He recalled advising Warner directly to sell when it seemed that a large publicly held company might be interested in acquiring Brandon. Warner at that time told Reynolds that he had no intention of selling the business and that he had no desires other than to continue as chairman of Brandon, to expand the business through developing new products, and through acquiring other companies.

Adherents of the chain of command philosophy might fault Warner for calling a meeting without first going through his chief operating officer. But such a philosophy presents an overly rigid notion of the significance of chain of command. It tends to obscure the motivational factors at play in this continuing conflict between superior and subordinate. In companies that run well, there is relatively little preoccupation with prescriptions for using authority.

In the Brandon case, the source of the conflict is Reynolds' rivalrous feelings toward his boss. His history demonstrates a marked trend in his desire (and ability) to overcome rivals, including his father and brother. He is uncomfortable with any hint that he may be dependent on another man. Therefore, he systematically works to control situations, including his boss' scope of activity. The game he plays is to make would-be authority figures dependent upon him.

Warner's complicity in this rivalry stems from his discomfort with aggression and his unwillingness to confront Reynolds directly around issues of authority and control. By giving in to his subordinate, and acting as though he is to blame for the disturbance, he only accentuates Reynolds' taste for power and his rivalrous feelings.

Power figures have to come to terms with the fact of their power. They must be willing to live with it comfortably and in the open. When competition for power arises, a tendency exists for it to become part of corporate mythology and ritual, as in the case of the head of the advertising agency who encouraged ritualistic behavior to repress aggression. The rivalry goes underground. New layers of mythology are erected to avoid confronting the legitimate sources and uses of authority and power. This communal repression appears most markedly on the heels of succession, when a charismatic leader leaves the scene.

When power-holders in a business incorporate in their psyches the mythology of a *once* successful leader and attempt to displace rational observation and analysis with a persisting mythological structure, the corporation becomes akin to a "totemistic community." Its cohesion depends upon the continuing worship of the representations of past leadership as these become cemented, first, in the corporate mythology and, second, in business policies and decisions. Case in point: the demise of the Curtis Publishing Company and its flagship publication, *The Saturday Evening Post*.

Successive management, along with the Curtis board of directors, rigidly adhered to the format, content, and image of *The Post,* which had been established by the company's founder, Cyrus Curtis, and long-standing editor, George Horace Lorimer. For these two men, their product represented America as it was at the turn of the century. Essentially rural, ethnocentric, and conservative in economic and political outlook, *The Post,* with its famous Norman Rockwell covers, became swamped by the changes occurring in the United States between the two world wars. Waves of immigration brought hundreds of thousands of Eastern and Southern Europeans to America. The Great Depression drove thousands from the farm to the city. The advent of the Second World War altered the isolationist outlook heralded in the magazine's pages.

Reflecting the deep-seated belief in the mythology handed down by Curtis and Lorimer—the sense of permanence of a Waspish, rural America—the company's management integrated backwards: it brought stands of timber, pulp mills, and expensive printing plants. Its capital thus became frozen in support of a dying image, one that no longer represented the consumers and advertisers who provided the revenues. The mythological structure prevented company management from seeing the significance of Henry Luce's new pictorial journalism (in *Life,* for example); it failed to appreciate the importance of radio, then television, broadcasting. Most of all, it didn't grasp the quickening pace of American life, which ran counter to the sleepy image of a docile country portrayed in the pages of *The Saturday Evening Post.*

An effective business leader who gains power in a nearly defunct corporation must ferret out the buried ideals in the company's mythology. He or she must destroy them as the fixed objects in constituents' psyches, and translate new images and visions into workable business strategies. Lee Iacocca, for example, had to restore product, manufacturing, and selling motifs instead of financial and real estate orientations, which had been reflected in Chrysler's own sense of permanence as the third partner in America's hegemony in the automotive industry. Focusing on finance and milking the business, Chrysler's leadership starved its factories. Iacocca aggressively led the company in reducing its break-even point by closing antiquated plants and upgrading capital equipment in those he intended to keep. By stimulating product engineers and designers to introduce low-priced knockoffs of luxury cars, he gained a renewed following among consumers. Because of his close association with dealers while at Ford and his understanding of what sold cars, Iacocca inspired his organization to do "real work." Indeed, manufacturing executives supported him wholeheartedly, even though he shrunk the manufacturing base by closing plants and subcontracting production.

But what price do such outsiders exact on a company? When the corporate "totem" and the underlying mythology are destroyed, what replaces them to maintain cohesion and self-esteem?

Organizations are hierarchies in which power is unevenly distributed. Despite experiments with reforms designed to narrow the gaps between levels of power, inequalities continue and probably always will. An organization's cohesiveness arises out of common identification with the leader as a person, the ideals that person represents, or the mythology that is a legacy of past leadership, as we have seen. Those who are included in the mythology maintain self-esteem through belonging. Institutions such as the church, the military, or a great university whose standing is linked to broad cultural needs and hopes include everyone, regardless of rank and relative power, in their mythology; the structure, moreover, provides a protective, enveloping cocoon to ward off anxiety and feelings of stress. Because such institutions are linked to universalistic values such as faith, patriotism, or truth, they express cultural hopes that belong to the society as a whole, not to the institution itself. The institutional myths are reflections of broader cultural wishes and values. As members of society, institutional participants have claim on and a stake in the institutional mythology as well.

Modern economic corporations, however, are instruments of ownership and capital appreciation. Where corporate leadership fails to link company efforts to broader cultural objectives and needs, the myths these leaders sustain are the myths and stories *surrounding* success itself, the stories of ambition, conquest, and status. These myths are by their very nature exclusive, so that lower-level employees cannot participate in them.

It is usually only the power elite that clings stubbornly to totem worship and faithful adherence to the corporate mythology. For those outside the main power structure, there is personal vulnerability from two sides. On one, the perpetuation of the mythology threatens their economic well-being—witness the hundreds of thousands of jobs recently lost in America's industrial heartland, which once appeared invulnerable to foreign competition. On the second side, the mythological structure produces psychological isolation for those excluded from it. This increases the risk of stress illnesses, as illustrated in the report of the Canadian Broadcasting study in chapter 9.

Individuals excluded from the dominant mythological structure tend to rely on their fantasy life to repair the damage that can occur with isolation. Fortunately, there are alternatives to falling ill as a result of stress. A strong case can be made that, in part, the mental process of effective leaders is contingent on their tolerance of separation from the group and its mythology. They rely on their fantasy as an instrument for formulating ideas (sometimes called visions) about an organization's future. Their exclusion from the group mythology, whether by personal choice or situational factors, often provides the impetus for fresh examination of familiar information. The resulting objectivity can set the stage for new work and the redefinition of an existing situation.

In chapter 9 we looked at an example that helped clarify distinctions between site/situation and accident/event. Let us look at this example again to illustrate that when a person lower down in the organization lacks the power to transform a private fantasy into a shared vision, the fantasy may not protect the person from stress. The result, the following example reveals, is the formation of stress symptoms and impaired ability to perform.

An air traffic controller in his early fifties slipped on the icy metal stairs of a control tower. For some time after the fall, he felt a sharp pain in his lower back. More than experiencing a physical mishap, however, the controller found himself engaged in a psychological accident in which his tendency toward isolated fantasy took a morbid turn toward depression and paranoid reactions.

This controller (call him Robert Graham) took pleasure in the thought that the superbly trained pilots flying large, high speed aircraft depended upon him to bring their planes and passengers to a safe landing. Pilots would at times go out of their way to compliment him on his performance, providing Graham with some real content to his fantasy that powerful people needed him.

This feeling of being needed contrasted sharply with the solitary quality of the work, the lack of association with his fellow controllers and supervisors, and the awareness that the mythology surrounding commercial aviation, while highlighting the dramatic role played by pilots, excluded the activity of aircraft controllers. This sense of being alone became pointedly real when Graham realized that his supervisor and fellow controllers seemed unaware of his accident. No one paid much attention to him until it became apparent that he could not carry out his duties, at which time his supervisor placed him on sick leave.

Besides a consciousness of being alone, Graham worried about the future. He was afraid he would not be able to keep up with the changes in technology, and that he would be placed on early retirement. He never had occasion to give voice to these fears until he began to see a psychiatrist for treatment of depression as well as for evaluation in a work-related compensation dispute. He was never able to resume work in the control tower. As a result, what he feared most actually occurred: He lived in a diminished capacity, incapable of taking on a skilled job that measured up to the responsibilities of an air traffic controller.

Modern corporate mythology, as we have seen through various examples, leads to a false sense of security that diminishes the intense scrutiny of a company's business environment; it engenders a complacency that dampens imagination and the aggressiveness needed to engage competitive issues long before they become manifest in financial results. Furthermore, the mythology speaks only to the members of the power elite, including those aspiring to it, protecting it from the ravages of stress.

Those with lesser status and power are excluded. Ironically, they may be more vulnerable to stress illnesses than those with the responsibility of actually running the organization.

When organizations encounter serious trouble, those included in the mythology find it exceedingly difficult to break out of the stereotypical thinking that belief in the mythology encourages. When problems become sufficiently grave to warrant drastic steps (usually under the threat of outside agendas), new leadership enters the scene. As "outsiders" not under the influence of the prevailing mythology, the new group or individual may be able to approach the business more objectively. New leadership thus has the opportunity to appeal to rationality and to the recognition that clinging to archaic images and ideas, no matter how self-gratifying, leads to disaster and runs counter to the impulses of self-preservation.

Endnotes—Chapter 10

1. David Halberstam, *The Reckoning* (New York: Morrow, 1986).

PSYCHOANALYSIS IN CHANGING ORGANIZATIONS

To do justice to the subject of using psychoanalysis to change organizations, it is necessary to explore the history of consulting in organizations. The term *consulting* is often used in psychoanalysis to refer to a patient's first encounters with an analyst for the purpose of diagnosis and arriving at a mutually agreeable recommendation for analysis or therapy. Consulting is also used when an analyst asks a colleague to review the course of treatment as a means of clarifying the dynamics and arriving at a clearer understanding of the treatment. Often in such consultations, countertransferences are involved and are impeding the progress of the treatment. It is a delicate and worthwhile task to ask for and receive such consultations in the interests of the patient.

In the business context, the term *consulting* has a broader definition than the one used commonly in psychoanalysis. In fact, consulting to management is a profession in its own right, although it contains a variety of schools of thought and types of practitioners.

The Association of Consulting Management Engineers defines "management consulting" in its 1968-1969 Directory of Membership and Services as follows:

> Management consulting is the professional service performed by specially trained and experienced persons in helping managers identify and solve managerial and operating problems of the various institutions of our society; in recommending practical solutions to these problems; and helping to implement them when necessary. The professional service focuses on im-

proving the managerial, operating, and economic performance of these institutions.

ASME's definition includes the notion of "counsel" to management on
managerial and operating problems of the enterprise, and these problems
are *action-oriented*, i.e., the "counsel" is directed toward improving managerial and economic performance and results for the client. In addition,
the *art* of this counsel goes beyond the knowledge possessed by the consultant, to include four distinct aspects: fidelity, understanding, persua-
sion, and education. These four aspects constitute the nature of the
consultant-client relationship.

Management consulting can also be defined as a *business*: consultants observe business life and provide what is missing, be it technological expertise, knowledge of organization, a creative approach to
finance, or something as general as "business advice." By recognizing
"what is missing," consultants match their products and services to genuine needs—their strategy is "market-driven."[1] What the client needs the
consultant provides.

Defining the boundaries and objectives of professional management consulting includes diverse and intriguing interpretations of the
consultant's role. As Seymour Tilles of the Boston Consulting Group
asks: Is the consultant a "seller of services," a "supplier of information,"
a "business doctor dispensing cures," or what?[2] History tells the story.

It was roughly contemporaneous with Freud's development
and application of his method of investigating the workings of the mind
that consulting in business began its history. At the turn of the twentieth
century, specific external factors prompted "outside advice": the population in the United States was growing rapidly and the work force was expanding.

Factories were incorporated into large-scale enterprises with
decentralized operations and diversified products. Mass production became commonplace, and as industries expanded, the communication and
transportation systems developed as well.

While the economy prospered, wages and productivity were
low. Industrial operations were inefficient relative to their potential.
Workers were asked to perform tasks that were not suited to their talents,
and managers gave little or no attention to the effects of fatigue on the
workers, or the effects of the sequence or tempo of work upon employees
and productivity. Management was not using their workers in the most
productive and efficient manner.[3] Both engineers and industrial managers began to examine the causes of inefficiency and sought improvements in factory operations.

Scientific management provided a solution to inefficiency in factories. Frederick Taylor, Henry Gantt and Harrington Emerson are familiar names associated with scientific management and the emerging field of engineering consultation. They cautioned against confusing the techniques of scientific management with its aims. Taylor explained scientific management as a mental revolution, both on the part of the workers and the management, "It is a complete change in the mental attitude of both sides towards their respective duties and towards their opponents."[4]

Briefly, Taylor's four principles of Scientific Management are:

"They are the development of a science to replace the old rule-of-thumb methods; the scientific selection and then the progressive teaching and development of the workmen; the bringing of the scientifically selected workmen and the science together; and then this almost equal division of the work between the management and the men."[5]

In his 1911 paper, entitled the *Principles of Scientific Management*, Frederick Winslow Taylor prescribed *systematic* management to cure inefficiency. The best management was based on laws, rules and principles—principles which could be applied to the simplest everyday acts, as well as to corporations requiring more complicated cooperation. The ideal engineer performs the best work at the lowest cost, so also, in industrial operations, the best manager organizes the forces under his control so that each person works at his best efficiency and shall be compensated accordingly. The *planning* of the work must be segregated from its *execution*. Trained experts possessing the right mental equipment, should be the planners, while the executors should have the right physical equipment for their respective tasks and a receptive attitude to expert guidance in their performance. Contrary to the popular opinion that scientific management, and the consultation derived from it is mechanistic, its founders were idealists. Frederick Winslow Taylor believed that scientific management would assure industrial peace and prosperity. By his objective approach to work and compensation, justice would prevail along with increased productivity and higher compensation in factories.

Public awareness of Scientific Management increased between 1910-1912, when Louis D. Brandeis represented the Traffic Committee of the Trade Organizations of the Atlantic Seaboard in the Eastern Rate Case in hearings before the Interstate Commerce Commission to establish rail freight rates on the Eastern Seaboard. Brandeis claimed that with the use of scientific management the railroads in the U.S. could save $1,000,000 per day. Brandeis had 11 engineers as witnesses (including Harrington Emerson) who testified that it was possible to raise wages and at the same time reduce costs in railroad operations.[6]

Management consulting soon after was to undergo changes. Edwin Booz attended Northwestern University where in 1906 he became intrigued with the studies of Walter Dill Scott, then chairman of the Psychology Department. Scott recognized the importance of finding the *right person* for the job rather than experimenting solely with time and motion of a task. In 1919, Booz left Scott to start his one-man consulting firm, Edwin G. Booz Business Engineering Service. In 1924 the firm became Edwin G. Booz Surveys, with George Fry as his assistant. Even during the 1920s, such firms were not yet referred to as professional management consultants, but were thought of as "business counselors," "management engineers" or "efficiency experts."

In 1929, two important events occurred: the Association of Consulting Management Engineers (ACME) was organized and James Lane Allen joined Booz's firm, which became Booz, Fry & Allen. (In 1935 Carl Lewis Hamilton joined the firm.)

ACME was formed for the purpose of establishing *professional* standards, creating a common sense of identity among members, promoting the "profession" of management, and protecting the public from unethical "practitioners." James Allen was to have a significant influence on the firm's direction and purpose. Allen hails Edwin Booz as the person who gave management consulting its greatest impetus: thinking in terms of *people* and the organization of them as being the key factors in successful management. While not undervaluing the scientific management model of consulting, Booz, from the beginning, was to emphasize *people*. Management consulting, according to Booz, could advise top management, could be instrumental in managerial succession, and in addition could provide management with ways of maximizing profits and minimizing costs. Thus the "engineering" model was expanded and the role of the consultants was to include a wider range of concerns. During the 1940s men were called to war and problems developed as people were left to run businesses without proper experience. Also, increased wartime production needs put additional pressures on industry and consultants were called upon more frequently for counsel.[7]

Like Booz, James O. McKinsey from the University of Chicago brought an innovative approach to management consulting. From his short career as a teacher of accounting and budgeting, McKinsey equated good budgeting with good management, and while at the University of

Chicago, he founded his own consulting firm, James O. McKinsey and Company in 1926.

The Depression brought business to his firm, as banks and other financial institutions had defaulted on loans. At a meeting in Chicago, McKinsey met Marvin Bower, then a corporate lawyer who was serving as secretary for bond holders' committees. Bower had firsthand knowledge of why companies had defaulted on their bonds, which afforded him direct insight on how *not* to run a business. Bower recognized a need for a consulting firm that could study a company as a totality—its competitive position, strategy, volume and profit outlook—and present objectively and knowledgeably analyses, just as a law firm analyzes the legal aspects of a reorganization. Both McKinsey and Bower agreed on the need for *independent* management consulting, and in 1933 they founded McKinsey and Company.[8]

In 1934, Marshall Field & Company hired the firm to study its business, which then included manufacturing, wholesaling, and retailing. McKinsey and Bower advised the company to focus solely on achieving retail leadership. Their recommendations were so comprehensive and well received as to prompt Mr. Field to offer McKinsey the position of company chairman. McKinsey accepted, stating that he wanted to become a "doer" and not just a "teller." He restructured the company, sold the less profitable factories, sold the high cost stores, and laid the foundation for a successful company. But this prodigious task exacted the ultimate price. An exhausted McKinsey succumbed to pneumonia at forty-eight years of age in 1937.

McKinsey the consultant was a "generalist," focusing attention on the organization as a whole. Managing was more than running an organization—it had to be viewed within a large context of politics and social issues. The business organization was conceptualized as a "system" of interdependent parts, functioning in the larger system. Executives must be aware of external forces which can influence the organization: "administration is as much an external profession as an internal one."[9] Once this perspective was understood, McKinsey maintained that the study of the processes of management should focus on the *specialized functions* that are usually found in all business organizations: marketing, production, finance, purchasing, personnel, etc.

The main goal of a manager was "to make a product of value to the human race and a profit to the producers."[10] To accomplish this, the manager participated in processes: formulated plans, established procedures for *implementing* them, and provided *controls* to see that they were carried out. To study management, one can focus on the major policies of the firm, the formal organization structure, and the operating procedures. This involves, in essence, the ways in which various activities (functional areas) are organized, directed and controlled.

Bower took over McKinsey & Company, and he had a great deal to do with the firm's image. He viewed consulting as a *profession* in which, as in law, the consultant applied knowledge that the client could not provide alone. He recognized what he called "perennial forces" which would expand and alter the profession over time.[11] During the Depression, companies had a "try anything" approach, and consultants were hired for independent managing advice. Once companies recognized the value of this advice, the image of the consultant as a professional was reinforced.

While the contributions of Booz, Allen, Hamilton, McKinsey and Bower have shaped professional management consulting since the 1920s, Alfred P. Sloan, Jr. must not go unrecognized. Sloan's concept became a model for the organization of multi-product businesses and consulting firms developed a healthy practice tailoring and implementing the Sloan model. Perhaps the Sloan model reached its peak in popularity when General Electric, with the help of McKinsey and Company, established the "strategic business unit" (SBU). As GE's former Chairman Reginald Jones said, "when it began in the early 1970's, our (strategic) system was an experimental idea. But it has since become a way of life for us at GE, enabling us to identify those businesses with the greatest potential for earnings growth, and to allocate them the resources needed for their full development."[12] Other companies followed General Electric's lead in merging strategy and structure in organization planning.

Bruce Henderson, formerly of Westinghouse, founded the Boston Consulting Group in 1963. Henderson refined the SBU concept, stressing its analytical aspects. He introduced the "experience curve," which showed that provided a *standardized* product is produced and is correctly managed, increasing production yielded a predictable decrease in per-unit production cost. Doubling volume or "experience" produced a 20–30 percent decrease in cost. The curve was even more attractive when BCG linked it with market share. With a large share, the company "slides" down the curve faster and undermines the competition, further increasing market share. The third concept Henderson introduced was the growth and market share matrix, plotting market share vs. market growth, permitting separation of business units into fast-growing high market share sectors versus "cash-cows" and "dogs," for example.[13]

Though strategic planning and experience curves may work well in the marketing of commodities, success was far from certain. The "implementation" problem fostered the growth of Bain and Company, split from Boston Consulting Group in 1973. The new firm disdained the "sea gull" approach to consulting, stressing the importance of continued presence at the company itself.

Strategic planning has been criticized by Richard T. Pascale of Stanford Graduate School of Business, who stated that "very often, procedures like the annual strategic planning cycle haven't been terribly effective, partly because strategy doesn't need to be changed every year. Strategy comes to be seen as rain dance, a fire drill, not to be taken seriously. The process ends up having the perverse effect of desensitizing people to strategic issues."[14]

The large consulting firms themselves have had their turbulent times as well. Plagued by a recession-bound economy, the firms stagnated as well in the 1970s. Appropriately James B. Farley, chairman of Booz, Allen and Hamilton called in a consultant. This individual recommended reduction in government business, expansion into the international sector, and, most importantly, directed the company into *specialty fields*. Broad, managerial efforts were replaced by projects involving problem solving in specific operations. The range of consultant service offered by Booz broadened considerably into new areas such as executive search and telecommunications. Farley called the approach "issue oriented." He further stated that "if you took a company's organization chart and built a consulting business covering the decisions people on the chart must make, you'd build a Booz-Allen. No consultant will be here five years from now who doesn't understand that issue orientation is the way to go."[15]

The philosophy seems quite timely in an era of increasing complexity in business practice engendered by seemingly disparate government regulation and deregulation. "Consulting is booming because the world is getting more complex," says Joseph J. Brady, executive vice-president of ACME. "Things are changing so rapidly that companies want specialists to come in and help."

C.S. Sloane noted that the change in governmental regulatory environment of the 1970s has encouraged the development of a whole new body of clients—those in energy, construction, chemicals, natural resources, agriculture, leisure and travel, to name a few. Each of these areas has witnessed significant shifts in government policy relevant to their businesses, and they have sought assistance in meeting the new challenges that these regulations create. These circumstances have helped to accelerate the departure from a "generalist" oriented consulting posture to a specialist-multispecialist orientation.[16]

Most consultations to management attempt to provide expert service to the client. The forms of expertise vary but in general they include collecting and analyzing data, and making recommendations which will produce beneficial results for the client. It is noteworthy that the expertise of most management consultants is not exclusive. In most instances the expertise is also present within the client's organization. For example, the client's production organization may understand and be capable of performing efficiency studies, or, the marketing department may have people who can perform market studies. But this nonexclusive position of the consultant may not diminish his contribution. The inside experts may not have the time to undertake special analyses. The claim for objectivity is important and the added authority of outside experts, a subject of much joking in organizations, may make it easier to embark on improvements where vested interests would prefer the status quo. It is also well-known that consulting studies are particularly necessary in dealing with political problems. A chief executive officer may wish to stand above the "battle" in deciding important strategic and structural directions. The consultants enable the CEO to carry out a process in which power conflicts will not revolve around his office. While the political factor is well-understood, professional management consulting firms lay no claim to observing or interpreting unconscious material.

Consultants from the social sciences, usually in universities, who represent themselves as competent to deal with the unconscious employ a theory that deals expressly with the concept of resistance. But unlike conventional consultants, who may be keenly aware of political forces that exist in the client organization and recognize that these forces have an effect on both the definitions of the problem at hand and the possible remedies, consultants using psychoanalytic models go beyond the manifest political forces. The resistances arise from unconscious processes within the group or organization. Models of consultation that consider these resistances propose that the client group has the resources to identify and deal with problems. Its failure to do so stems from unconscious group process. By interpreting the unconscious, the resistances to "work" disappear and the group is able to progress in dealing with reality issues. W. R. Bion, whose work we first considered in chapter 9 on Organizations, employed the terms *basic assumption* and *work groups* to distinguish the condition where unconscious forces dominate from those conditions in a group where the defenses are unnecessary and energy can now move toward reality.[17]

For such therapeutic work to occur, a setting is required in which a group can examine, with the help of the consultant, its own process and deal with the basic assumption modalities that prevent effective work from being performed. It is easy to visualize this setting in group psychotherapy from which Bion derived his theory of group psychology.

It is more difficult to envision how this setting gets established and what the operative effects are in producing and interpreting data.

Let us use as an example a consultation in business. The narration has been disguised to protect confidences, but without distorting the issues under consideration.

A large family-owned manufacturing company was in the throes of a management succession problem. There were significant conflicts between and within the generations running this profitable enterprise.

The older generation believed the younger had not taken responsibility for the direction of the business, were not showing initiative in operations, let alone policy and planning, and despaired over whether fresh leadership would ever be forthcoming from this group. The younger generation (their average age was 40) believed the older generation had stifled them, trampled on their initiatives, and were intent on keeping them relatively powerless in this organization.

Among the older generation, rivalries and conflicts were in abundance. The most powerful individual in this older group wanted nothing to do with succession planning, opposed using an outside consultant, and in general went his own way in performing his executive duties. He was a talented man, who conceived new product ideas and mobilized engineers and production people to carry them through to fruition, usually not involving members of either generation. He was a powerful "loner" with a reputation for brilliance as well as harshness. He had become a shadowy presence in this succession problem and refused to enter into the deliberations. Observation of the situation led the consultant to the conclusion that despite the myth of equality, there was a code in this family that permitted any individual to take initiatives so long as he had the drive, enthusiasm, and courage to assume leadership. Thus, one of the junior members of the younger generation, withdrew from his peer group and started a new division. He lobbied the older generation for support, which he received without difficulty and launched his new venture successfully. The response of his peers was to ignore him and the significance of his behavior, which violated their belief that they were capable of great achievement if only the older generation would free them from the constraints of their dominance and control.

The belief systems of both generations were neither unconscious nor, which amounts to the same conclusion, repressed. Using the venerable, but still valuable, topological model, perhaps these beliefs existed in the system preconscious, and were easily accessible to consciousness.

In any case, the consultant decided to deal with the substance of the succession and organizational problems, without attempting to uncover what lay behind the beliefs of the two generations. The consultant believed that probing for unconscious material would have revealed a great deal about sibling rivalry, displaced oedipal conflicts, and homosexual anxiety. There was undoubtedly much to defend against in this aggregation of unconscious material. Instead of interpreting the unconscious, the consultant wrote a report addressed to members of both generations in which he described their beliefs, and showed how these beliefs had created the stand-off in the conflicts between and within generations. He continued his report with a number of recommendations, including the naming of a chairman of the board from the younger generation, the naming of a president from the younger generation and steps that would enable them to reconstitute the board of directors to assure accountability to, and responsibility on the part of, both directors and operating executives.

He submitted his report and met with the two generations. The "real leader" refused to attend the meeting and expressed despair that the report would spell the end of the family business. It is interesting that his claim for family unity and harmony ignored his part in exacerbating conflict and disarray. The wife of one of the second generation appeared at the meeting and asked to attend and participate. When asked for his opinion, the consultant said she should not be allowed to attend, that the issues belonged to the executives who were there.

Most of the second generation greeted the consultant's findings and recommendations with hostility. None of the older generation joined in this attack. It was clear that the report had confronted a dominant belief that all executives in each generation were equal. They were paid the same, enjoyed the same benefits and perquisites of executive rank. The report stated explicitly that there were significant differences in ability, and, indeed the recommendations, by singling out designees for the chairmanship and presidency, reflected these differences.

After substantial discussion, the group excused the consultant from the meeting and continued with their deliberations. Representatives were delegated to report back to the consultant the conclusions reached. First, they agreed to destroy all copies of the consulting report, and second they agreed to do nothing to alter the organization structure. About one year later seniors and juniors accepted and implemented all of the consultant's recommendations. Several senior and junior members called or wrote to the consultant to express their appreciation for his contribution, claiming that they would not have been able to face the realities of succession without his work. At latest reports, the company is thriving, although some of the juniors who were not promoted continue to feel hurt, as do their wives.

Assume that the consultant's recommendations were substantively sound and were beneficial to the company. Would there have been an alternative way to reach this end point, assuming that the group was prevented from dealing with reality because it existed in one or several of the basic assumption modalities instead of a work modality? This is not a trivial question, and it evokes another. Would a Bionesque group leader have been able to interpret unconscious material, remove repressions, lift defenses, guide the group to a work modality which would have developed realistic solutions, without the disaffections that were a legacy of the consultation? Perhaps there would have been even better solutions than the ones proposed if a work group, freed from neurotic struggles, had been operative.

Consideration of these questions about consultation and change in organizations suggests a reading of Freud's important paper, "Analysis, Terminable and Interminable" in which he considers analogous issues applied to clinical psychoanalysis. As with many of Freud's other works, the reading of "Analysis, Terminable or Interminable"[18] requires an historical perspective. The paper was published in 1937. Freud was 81, suffering from cancer of the jaw, and the loss of some of his best and favorite pupils. Otto Rank had joined the defectors claiming the birth trauma as a discovery of the underlying cause of neurosis.

Rank experimented with a brief therapeutic procedure that would uncover the birth trauma, thereby removing the source of all neurotic conflict. In opening "Analysis Terminable and Interminable," Freud wryly remarked about Rank's treatment:

"We have not heard much about what the implementation of Rank's plan has done for cases of sickness. Probably not more than if the fire-brigade, called to deal with a house that had been set on fire by an overturned oil-lamp, contented themselves with removing the lamp from the room in which the blaze had started. No doubt a considerable shortening of the brigade's activities would be effected by this means."[19]

The general tenor of this paper suggests that the termination of analysis and the concept of a cure is elusive. The decision to terminate reflects the analyst's and the patient's agreement that the progress is substantial (reflected, for example, in the amelioration of major psychological symptoms and the reduction of the anxiety level), but that depending on circumstances, it is possible that the patient will seek further treatment at a later date. The idea of cure is an alteration of the ego so that the structure of defenses are less costly, the superego does not dominate the ego, and the individual is capable of acting in the service of pleasure as well as reality. In Freud's words, "The business of the analysis is to secure the best possible psychological conditions for the functions of the ego; with that it has discharged its task."[20]

Freud was propelled into this paper not only by questions concerning shortening the length of analyses, but also by questions of preventing future neurotic disturbances by stimulating latent conflicts and dealing with them as part of the analysis to prevent their future eruption. In considering a preventive or prophylaxis analysis, Freud became even more cautious than his aversion to therapeutic zeal would explain.

Another of his students, the gifted analyst Sandor Ferenczi, reproached Freud for having neglected to uncover the negative transference and analyzing it during the brief analysis Freud undertook with Ferenczi to deal with some disturbances in relation to women and male rivals. For years after this treatment, Ferenczi was able to maintain a good marriage and be a valuable teacher to men who could easily have been perceived as rivals. Later, Ferenczi felt hostile to Freud and reproached him for neglecting the negative transference.

The questions Freud posed in "Analysis, Terminable and Interminable" were expressly directed to clinical psychoanalysis, but offer thoughtful questions to those who seek to apply psychoanalytic psychology to consultation in organizations. There is a principle in psychoanalytic technique that directs the analyst's attention to interpretation from the surface. Instead of plunging into id interpretations, observe what conflicts and defenses are in play, and direct interpretations to them. The aim is to alter the defenses, permit regression to occur at a rate that is tolerable to the patient, thereby deepening the analysis to expose conflicts that are being repressed at the cost of debilitating symptoms. This same principle avoids stimulating conflicts by maneuvers and manipulations on the analyst's part. The conduct of psychoanalysis implies no active measure to deprive, withhold, or otherwise frustrate the patient in order to bring about conflict.

In consultations that draw on principles of group therapy, the relationship between conflict present and conflict induced by the procedure is murky at best. When the consultant convenes a group and then withdraws into the leaderless group situation, regression will occur at a rapid pace. Predictably, anxiety levels will mount rapidly and defenses will be activated, including the types of defenses that are group determined in the group dynamics.

Bion's theory, which is derived from the work of the child psychoanalyst Melanie Klein, is a conflict-defense model of group psychology. But in his experiences with groups, Bion believes that what Freudians would consider primitive defenses appear regularly in groups, leading him to comment, "The apparent difference between group psychology and individual psychology is an illusion produced by the fact that the group brings into prominence phenomena that appear alien to an observer unaccustomed to using the group."[21] Bion explains what he means in a footnote, "It is also a matter of historical development; there are aspects of group behavior which appear strange unless there is some understanding of Melanie Klein's work on the psychoses. See particularly papers on symbol formation and schizoid mechanisms."[22]

Bion draws certain differences between his theories of group psychology and those of Freud, particularly as developed in *Group Psychology and the Analysis of the Ego*.[23] For Freud, group psychology was a derivative of the followers' common identification with the leader. The incorporation of the image of the leader results in a common representation in the egos of the followers. This commonly held representation becomes the basis of group cohesion. In Bion's view, the leader is a result of the projective identifications of the followers, which he explicitly attributes to the basic assumption groups, allowing for the fact that the leader of work groups may be closer to external reality than the followers. Bion states,

"It is clear that between the theories advanced by Freud and those I have sketched out here there is a gap. It may appear to be more considerable than it is because of my deliberate use of a new terminology with which to clothe the apparatus of mechanisms that I think I have detected. It will be necessary to test this by looking at the group more from the standpoint of the individual. But before I do this, I shall sum up by saying

that Freud sees the group as a repetition of part-object relationships. It follows from this that groups would, in Freud's
view, approximate to neurotic patterns of behaviour, whereas
in my view they would approximate to the patterns of psychotic behaviour."[24]

Bion may be correct in connecting group behavior to underlying psychotic patterns. But the correctness of this view may be a function of the
observer and what the observer does to produce the psychotic effect. In a
wonderfully ambiguous statement that seems to anchor itself at once in
the observation of groups made up of "patients," of "sick" groups of any
kind, and even of all groups, Bion clearly forces a central issue. He states,

"This does not mean that I consider my descriptions apply
only to sick groups. On the contrary, I very much doubt if any
real therapy could result unless these psychotic patterns were
laid bare with no matter what group. In some groups their
existence is clearly discernible; in others, work has to be done
before they become manifest. These groups resemble the analytic patient who appears much more ill after many months of
analysis than he did before he had had any analysis at all."[25]

Put aside consideration of the methods of conducting group psychotherapy. Assume that group psychotherapy is a procedure that takes place
with a number of individual patients who enter the group as part of their
personal therapy. Assume also that we can exclude from consideration all
didactic group procedures, whether conducted in small groups or large
assemblies, where the purpose is education through experimental training
methods. Focus instead on consultation, which consists of a client engaging a professional to apply some expertise in the solution of the client's
problem for which the client pays an agreed upon fee. What are the conditions that call for the interpretation of unconscious material as a part
or all of the work of consultation? What is the nature of the consultant's
expertise that is the foundation for such work? What are the data that
lead to interpretations, and what are the sources of the data?
Five guidelines warrant consideration:

1. Unconscious material becomes accessible through regression. There is natural and induced regression. The natural regression defines the psychological state of individuals who make up the focal group
for the consultation, the state which the consultant may observe as a condition resembling the natural state of the dynamics affecting the client

without activity, intervention, or prescription on the part of the consultant. The picture of this natural state of regression is formed in part as a description of the presenting complaints. Why is the client seeking consultation? What is the distress, and how is it distributed within the client organization? In some cases, there may be very little regression, when, for example, a Board of Directors asks for consultation on the naming of a new Chief Executive Officer in an expected succession in management. In other cases, such as that described by Bidier Anziev,[26] the degree of regression may be considerable. In this case, the group was leaderless, since the designated successor did not, or could not, assume his role, leading to substantial interpersonal conflict that seemed to have been fed by fantasies about the old leader and his son. The consultant assumed leadership when he accepted the engagement and effectively convinced the designated successor that it was his job to run the business, while convincing the subordinates of the legitimacy of this appointment. Regression will occur when there is a leadership vacuum. The consultant can stem the regression or exacerbate it by what he or she does to fill the vacuum temporarily and permanently.

2. A consultant should observe, but not induce, regression. If a consultant establishes a "group" of which he is the leader and then withdraws, he will induce regression fulfilling W. R. Bion's expectation of psychotic behavior attending this regression. Should a consultant induce regression by withdrawing leadership or assert leadership to stem regression? In one case where projective identification was present as a natural condition of the regression that was underway, the consultant persuaded the central figure in this case to enter individual psychotherapy. He was strongly affected by a continuing idealization of his father, and, by projective identification, was creating a set of roles for his subordinates equivalent to a good son and bad son while he enacted the dual roles of the idealized and hated father. The consultant decided that the group was not in place to resolve such conflicts.

3. Interpreting unconscious material in organizations tends to induce regression with probable harm. The obverse of this guideline is that by representing reality, the consultant helps stem regression, and mobilizes energies to solve problems. The ability of the consultant to observe regression and other manifestations of unconscious material helps him or her understand reality issues in order to present them more lucidly and with conviction. By a cycle of inducing regression and interpreting unconscious material, which further induces regression, the consultant becomes part of the problem and not the means toward solutions.

4. The use of the Bion model in consultations is an unreliable instrument for the observation of unconscious mental process in organizations. It tends strongly to produce what the consultant expects, and therefore interferes with the observation of what exists at conscious, preconscious, and unconscious levels. Freud's paper, "Analysis, Terminable, and Interminable" sets the stage for consideration of the role of the psychoanalyst as a "naturalist," an observer of what is there rather than an "experimenter" who induces certain effects in the pursuit of a theoretical position. In consultation, whether or not the consultant is a psychoanalyst, it is extremely important to observe the situation as a "naturalist," despite the philosophical argument that the presence of an observer already disturbs a situation.

5. Transference reactions provide a good vantage point for psychoanalytic observation in consultation. Perhaps it would be more accurate to state that how members of the client organization relate to and use the consultant provides the observational focus. Whether this material is in the nature of real transference remains to be seen. It should not be prejudged, nor should it be interpreted. The purpose of observation is to understand the problems contained in the client's experience. Whether unconscious mental life enters significantly into these problems remains to be seen and should not be presumed.

A client enlists a consultant with certain positive expectations. These expectations may contain elements of transference, but they also should be driven by rational motives. It is sensible at times to engage professionals to help solve problems. Consultants should build on these positive expectations as part of their being a "leader" in the solution of problems.

A chief executive officer of a company sought consultation. His initial complaint was uncertainty about his subordinates' views of him, particularly since the company was facing severe financial problems as a result of losses generated in one division. It struck the consultant that the CEO's first complaint referred to his subordinates' views of him rather than to the financial problem, but he said nothing about this thought. He also observed during this first meeting that the CEO had certain characteristics associated with excessive use of alcohol, but he also did not comment about these thoughts nor did he ask about the CEO's drinking habits.

At the start of the second meeting, the CEO described *his* concerns about excessive drinking. He reported how much he was drinking and it became clear that his slurred speech, florid face, and difficulties in remembering probably were connected to his drinking. The consultant asked the CEO when he had last seen a doctor and urged him to have a physical examination. The consultant also suggested to the CEO that he stop his drinking and see what effects alcohol was having on his behavior. He agreed to take the consultant's advice and the consultant began individual interviews with key executives throughout the company. As a result of the study, the consultant soon concluded that a crisis existed. The case presented a classic instance of a Chief Executive Officer who was not functioning in that capacity.

In a written report, the consultant presented a description of the critical condition of the company and offered recommendations which included liquidating the division generating losses, restructuring the key management group in order to restore the integrity of the authority structure, and consolidating various activities once the liquidation had taken place.

Following a number of meetings to discuss the report, the CEO decided to implement the recommendations. Follow-up meetings showed that he had taken the consultant's advice and felt that the company and he personally were moving in a favorable direction. Later follow-up established that the losing division had been liquidated, the financial situation had improved, and the new role distributions provided leadership to everyone's satisfaction.

While we might be tempted to reach the conclusion that this client had focused his dependency on to the consultant, we should not hastily reject fulfilling needs as the basis for beneficial changes. In this sense, psychoanalytic consulting in organizations may resemble in part the age old practice of giving advice.

One of the great pleasures psychoanalysis can offer is the aesthetics of overcoming confusion with clarity. To understand what is going on but also to know what one does not know wards off hubris. To enjoy the surprise of fresh and unanticipated questions may even approach ecstasy. To discover that a seemingly new application of psychoanalysis is historically rooted in some venerable aspects of human relations should be a cause for celebration because it is an antidote to mystification. While psychoanalysis is the science of the unconscious, it is not a vehicle for mystification. That is probably one reason why Freud clung with fervent hope to his metapsychology as a stable structure for new discoveries. It helps from time to time to take a purely human view of even the most sophisticated theory of human motivation. In the end, the aim of psychoanalysis, clinical or applied, is to encourage rationality.

Endnotes—Chapter 11

1. Tierno, David A., "Growth Strategies for Consulting in the Next Decade," *Sloan Management Review*, Winter 1986, p. 61.

2. "Understanding the Consultant's Role." Seymour Tilles, *Harvard Business Review*, November-December 1961, p. 87.

3. *Encyclopedia of Management*, (NY: Van Nostrand, Reinhold Company, 1982), 2nd ed., edited by Carl Heyel, p. 1083.

4. *Ibid.*

5. *Ibid.*

6. *Ibid.*

7. Higdon, Hal, *The Business Healers*, (New York: Random House, 1960), pp. 112-131.

8. Bower, Marvin, "The Focuses That Launched Management Consulting Are Still at Work," *Journal of Management Consulting*, Winter 1982, p. 4.

9. Wolf, William B., *Management and Consulting: An Introduction to James O. McKinsey*, Ithaca: New York: State School of Industrial and Labor Relations, Cornell University, 1978, (ILR paperback; no. 17), pp. 20-53.

10. McKinsey, James O., *Business Adminstration*, (Cincinnati, OH: South-Western Publishing Company, 1924).

11. Bower, *op. cit.*, p. 4.

12. *Ibid.*

13. Kiechel, Walter, "The Decline of the Experience Curve," *Fortune*, October 5, 1981, p. 139.

14. *Business Week*, May 21, 1979, p. 101.

15. *Ibid.*

16. *Sloan, Carl S., "The Road Ahead for Consulting," Journal of Management Consulting*, Volume 3, Number 1, pp. 13-14.

17. W. R. Bion, *Experience in Groups*, (New York: Basic Books, 1961).

18. *The Standard Edition of The Complete Psychological Work of Sigmund Freud*, Vol. XIII, pp. 211-253.

19. *Ibid.*, pp. 216-217.

20. *Ibid.*, p. 250.

21. *Ibid.*, p. 169.

22. *Ibid.*

23. *The Standard Edition*, Vol. XVIII (1955), pp. 67-110.

24. Bion, op. cit., pp. 180-181.

25. *Ibid.*, p. 181.

26. Bidier Anziev, *The Unconscious*, (London: Routledge, Kegan Paul, 1984), pp. 206-215.

THE LAST WORD

If you're anything like my students at the Harvard Business School, you are probably looking forward to this "last word," much as they anticipated my final lecture. It's a kind of "wrap up," a commentary on what the course (in this case, the book) is all about, and how the theory can be applied to real problems executives face in their human relations.

As for me, I never looked forward to the final lecture. It's not that I lacked appreciation for their need for a summary, a pulling together of the many threads that make up the fabric of this work. Instead, it's a personal matter. I dislike endings, almost as much as I dislike beginnings. For if the truth were to be told, there is no such thing as a beginning or an ending to the exploration of human motivation. So what I would do for my final lecture was to open up some new avenues to stimulate thinking, shake up the filing cabinets into which we tend to compartmentalize and store knowledge gained. I'm inclined to the same position here.

You already can tell that applying psychoanalytic knowledge to human affairs is no simple matter. You can't stand at a distance from human problems and expect to cure them with a few techniques or formulae. As soon as you step into a problem, your intentions and desires become part of the problem, and, let us hope, ultimately part of the solution.

I remember a few years ago I was asked to consult on a problem involving a corporation that had successfully taken over a company in a hostile action. Management of the "target" corporation had resisted bitterly. Management finally had to acquiesce to a bid, which exceeded shareholders' expected value by a considerable margin. The board of the target agreed to the acquisition. The problem for the acquirer was how to integrate the two organizations, which were in allied businesses and former competitors. The chief executive of the acquirer described the intricate process he was on the verge of establishing to bring about this integration. He was about to appoint task forces, strategy committees, and steering committees made up of representatives of both managements to work on plans for organization structure, duplicate functions in manufacturing, sales, management information, financial management, and controllership. Executives in both organizations were waiting for the other shoe to drop, the first shoe being the successful takeover bid. Who was to gain and lose power in the new integrated organization? Who would lose his or her job, what sales offices were redundant and slated for elimination, and what plants were to be closed, with jobs lost and personal lives in disarray?

In an atmosphere fraught with anxiety, both in the acquirer's and the acquired's organization, does the instigation of process (a method ostensibly designed for reaching decisions) rather than substantive decisions to problems that were already on the table, at least in the minds of the people, make sense? In my judgment, based on some ideas of what happens when anxiety begins floating in organizations the answer is no. Leadership that is timely, direct, and substantive will allay anxiety and energize people, while process will delay important decisions, make a mystery of the power at hand, and disconcert people because they really will not know who is in charge, and where the new organization is heading.

My recommendations in this case were grounded in certain insights derived from group psychology and theories of anxiety (in times of crisis, leadership must be present, visible, and right, wrong, or indifferent, willing to take responsibility for actions). The client, in this case the acquirer's CEO, did not take my advice, although his subordinates were inclined strongly to do so. Instead, he decided to go with his methodology. While it may sound self-serving to report that the CEO soon stepped down from his position, the point to be made is that people in positions of power are part of the problem as soon as the ball lands in their court. To bat it away to someone else's court, either directly by avoidance, or indirectly by establishing elaborate process, is usually bad use of power. We could speculate, and we wouldn't be far wrong, that the problem of integrating two former competitors had become confounded by the boss's own anxiety and heightened defensiveness. It is not unusual to become anxious in times of crisis. But for a leader to institute obsessional defenses in the form of substituting ritual for action, is to confound the problem. I guess that's why Socrates urged leaders to "know thyself."

When I speak of "acting" and of leaders as "actors," I easily visualize myself causing some misunderstanding. A favorite posture of executives and would-be executives is to imagine that in power positions they are role players or actors. The real "me" is hidden behind the mask encapsulated in a role of "chief executive officer" or whatever title. Great actors, and now I mean those gifted people who bring profound truth to life in dramatization on stage, face the grave problem of overcoming disbelief. But the overcoming of disbelief initially is never the problem of the audience. It is always the problem of the actor. What will render the part authentic in his or her own eyes? Why should the actor believe in the drama and in the character? The bridge from pure selfhood to submergence in the idea of the other as cast in the mind of the playwright, is the sense of the truth contained in the drama itself and the character's crucial position in making the truth known. So the first thing that happens is the knowing and experiencing of the truth, and then finding the inspiration to convey this unfolded truth to a wider audience. In this sense, acting on the stage is no make believe.

More often than not as I observe the use of power in real life, it becomes more pretense and make believe than an acted play on the stage with script, precise stagecraft, and pure technique designed to overcome the audience's disbelief. The use of power usually includes a secret hostility to those who represent some truth about to be revealed.

While I may not have been as explicit as you would have liked in this book, you should realize that thinking with psychoanalysis as a frame of reference puts you in a position of despising pretense. Why else go to the pains of decoding the often obscure and confusing information people provide as they go about their daily work? The message is try to understand what is going on, and speak and act in direct relation to your assessment of the situation. Differentiate between the problems in the real world (I'm speaking here of the marketplace) and the infinite variety of ways people have of obscuring and obfuscating what is real. Too many executives are frightened of their responsibility and of the notion that other people are counting on them to preserve the health and vigor of the corporate enterprise. They would just as soon deflect this responsiblity, get out of the position of being depended upon, and create their alibis well in advance of knowing the final outcome. For this reason too many executives position themselves to avoid errors of commission. They prefer instead to rely on the hope that their errors of omission will escape the sharp eyes of historians who someday will review their tenure and ask, "What were the consequences of this person's use of power?"

Psychoanalysis offers the clearest view of the human scene that I have ever encountered. For this psychoanalysis doesn't necessarily evoke gratitude. It takes resoluteness of mind and spirit to look at the world as it is, even while hoping to change if for the better.

As you have already discerned, I am suggesting that the use of psychoanalytic knowledge intensifies rather than diminishes your involvement in the affairs of your organizations. It makes of leadership a personal as well as professional venture. But in the interests of clarity, let me warn you that other schools of thought purport to do the same thing, that is, to intensify and make personal your professional activity.

On the serious side, these other schools of thought stress experiential rather than cognitive approaches to learning about human motivation. You have probably been invited to participate in such learning programs, sometimes referred to as "T" groups, encounter groups, and the like. Less seriously, perhaps even derisively, these experiential modes are called "touchy/feely" events, hence the term encounter group. Sometimes these events draw on the theories of group psychology, even Freudian theories, as the backdrop to support the intense emotions such activity evokes. I experimented with experiential learning in the 1950s and decided it was indeed psychodynamically charged, but not for intended reasons. Hence my decision to go for the intellect of my audience rather than their emotions. I was never a strong believer in the idea that emotions are more powerful than ideas. While experience indicates strongly that emotions can at times swamp the intellect (with disastrous results), it is only by strengthening the intellect (read here ego) that enduring improvements can occur in human affairs.

Let me suggest briefly what I think is wrong with experiential learning and what I mean about an event that is psychodynamically charged with a lot of unforeseen consequences, most of which I believe to be harmful.

Plainly put, most group training activities involve serious manipulations. While the manipulations, such as the withdrawal of leadership in the group and the consequent evoking of intense anxiety, are usually intended to illustrate the common expectations of a leader, the subtle pressures the "absent" leader creates to conform to certain norms also creates a double bind situation for participants. The formal leader's authority does not disappear. It merely goes underground to arise when the need to punish nonconformists surfaces. If someone wants to fill the leadership gap, the group punishes, not only from unconscious fears about displacing the "father" of the group, or from rivalrous feelings, but also because of the leader's subtle indications that the culture of the group *should* induce egalitarian, trusting, and caring attitudes rather than assertive, differentiating (as a leader surely does), and objective attitudes toward other people. I don't now know, nor have I ever, why a group of strangers should trust, care, and selflessly approach one another in the face of little knowledge about who is present, why they are there, and the purposes that bring them together. In short, the leader manipulates to the point where he becomes the superego of the group, rewarding and punishing, embracing and rejecting, and attacking and defending while acclaiming the event as a rebirth, a transformation of personality and character from authoritarian to democratic norms.

The versions of this conversion experience differ according to the tastes and ideologies of the various experiential camps, but make no mistake about the aim. It's to get into your head and remake the image you have of yourself and of the world in which you live. In my view, what passes for experiential learning is a coarse ideology propounded by people with the least self knowledge I have encountered, yet dominated by the arrogance that can only come from people who believe they have discovered the road to a new utopia and will settle for nothing less than heaven on earth. What is astonishing in our recent past is not the presence of this form of psychologizing a new ideology, but of the support afforded this effort from the most unlikely sources: hard-headed executives who appear determined to stir people up without the slightest sophistication on their part as to what they are supporting, what the end result is to be, and the implications, moral as well as psychological, of drawing others into a program for manipulation and control.

All human activity embodies certain ideals, psychoanalysis included. But it is a far cry from fostering ideals (such as respect for what is true and real about the human condition) to creating an ideology, a world view, which contains both the diagnosis and cure, in highly charged and abstract terms, for what ails human beings and their organized relations. In the end, the ideal of psychoanalysis, embodied in this book, is a rather old-fashioned one: that human progress depends on strengthening our rational faculties. As Freud put the issue, where id was, ego shall be. If psychoanalysis hasn't already struck you as being filled with irony, think about this: a science of the irrational takes as its purpose the enhancement of man's rational capacities. On that note, I send you my regards and best wishes.

INDEX